2014 ANNUAL
INTERIOR DETAIL

foreword

2014년 Annual Interior Detail이 발행되었습니다. 사진 위주의 작품집에 상세 도면을 함께 수록하여 실무에 접근성을 더하였습니다. 매년 1회씩 발행되는 본 연감은 60여개의 작품을 카페·레스토랑 / 업무·교육·전시 / 클럽·바·라운지 / 상업 / 의료 / 호텔·주거 등으로 구분하여 설계시 초기 작품 구상에 편리하도록 구성하였습니다. 인테리어의 트렌드는 매년 빠른 주기로 변화되므로 당 해년도의 작품을 도면과 함께 정리함으로써 연도별로 작품을 한눈에 비교할 수 있는 좋은 자료가 되리라 사료됩니다. 이러한 기획 하에 발행되는 연감이 실무에 많은 참고가 되기를 바라며, 끝으로 자료 협조에 노력을 아끼지 않으신 작가 및 실무진여러분들께 감사드립니다.

Contents _2014 ANNUAL INTERIOR DETAIL 20

2014 ANNUAL INTERIOR DETAIL 20

발행	에이엔씨출판 주식회사
등록	제2004-000166호
발행인	정흥채
진행	출판기획부
출력·인쇄	삼성문화인쇄(주)
주소	서울특별시 강남구 테헤란로22길 15 에이엔씨빌딩 10층
전화	02-538-7333

ⓒ에이엔씨출판 주식회사

한국간행물 윤리위원회의 윤리강령 및 실천요강을 준수합니다.
본지에 게재된 내용을 사전허가 없이 무단 복제 및 전제를 금합니다.

값 68,000원

COMMERCE 상업

- 010 WONDERPLACE_CHEONGJU 원더플레이스_청주
- 018 KKUN NORI 꾼 노리
- 028 KWANPEN VER.2 콴펜 2
- 034 BONBONROUGE AT ROOFTOP 봉봉루즈 루프탑
- 042 JACQUELINE 재클린
- 050 HAIR MARUNI 헤어 마루니
- 056 IL LAGO BAKERY & WINE SHOP IN MVL HOTEL 엠블호텔 일라고 베이커리 & 와인숍
- 064 MAINZDOM BÄKEREI 마인츠돔 베이커리
- 080 ANGSEE HAIR SHOP 앙시 헤어숍
- 088 RAKU IZAKAYA & SAKE PUB 라쿠
- 094 SALON DE H 살롱 드 에이치
- 100 JEO-JIP 저 집
- 106 VB DIET LAB VB 다이어트 랩
- 118 9 TOPAZ 나인 토파즈

CLINIC 의료

- 130 MIRAE MEDICAL FOUNDATION HEALTH IMPROVEMENT CENTER 미래의료재단 건강증진센터
- 138 OLIVE PLASTIC SURGERY 올리브성형외과
- 148 GOOD FLOWER DERMATOLOGY CLINIC 굿플라워 피부과
- 154 E.EUM ANIMAL MEDICAL CLINIC 이음동물병원
- 162 INURI ORIENTAL MEDICAL CLINIC 아이누리 한의원
- 176 HOSAN HOSPITAL POSTNATAL CARE CENTER 호산병원 산후조리원
- 184 PYUNKANG ORIENTAL CLINIC_SEOMYUN 편강한의원_서면
- 194 SUUM SLEEP CLINIC 숨 수면클리닉
- 200 AGAON FERTILITY CLINIC 아가온 여성의원
- 206 SEOUL BEST DENTAL CLINIC 서울 베스트 치과
- 214 DREAM DENTAL CLINIC 드림 치과
- 226 KOWON PLASTIC SURGERY 코원 성형외과
- 232 SHINSEGAE DENTAL CLINIC 신세계 치과
- 242 S PEDIATRICS (HOUSE IN HOUSE) S 소아과(집 속의 집)

HOTEL · HOUSING 호텔 · 주거

- 250 HOTEL MANU 마누 호텔
- 266 FUNCTION HOUSE 기능적인 집
- 276 YANGPYEONG HOUSE 양평주택

Contents _2014 ANNUAL INTERIOR DETAIL 19

2014 ANNUAL INTERIOR DETAIL 19

Publication	A&C Publishing Co., Ltd.
Registration	2004-000166
Publisher	Jung Heung Chae
Edit	Publishing Division
Process · Printing	Samsung Munwha Printing Co., Ltd.
Address	10F, 15, Teheran-ro 22-gil, Gangnam-gu, Seoul, Korea
Tel	+82-2-538-7333

Copyright © 2014 by A&C Publishing Co., Ltd., and may not be reproduced in any manner or from without permission

The exclusive distributorship in Taiwan is offered to ArchiHeart Corporation. Any infringement shall be subject to penalties.

Price 68 $

CAFE · RESTAURANT 카페 · 레스토랑

- 010 **MANOFFIN** 마노핀
- 018 **COCOBRUNI_PANGYO** 코코브루니_판교
- 028 **COCOBRUNI_SEOLLEUNG** 코코브루니_선릉
- 038 **53 BREAD KITCHEN** 53 브레드 키친
- 044 **THE MORE** 더 모어
- 050 **BURANO ISLAND CAFÉ** 부라노 아일랜드 카페
- 058 **LAZY MINT COFFEE BAR** 레이지 민트
- 066 **CAFÉ ONE FINE DAY** 카페 어느 멋진 날
- 074 **BRUNCH CAFE JEEZLE** 브런치 카페 지즐
- 086 **KITCHEN 131** 키친 131
- 094 **HARUENSOKU** 하루엔소쿠
- 104 **PLAY POT** 플레이팟
- 112 **NOODLE CCOCCO_GANGNAM** 누들꼬꼬_강남
- 120 **ONE PLATE STANDARD KITCHEN** 원플레이트 스탠다드 키친
- 126 **KKOTMAREUM_CHELSAN** 꽃마름_철산

OFFICE · EDUCATION · EXHIBITION 업무 · 교육 · 전시

- 138 **CITRIX SEOUL OFFICE** 시트릭스
- 152 **ALMOST HOME** 올모스트 홈
- 172 **POSTECH CITE CREATIVE SPACE** 포항공대 창의IT융합공학과 창의공간
- 176 **KOREA NATIONAL OPEN UNIVERSITY ATRIUM** 한국방송통신대학교 아트리움
- 188 **ENGLISH INSTITUTE PLATO** 플라토 어학원
- 198 **AVION** 아비온
- 212 **TO MAKE CUBE WEIGHTLESS** 무중력의 육면체
- 218 **SAIT INFINITE RESEARCH HALL** 삼성종합기술원 무한탐구관

CLUB · BAR · LOUNGE 클럽 · 바 · 라운지

- 232 **B-ONE LOUNGE CLUB** 비원 라운지클럽
- 246 **CLUB THE A** 클럽 디에이
- 258 **SOO BAR** 수(秀) 바
- 264 **CHARLS HOUSE** 찰스하우스
- 272 **KATAKOMB** 카타콤

2014 ANNUAL INTER DETAI

COMMERCE

010	**WONDERPLACE_CHEONGJU**	원더플레이스_청주
018	**KKUN NORI**	꾼 노리
028	**KWANPEN VER.2**	콴펜 2
034	**BONBONROUGE AT ROOFTOP**	봉봉루즈 루프탑
042	**JACQUELINE**	재클린
050	**HAIR MARUNI**	헤어 마루니
056	**IL LAGO BAKERY & WINE SHOP IN MVL HOTEL**	엠블호텔 일라고 베이커리 & 와인숍
064	**MAINZDOM BÄKEREI**	마인츠돔 베이커리
080	**ANGSEE HAIR SHOP**	앙시 헤어숍
088	**RAKU IZAKAYA & SAKE PUB**	라쿠
094	**SALON DE H**	살롱 드 에이치
100	**JEO-JIP**	저 집
106	**VB DIET LAB**	VB 다이어트 랩
118	**9 TOPAZ**	나인 토파즈

WONDERPLACE_CHEONGJU

TTAE | Yoon Young Kweon

청주 상권의 중심에 위치한 원더플레이스 청주점은 외부의 복잡한 도로를 고려하여 내부가 시원하게 들여다보이는 과감하고도 단순한 파사드를 시도하였다. 매장의 전체적인 콘셉트는 금속 소재와 현대적인 검은색을 사용하여 산업적 분위기를 유도하였다. 2, 3층을 연결하는 넓은 보이드 공간에는 내부와 상품을 진열할 수 있는 계단을 연결하여 시각적 확장성과 수직적 역동성을 부여하고, 초현실적인 말 그래픽을 통해 소비자의 호기심을 유발하도록 하였다. 잡화류가 있는 1층은 청녹색을 포인트로 노출콘크리트, 열연강판, 컨테이너 등의 소재를 사용하였다. 2층과 3층은 각각 오렌지와 아쿠아 블루의 포인트 색상을 통해 여성과 남성의 공간으로 구분하였다. 또한 자칫 딱딱하고 차가워 보일 수 있는 금속 소재들 사이에 생화나무를 두어 온화하고 몽환적인 분위기를 연출하였다.

Wonderplace Cheongju branch, located at the heart of Cheongju business district, went for a daring but simple facade that allows clear view of the interior considering the complex street atmosphere outside. The overall concept of the design leaned towards an industrial ambiance using metal materials and modern black. The wide void space that connects the 2nd floor and the 3rd is turned into stairs that displays the interior and the products, granting visual expansion and vertical dynamic and attracting customer's curiosity with a surrealist horse graphic.

The 1st floor where miscellaneous goods are displayed and sold is planned out with bluish green accents along with exposed concrete wall, hot rolled steel sheets, and containers. The 2nd and the 3rd floor are respectively highlighted with orange and blue to separate the space for women and men. In addition, live plants and flowers are decorated in between the metallic materials that can feel rather harsh and cold creating a dreamlike atmosphere.

디자인 윤영권 / 때
위치 경기도 성남시 분당구 정자동 163
용도 의류매장
면적 580㎡
마감 바닥 – 셀프 레벨링, 합판, 투명 에폭시 / 벽 – 솔리톤, 가문비나무 목재, 시멘트 블록, 컨테이너, 비닐 페인트 / 천장 – 노출천장, 비닐 페인트
시공팀 심진성, 김진철, 한송희
사진 남궁선, 윤영권

Location 163, Jeongja-dong, Bundang-gu, Seongnam, Gyeonggi-do
Use Fashion shop
Area 580㎡
Finishing Floor - Self leveling, Plywood, Clear epoxy / Wall - Solitone, Spruce, Cement block, Container, Vinyl paint / Ceiling - Exposed ceiling, Vinyl paint
Photographer Namgoong Sun, Yoon Young Kweon

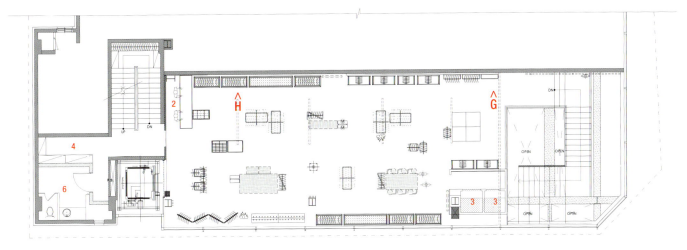

3층 평면도 / 3rd floor plan

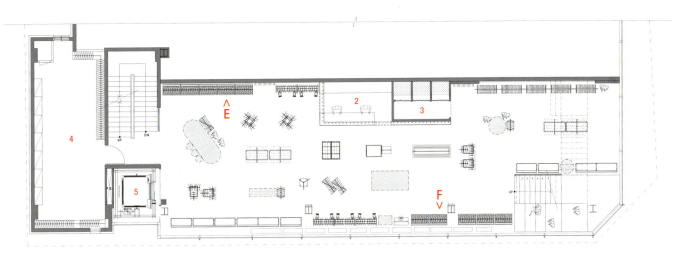

2층 평면도 / 2nd floor plan

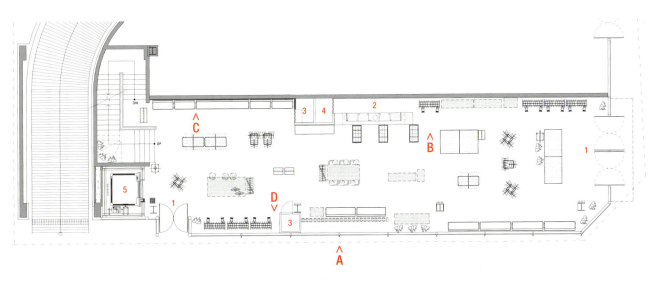

1층 평면도 / 1st floor plan

1 입구 2 카운터 3 피팅룸 4 창고 5 엘리베이터 6 화장실   1 Entrance 2 Counter 3 Fitting room 4 Storage 5 Elevator 6 Toilet

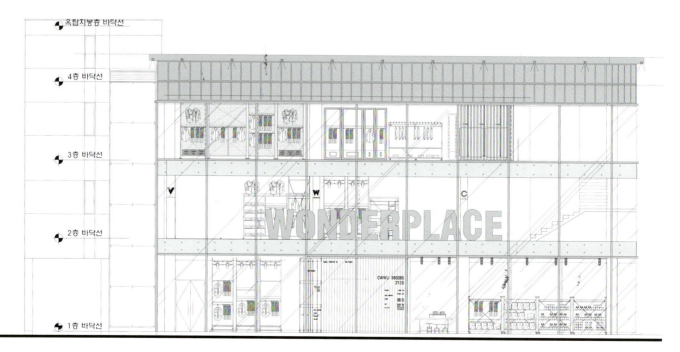

파사드 A / facade A

1 지정 무늬목 2 로고 : LED 조명형 3 선반 : 지정 무늬목 / 프레임 : 열연강판 4 프레임 : 열연강판 5 조명 : 지정 분체도장 6 벽 : 석고보드 위 지정 파벽돌 7 지정 무늬목 / 선반 : 열연강판 8 열연강판 9 조명 : 기성품

1 App. wood veneer 2 Logo : LED lighting type 3 Shelf : app. wood veneer / frame : hot rolled steel sheet 4 Frame : hot rolled steel sheet 5 Lighting : app. powder coated 6 Wall : app. used brick on gypsum board 7 App. wood veneer / shelf : hot rolled steel sheet 8 Hot rolled steel sheet 9 Ready-made lighting

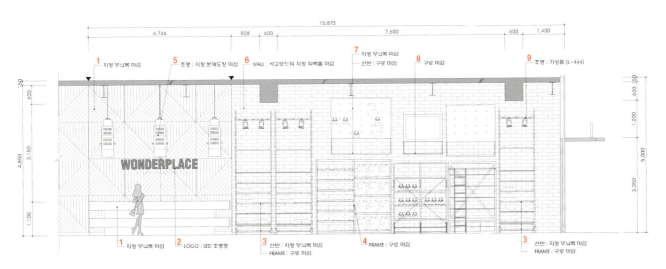

1층 매장 입면 B / 1F store elevation B

1 벽 : 석고보드 위 지정 파벽돌 2 행거 : 열연강판 / 선반 : 지정 무늬목 3 프레임 : 열연강판 4 커튼 : 지정 패브릭 5 파이프 : 열연강판 / 조명 : 기성품 6 파이프 : 열연강판 7 행거 : 열연강판 8 거울 9 선반 : 지정 무늬목 / 프레임 : 열연강판 10 지정 도장 11 벽 : 석고보드 위 지정 파벽돌 / 텍스트 : 지정 도장 12 열연강판 / 벽 : 지정 도장 13 조명 : 기성품 14 창호 : 건축마감 15 프레임 : 지정 분체도장 16 벽 : 지정색 도장 / 카운터 : 폴리카보네이트 조명형 17 계단 : 지정 원목 18 기둥 : 지정 도장 19 텍스트 : 지정색 시트 20 벽 : 지정색 도장

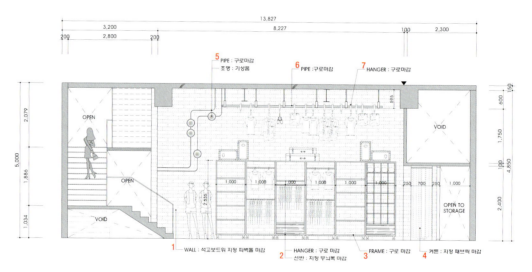

1층 매장 입면 C / 1F store elevation C

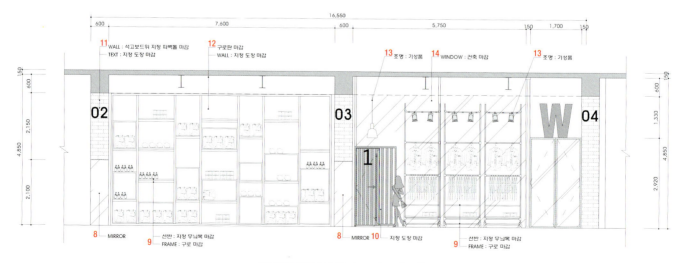

1층 매장 입면 D / 1F store elevation D

1 Wall : app. used brick on gypsum board 2 Hanger : hot rolled steel sheet / shelf : app. wood veneer 3 Frame : hot rolled steel sheet 4 Curtain : app. fabric 5 Pipe : hot rolled steel sheet / lighting : ready-made lighting 6 Pipe : hot rolled steel sheet 7 Hanger : hot rolled steel sheet 8 Mirror 9 Shelf : app. wood veneer / frame : hot rolled steel sheet 10 App. painting 11 Wall : app. used brick on gypsum board / text : app. painting 12 Hot rolled steel sheet / wall : app. painting 13 Ready-made lighting 14 Window : building finishing 15 Frame : app. powder coated 16 Wall : app. color painting / counter : polycarbonate lighting type 17 Stairs : app. wood 18 Column : app. painting 19 Text : app. color sheet 20 Wall : app. color painting

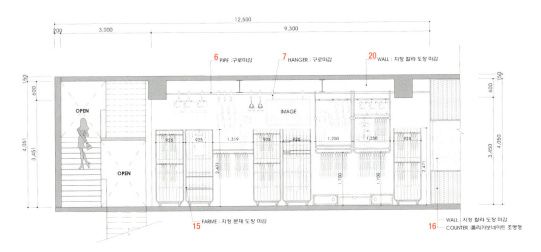

2층 매장 입면 E / 2F store elevation E

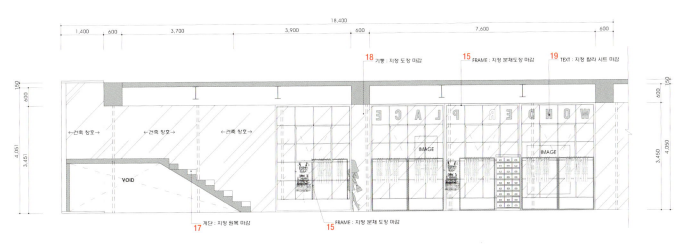

2층 매장 입면 F / 2F store elevation F

1 프레임 : 열연강판 2 벽 : 석고보드 위 지정 파벽돌 3 조명 : 지정 분체도장   1 Frame : hot rolled steel sheet   2 Wall : app. used brick on gypsum board   3 Lighting : app. powder coated

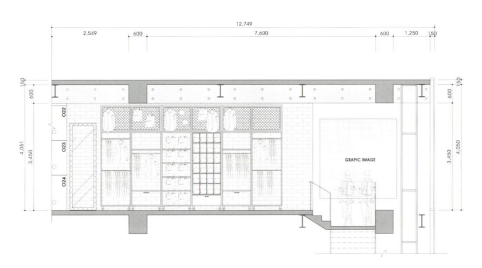

3층 매장 입면 G / 3F store elevation G

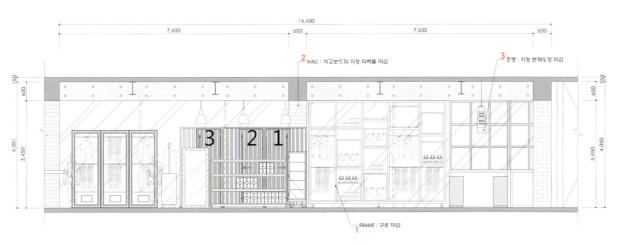

3층 매장 입면 H / 3F store elevation H

KKUN NORI

Friend's Design | Yang Jin Young, Kwon Il Kwon

꾼 노리의 콘셉트는 1920년대 미국에서 금주법을 피해 지하벙커와 같은 자신들만의 아지트를 만들어 음주를 즐긴 것에서 출발하였다. 전반적으로 어두운 분위기의 공간에 방을 넣어줌으로써 1920년대의 아지트를 현대적으로 각색하였다. 공간의 다양성을 위해 각 방의 재료와 형태를 달리하고, 공간을 분할하여 연출하였다. 각 방들은 반폐쇄적인 분리로 독립성을 가지는 동시에 답답한 느낌을 줄였으며, 복도는 천장을 노출시켜 더 넓어 보이는 효과를 주었다. 방들은 획일화된 디자인이 아닌 서로 다른 분위기를 연출하면서, 하나로 어우러질 수 있는 소재를 사용하였다. 철망, 유리, 목재 등 친숙한 재료를 통해 편안함을 주고자 하였다. 또한 공간마다 다른 소재로 호기심을 자극하여 다시 찾고 싶은 공간으로 계획하였다.

The concept of KKUN NORI came from the historical fact that, in the United States during the 1920s, people made their own hiding place like underground bunkers to get around the liquor prohibition law and enjoy drinking. The hideouts from the 1920s were adapted for this modern time pub by putting rooms in a space that has an overall dark ambiance. To add variety to the space, the space is divided up for styling and the shape and materials for each room were differentiated from one another. Each room is half-closed granting independence and eliminating crampedness at the same time. The hallway is designed with an exposed ceiling to make it look more spacious. Instead of a uniform design, each room is styled with different atmosphere. Yet, materials are used to bring all of the rooms in harmony. To create a comfortable atmosphere, familiar materials are used such as wire mesh, glass, and wood. In addition, by using different materials that spark curiosity, the establishment is designed to make the visitors want to come again.

디자인 양진영, 권일권 / (주)프랜즈디자인
위치 경기도 고양시 일산동구 장항동 859
용도 상업
면적 351㎡
마감 바닥 – 타일 / 벽 – 목재, 금속, 도장, 벽돌, 유리, 벽지 / 천장 – 도장
디자인팀 박안나, 노지은
완공 2013. 5
사진 최정복

Location 859, Janghang 2-dong, Ilsandong-gu, Goyang, Gyeonggi-do
Use Commerce
Area 351㎡
Finishing Floor - Tile / Wall - Wood, Metal, Painting, Brick, Glass, Wallpaper / Ceiling - Painting
Completion 2013. 5
Photographer Choi Jeong Bok

천장도 / ceiling plan

평면도 / floor plan

1 입구 2 카운터 3 주방 4 보조 주방 5 창고   1 Entrance 2 Counter 3 Kitchen 4 Sub kitchen 5 Storage

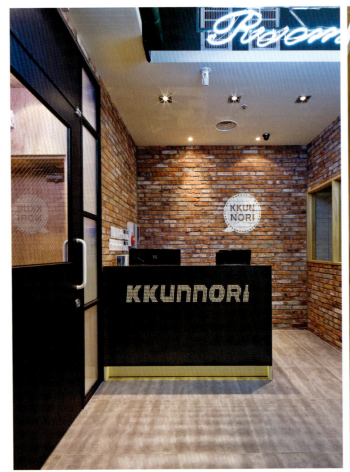 

1 T5 무늬유리 / 목재 프레임 위 투명 래커 / 240X55 고벽돌, 시멘트 줄눈 2 240X55 고벽돌 위 그래픽 이미지 부분 도장 3 500X500 이미지 패널 설치, 30° 기울여 시공 4 500X850 문 타공, T7 망입유리 / 목재 도어 위 크림색 도장 5 타공판 위 크림색 도장 / T5 무늬유리 6 노출천정 : 수성 도장 / 간접 등박스 시공, 비닐 페인트 도장 7 OBS 합판, 투명 래커 / 20X20 철제 위 크림색 도장 8 카운터 : 열연강판 위 투명래커 9 글씨 타공(내부 : LED 조명 글씨 상하부에 매입) 10 T7 망입유리 시공 / 240X55 고벽돌, 시멘트 줄눈 11 노출천정 : 수성 도장 12 간접 등박스 시공, 비닐 페인트 도장 / 갈바륨 철판 레이저 타공판 위 T10 아크릴 부착 13 상부 : 스포트 라이트 시공, 하부 : 할로겐 시공

1 T5 pattern glass / clear lacquer on wood frame / 240X55 old brick, cement masonry joint 2 Graphic image partial painting on 240X55 old brick 3 500X500 image panel gradient of 30° installed 4 500X850 door perforated, T7 wired glass / cream color painting on wood door 5 Cream color painting on perforated plate / T5 pattern glass 6 Exposed ceiling : water painting / indirect lighting box installed, vinyl paint painting 7 OBS plywood, clear lacquer / cream color painting on 20X20 steel 8 Counter : clear lacquer on hot rolled steel sheet 9 Letter perforated (inside : LED lighting embedded at the bottom and the top of letters) 10 T7 wired glass installed / 240X55 old brick, cement masonry joint 11 Exposed ceiling : water painting 12 Indirect lighting box installed, vinyl paint painting / T10 acryl attached on laser perforated galvalume plate 13 Top : spot light installed, bottom : halogen installed

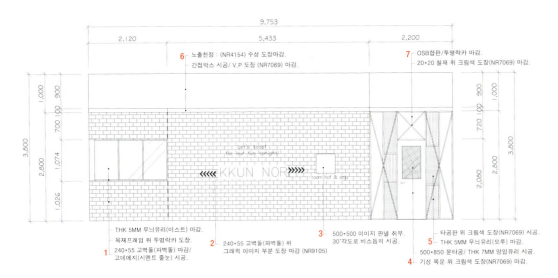

복도 입면 A / corridor elevation A

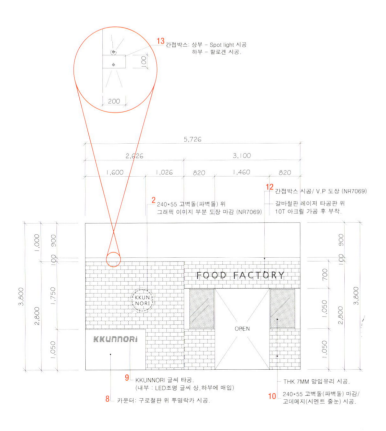

리셉션 입면 B / reception elevation B

리셉션 입면 C / reception elevation C

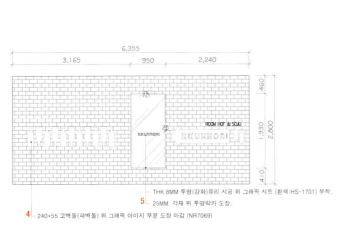

복도 입면 D / corridor elevation D

복도 입면 E / corridor elevation E

복도 입면 F / corridor elevation F

복도 입면 G / corridor elevation G

복도 입면 H / corridor elevation H

1 30X60 각파이프 위 흑색 래커 도장 / T5 무늬유리   2 입구문 : 열연강판 위 투명 래커, T7 망입유리   3 열연강판 위 투명 래커 / 네온간판 시공   4 240X55 고벽돌 위 그래픽 이미지 부분 도장   5 T8 투명 강화유리 위 그래픽 시트 / 25mm 각재 위 투명 래커   6 T10 투명 폴리카보네이트 시공 / 30X60 각파이프 위 크림색 래커 / T8 투명 강화유리 위 솔벤 시트 설치   7 500X850 문 타공, T7 망입유리 시공 / 목재 도어 위 크림색 도장   8 창틀 : 20X20 각파이프, 크림색 래커   9 240X55 고벽돌 / 시멘트 줄눈 / 카운터 : 열연강판 위 투명 래커   10 열연강판 위 투명 래커   11 노출천장 : 수성 도장 / 간접 등박스 시공, 비닐 페인트 도장   12 450X850 문 타공, T7 망입 유리 시공 / 우드 도어 위 크림색 도장   13 T10 흰색 폴리카보네이트 시공 / 30X60 각파이프 위 흑색 래커 / T8 투명 강화유리 위 솔벤 시트   14 창틀 : 20X20 각파이프, 흑색 래커(T5 유리 시공)   15 크림색 도장 마감 / 디자인 그래픽 부착 / 30X60 각파이프 위 흑색 래커   16 MDF 위 열연강판   17 MDF 위 인테리어 필름   18 T5 투명유리 / T18 MDF 위 인테리어 필름 / 서랍 : T18 MDF 위 크림색 도장

1 Black lacquer painting on 30X60 square pipe / T5 pattern glass   2 Entrance door : clear lacquer on hot rolled steel sheet, T7 wired glass   3 Clear lacquer on hot rolled steel sheet / neon sign installed   4 Graphic image partial painting on 240X55 old brick   5 Graphic sheet on T8 clear tempered glass / clear lacquer on 25mm square timber   6 T10 clear polycarbonate installed / cream color lacquer on 30X60 square pipe / solvent sheet on T8 clear tempered glass   7 500X850 door perforated, T7 wired glass installed / cream color lacquer on wood door   8 Window frame : 20X20 square pipe, cream color lacquer   9 240X55 old brick / cement masonry joint / counter : clear lacquer on hot rolled steel sheet   10 Clear lacquer on hot rolled steel sheet   11 Exposed ceiling : water paint / indirect lighting box installed, vinyl paint painting   12 450X850 door perforated, T7 wired glass installed / cream color lacquer on wood door   13 T10 white polycarbonate installed / black lacquer on 30X60 square pipe / solvent sheet on T8 clear tempered glass   14 Window frame : 20X20 square paipe, black lacquer (T5 glass installed)   15 Cream color painting / design graphic attached / 30X60 square pipe   16 Hot rolled steel sheet on MDF   17 Interior film on MDF   18 T5 clear glass / interior film on T18 MDF / shelf : cream color painting on T18

카운터 평면 I1 / counter top view I1

카운터 후면 I2 / counter rear view I2

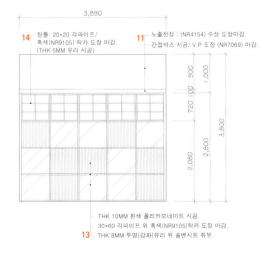

복도 입면 J / corridor elevation J

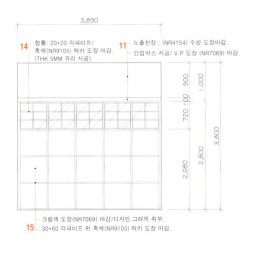

복도 입면 K / corridor elevation K

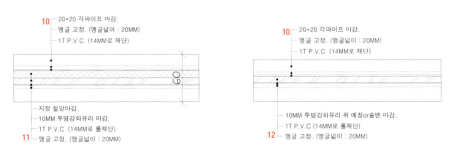

단면 M / section M   단면 N / section N

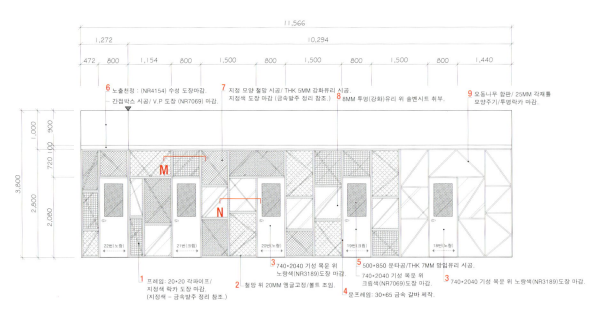

복도 입면 L / corridor elevation L

1 프레임 : 20X20 각파이프, 지정색 래커 도장   2 철망 위 20mm 앵글 고정, 볼트 조임   3 740X2040 우드 도어 위 노란색 도장   4 도어 프레임 : 30X65 금속 갈바륨 제작   5 500X850 도어 타공, T7 망입유리 시공   6 노출천장 : 수성 도장 / 간접 등박스 시공, 비닐 페인트 도장   7 지정 모양 철망, T5 강화유리, 지정색 도장   8 T8 투명 강화유리 위 솔벤 시트   9 오동나무 합판, 25mm 프레임, 투명 래커   10 20X20 각파이프 / 20mm 앵글 고정 / 14mm PVC   11 지정 철망 / T10 투명 강화유리 / 14mm PVC / 20mm 앵글 고정   12 10mm 투명 강화유리 위 에칭 또는 솔벤 마감 / 14mm PVC / 20mm 앵글 고정   13 500X850 도어 타공, T7 망입유리 시공 / 740X2040 우드 도어 위 오동나무 합판, 투명 래커

1 Frame : 20X20 square pipe, app. color lacquer painting   2 20mm angle fix on mesh, bolt tighten   3 Yellow painting on 740X2040 wood door   4 Door frame : 30X65 metal galvalume making   5 500X850 door perforated, T7 wired glass installed   6 Exposed ceiling : water painting / indirect lighting box installed, vinyl paint   7 App. shape mesh, T5 tempered glass, app. painting   8 Solvent sheet on T8 clear tempered glass   9 Paulownia coreana plywood, 25mm frame, clear lacquer   10 20X20 square pipe / 20mm angle fix / 14mm PVC   11 App. mesh / T10 clear tempered glass / 14mm PVC / 20mm algle fix   12 Etching or solvent on 10mm clear tempered glass / 14mm PVC / 20mm angle fix   13 500X850 door perforated, T7 wired glass / Paulownia coreana plywood on 740X2040 wood door, clear lacquer

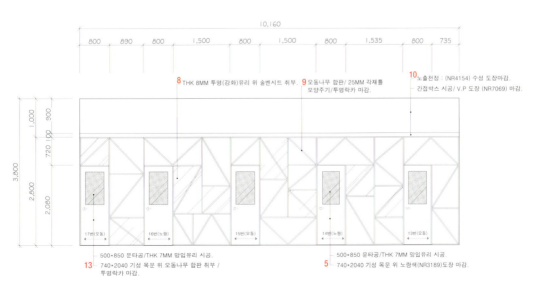

복도 입면 O / corridor elevation O

테이블 측면 S1 / table side view S1

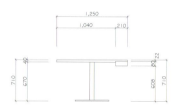

테이블 정면 S2 / table front view S2

룸 입면 P / room elevation P

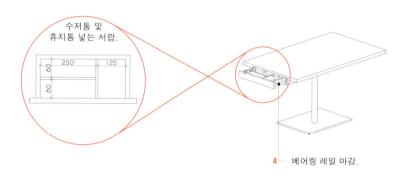

테이블 투시도 / table perspective view

룸 입면 Q / room elevation Q

룸 입면 R / room elevation R

1 벽 : 콘센트 2 창틀 : 20X20 각파이프, 흑색 래커 도장 3 팬던트 조명 4 베어링 마감 5 상부 : 25mm 각재, T5 투명 유리 6 지정색 도장 7 벽등 시공 / 지정색 도장 8 슈퍼화인 도장

1 Wall : socket 2 Window frame : 20X20 square pipe, black lacquer painting 3 Pendant 4 Bearing finish 5 Top : 25mm square timber, T5 clear glass 6 App. color painting 7 Bracket installed / app. color painting 8 Super fine painting

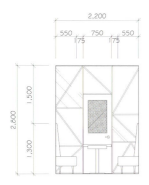

룸 입면 T / room elevation T

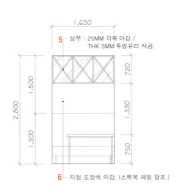

룸 입면 U / room elevation U

룸 입면 V / room elevation V

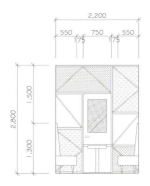

룸 입면 W / room elevation W

룸 입면 X / room elevation X

룸 입면 Y / room elevation Y

KWANPEN VER.2

Betwin Space Design | Kim Jung Gon, Oh Hwan Woo

콴펜은 명품 싱가포르 핸드메이드 악어가죽 핸드백 브랜드로, 3년 전 국내에 처음 개장한 매장의 이전에 따른 두 번째 디자인 작업을 진행하였다. 매장이 빌딩 내부에 위치하여 외부에서의 가시성이 떨어지므로, 매장 외부의 별도 공간에 악어가죽의 패턴을 음각형태의 입체 패턴타일로 제작한 전작 파사드의 미니어처 버전으로 독립 쇼윈도를 제작하였다. 내부 공간은 '반전' 이라는 키워드를 가지고 전작에서 갖고 있던 디자인 요소와 함께 클래식한 장식의 어두운 벽면을 따라 상품을 진열하였다. 중앙의 미니멀한 백색의 홀 공간을 따라 복도식 구조로 동선을 분리하고, 원웨이 유리를 사용하여 상품에 대한 고객의 집중도를 높이고자 하였다.

Kwanpen is a luxury handmade crocodile handbag brand of Singapore. This project is the second design work following the first establishment, which opened in Korea for the first time three years ago. Since the shop is located inside the building and lacks visibility from the outside, an independent show window was installed at a separate place outside the shop. The show window is a miniature version of the previous facade built with intaglio-style three-dimensional pattern tiles patterned after crocodile leather. Applying the keyword 'reversal' into the design, the interior of the shop was displayed with products along the dark and classically decorated wall in addition to design elements used in the previous project. From the minimal white hall space at the center, the moving line was separated in a hallway system. Also customer's attention for the products was heightened using a one-way glass.

디자인 김정곤, 오환우 / 비트윈스페이스디자인
위치 서울특별시 강남구 청담동 100 1층
용도 상업
면적 120㎡
마감 바닥 - 우드 플로링, 타일 / 벽 - 목재 패널, 원웨이 유리 / 천장 - 비닐 페인트
완공 2013. 3
디자인팀 임희상, 장준이, 정석병
시공 비트윈스페이스디자인
사진 이표준

Location 1F, 100, Cheongdam-dong, Gangnam-gu, Seoul
Use Shop
Area 120㎡
Finishing Floor - Wood flooring, Tile / Wall - Wood panel, One way glass / Ceiling - Vinyl paint
Completion 2013. 3
Photographer Lee pyo Joon

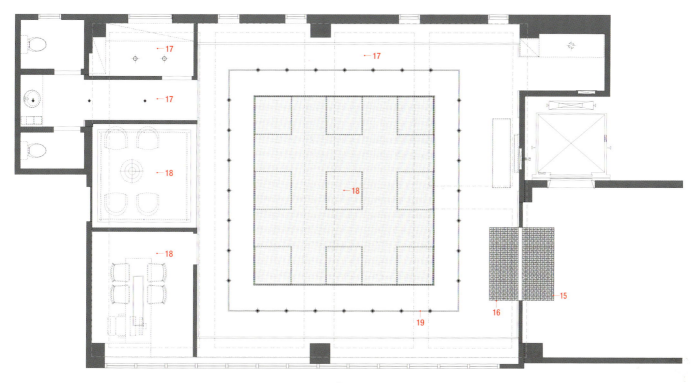

천장도 / ceiling plan

평면도 / floor plan

1 로비 2 입구 3 복도 4 계산대 5 홀 6 창고 7 화장실 8 휴게공간 9 사무실 10 재고함 & 진열장 11 재고함 12 지정 백색 대리석 13 1,000X1,000X700 아일랜드형 가구 14 지정 검은색 우드 플로링 15 주물성형 금속 패턴 위 지정 백색 도장 16 주물성형 금속 패턴 위 지정 검은색 도장 17 노출천장 위 지정 비닐 페인트 18 지정 스트레치 천장 시스템 19 트랙 조명

1 Lobby 2 Entrance 3 Corridor 4 Counter desk 5 Hall 6 Storage 7 Toilet 8 Rest zone 9 Office 10 Stock & display 11 Stock 12 App. white marble 13 1,000X1,000X700 Island furniture 14 App. black wood flooring 15 App. white painting on casting forming metal pattern 16 App. black painting on casting forming metal pattern 17 App. vinyl paint on exposed ceiling 18 App. stretch ceiling system 19 Track lighting

1 노출 천장 : 지정색 도장　**2** T1.2 갈바륨 절곡 후 백색 래커 도장, 지정색 도장　**3** T6 원웨이 유리　**4** 프레임 : 주물성형 금속 패턴 위 지정 검은색 도장　**5** 지정 무늬목 위 무광 검은색 오일 스테인　**6** 진열장 문 : 지정 무늬목 위 무광 검은색 오일 스테인

1 Exposed ceiling : app. color painting　**2** White lacquer painting after T1.2 galvalume bending, app. color painting　**3** T6 one way mirror glass　**4** Frame : app. black painting on casting forming metal pattern　**5** Matt black oil stain on app. wood veneer　**6** Display door : matt black oil stain on app. wood veneer

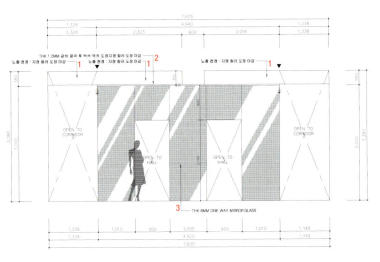

홀 입면 A / hall elevation A

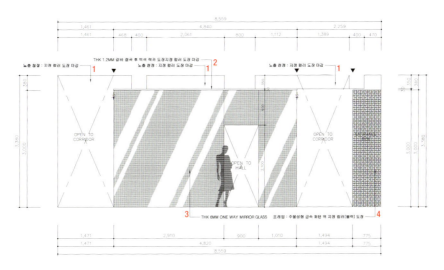

복도 입면 B / corridor elevation B

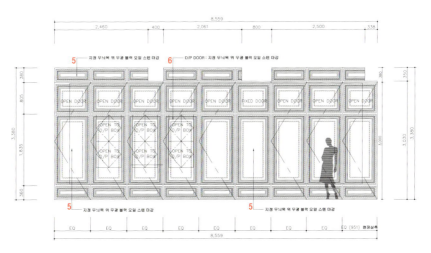

복도 입면 C / corridor elevation C

1 지정 무늬목 위 무광 검은색 오일 스테인   2 T5 은경 부착   3 액자 타입 거울   4 프레임 : 주물성형 금속 패턴 위 지정색 도장   5 T12 강화유리 문   6 지정색 도장   7 T1.2 갈바륨 절곡 후 백색 래커 도장, 지정색 도장
8 노출 천장 : 지정색 도장   9 T6 원웨이 유리   10 문 : 지정 무늬목 위 무광 검은색 오일 스테인   11 측면 수납장 : 지정색 도장

1 Matt black oil stain on app. wood veneer   2 T5 silver mirror attached   3 Frame-type mirror   4 Frame : app. color painting on casting forming metal pattern   5 T12 tempered glass door   6 App. color painting   7 White lacquer painting after T1.2 galvalume bending, app. color painting   8 Exposed ceiling : app. color painting   9 T6 one way mirror glass   10 Door : matt black oil stain on app. wood veneer   11 Side storage closet : app. color painting

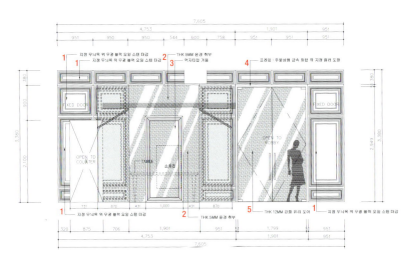

복도 입면 D / corridor elevation D

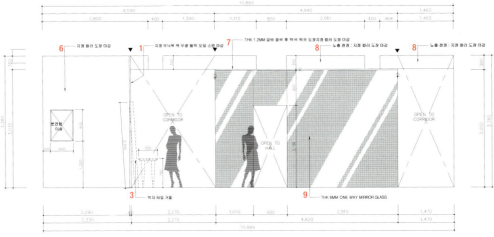

복도 입면 E / corridor elevation E

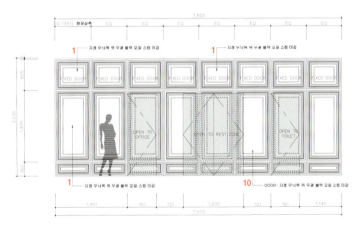

복도 입면 F / corridor elevation F

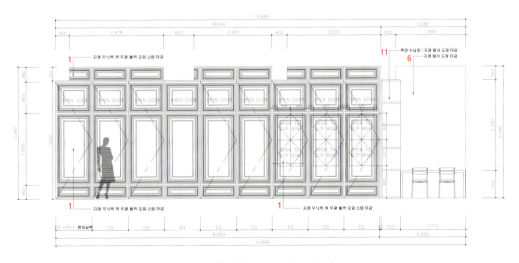

복도 입면 G / corridor elevation G

BONBONROUGE AT ROOFTOP

melloncolie fantastic space LITA | Kim Jae Hwa

컵케익 카페 봉봉루즈의 낡고 오래된 옥탑층에 쿠킹스튜디오 봉봉루즈 루프탑이 새롭게 자리 잡았다. 공간은 메인 키친공간과 음식을 먹으며 작은 모임을 할 수 있는 프라이빗룸, 쉐프 작업실의 용도로 분리된다. 오픈된 메인 키친은 요리를 시연할 수 있는 공간과 수업할 수 있는 공간으로 나누어져 있으며 정갈한 주방공간과 기능성을 살리기 위하여 금속을 주로 사용하였다. 또한 차가워 보이지 않도록 원목 오크 재질을 긴 테이블과 작업대에 적절히 사용하여 전체적으로 모던한 쿠킹스튜디오를 연출하였다. 톤다운된 벽체를 따라 금속 프레임의 유리 슬라이딩 도어를 밀고 들어가면 다른 컨셉의 프라이빗룸이 나타난다. 클래식한 분위기의 프라이빗 룸은 전체적인 몰딩마감으로 공간을 정갈하게 연출하였으며, 화이트톤과 그레이톤의 컬러믹스와 스케일감있는 오크 원목 및 린넨소재의 원단을 매치하여 전반적인 공간의 분위기를 부드럽게 연출하였다.

A cooking studio Bonbonrouge at Rooftop settled in on the old and worn out roof top of cupcake cafe Bonbonrouge. The space is divided into three sections: the main kitchen area, a private room where people can have a small gathering while eating, and a chef's studio. The main open-kitchen is divided into an area where cooking demonstrations take place and an area for cooking classes. It is designed mainly with metals to deliver a clean and neat kitchen environment and heighten its functionality. Preventing it from appearing cold, oak hardwood was appropriately applied on the long table and work surface giving an overall modern look to the cooking studio. Opening the metal framed glass sliding door along the toned down wall, one can step into the private room built with a different concept. The private room presenting a classical atmosphere is neatly styled with molding finishing. The overall space ambiance delivers a soft touch with the combination of white and gray-tone colors and the matching of oak hardwood and linen fabrics.

디자인 김재화 / 멜랑콜리 판타스틱 스페이스 리타
위치 서울특별시 양천구 신정동 900-1
용도 카페 & 쿠킹 스튜디오
면적 81㎡
마감 바닥 – 무기질 도장 / 벽 – 비닐 페인트 / 천장 – 비닐 페인트
설계기간 2012. 9 ~ 2012. 11
완공 2012. 11
사진 김주원

Location 900-1, Sinjeong-dong, Yangcheon-gu, Seoul
Use Cafe & Cooking studio
Area 81㎡
Finishing Floor - Inorganic painting / Wall - Vinyl paint / Ceiling - Vinyl paint
Design period 2012. 9 ~ 2012. 11
Completion 2012. 11
Photographer Kim Ju Won

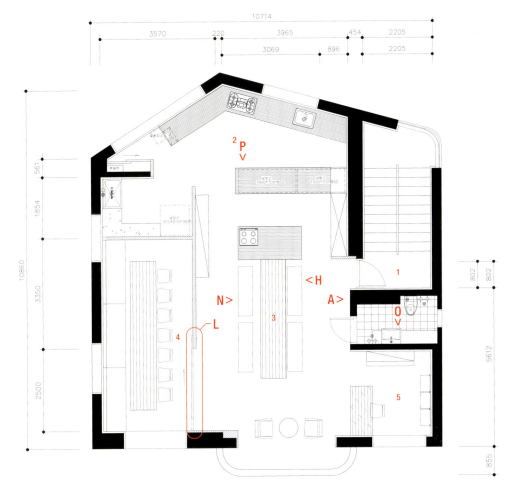

1 입구 2 오픈 키친 3 쿠킹 클래스존 4 프라이빗룸
5 작업실

1 Entrance 2 Open kitchen 3 Cooking class zone
4 Private room 5 Work area

평면도 / floor plan

1 T5 MDF 위 무늬목 / T24 MDF 위 무늬목 / T5 MDF 위 무늬목 / T24 MDF 위 무늬목 / T5 MDF 위 무늬목 / T24 MDF 위 무늬목 / T5 MDF 위 무늬목 / T9 MDF 위 T1.2 스테인리스 스틸 / 30X30 각재 위 T18 원목 2 T15 MDF 위 지정색 에나멜 도장 / T15 MDF 위 지정 무늬목 3 지정색 수성 도장 / T1.2 갈바륨 위 지정색 에나멜 도장 / T9 강화유리 / 지정색 소부도장 4 지정색 수성 도장 / 지정색 에나멜 도장 / 지정색 에나멜 도장 5 지정색 수성 도장 6 T9 MDF 위 T1.2 스테인리스 스틸 / T18 지정 원목 7 T9 MDF 위 T1.2 스테인리스 스틸 / T18 MDF 위 우레탄 도장 8 T18 MDF 위 우레탄 도장 9 30X30 각재 10 T9 MDF 위 T1.2 스테인리스 스틸 11 T1.2 갈바륨 위 지정색 에나멜 도장 / T9 강화유리 / 제작 손잡이 지정색 소부도장 / T1.2 갈바륨 위 지정색 에나멜 도장

1 Wood veneer on T5 MDF / wood veneer on T24 MDF / wood veneer on T5 MDF / wood veneer on T24 MDF / wood veneer on T5 MDF / wood veneer on T24 MDF / wood veneer on T5 MDF / T1.2 stainless steel on T9 MDF / T18 wood on 30X30 square timber 2 App. wood veneer on T15 MDF 3 App. water painting / app. enamel painting on T1.2 galvalume / T9 tempered glass / app. color baked painting / app. color enamel painting on T1.2 galvalume 4 App. water painting / app. color enamel painting / app. color enamel painting 5 App. color water paint 6 T1.2 stainless steel on T9 MDF / App. T18 wood 7 T1.2 stainless steel on T9 MDF / urethane painting on T18 MDF 8 Urethane painting on T18 MDF 9 30X30 square timber 10 T1.2 stainless steel on T9 MDF 11 App. color enamel painting on T1.2 galvalume / T9 tempered glass / customized handle, app. baked painting / app. color enamel painting on T1.2 galvalume

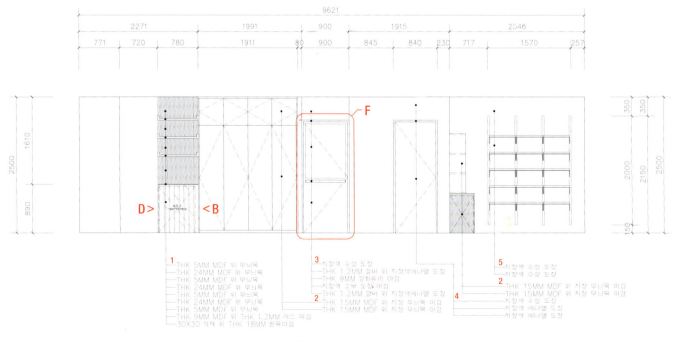

홀 입면 A / hall elevation A

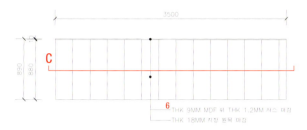

가구 정면 B / furniture front view B

가구 단면 C / furniture section C

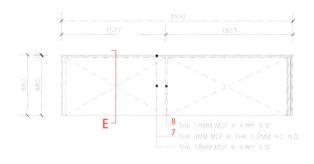

가구 후면 D / furniture rear view D

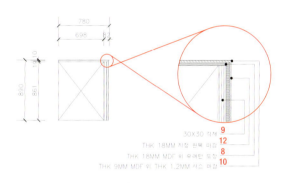

가구 단면 E / furniture section E

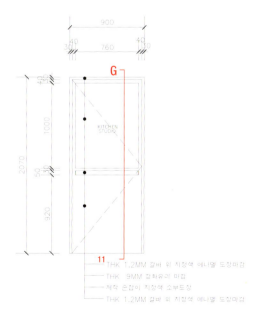

문 정면 F / door front view F

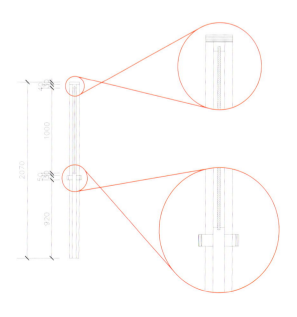

문 단면 G / door section G

1 T9.5 석고보드 위 지정색 수성 도장 / 20X40 각파이프 위 T18 원목 / T9.5 석고보드 위 지정색 수성 도장 / 20X40 각파이프 위 T18 원목 / T9.5 석고보드 위 지정색 수성 도장   2 T9 MDF 위 T1.2 스테인리스 스틸   3 20X40 금속 각프레임 위 지정 원목   4 T5 평철 위 지정색 도장   5 T10 평철   6 T1.2 갈바륨 위 지정색 에나멜 도장   7 T12 강화유리

1 App. color water painting on T9.5 gypsum board / T18 wood on 20X40 square pipe / app. color water painting on T9.5 gypsum board / T18 wood on 20X40 square pipe / app. color water painting on T9.5 gypsum board   2 T1.2 stainless steel on T9 MDF   3 App. wood on 20X40 metal square frame   4 App. color painting on T5 flat steel bar   5 T10 flat steel bar   6 App. color enamel painting on T1.2 galvalume   7 T12 tempered glass

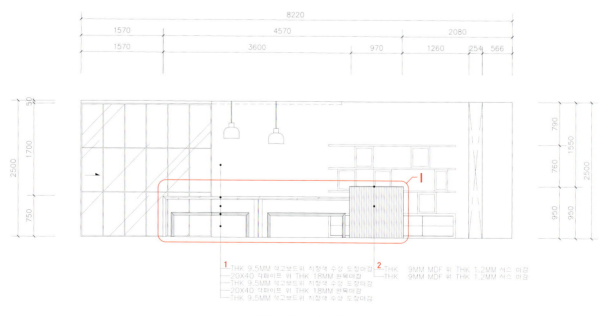

홀 입면 H / hall elevation H

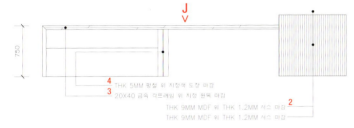

가구 정면 I / furniture front view I

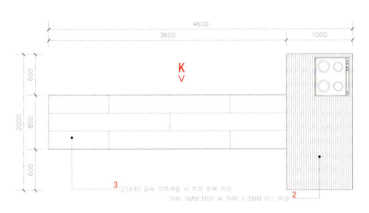

가구 평면 J / furniture top view J

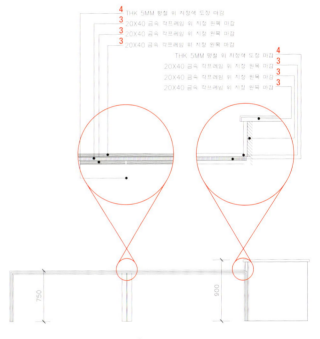

가구 후면 K / furniture rear view K

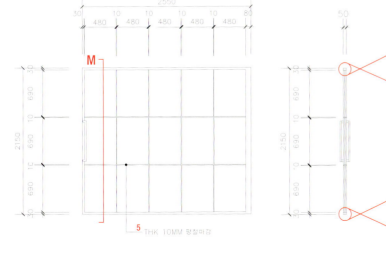

슬라이딩 도어 정면 L / sliding door front view L

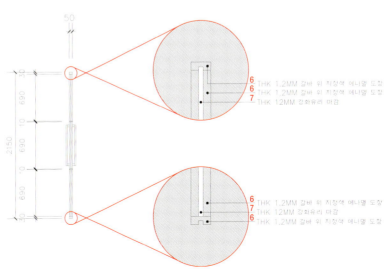

슬라이딩 도어 단면 M / sliding door section M

1 T5 MDF 위 무늬목 / T24 MDF 위 무늬목 / T5 MDF 위 무늬목 / T24 MDF 위 무늬목 / T5 MDF 위 무늬목 / T24 MDF 위 무늬목 / T5 MDF 위 무늬목 / T9 MDF 위 T1.2 스테인리스 스틸 / T9 MDF 위 T1.2 스테인리스 스틸 2 T9 MDF 위 T1.2 스테인리스 스틸 3 20X40 금속 각재 위 T18 원목 4 T5 평철 위 지정색 에나멜 도장 5 지정 타일 / 제작 유리 수납장 설치 / 지정 타일 / 30X30 금속 프레임 위 T9 MDF 위 지정 무늬목 / 지정 타일 / 30X30 금속 프레임 위 T9 MDF 위 지정 무늬목 / 지정 타일

1 Wood veneer on T5 MDF / wood veneer on T24 MDF / wood veneer on T5 MDF / wood veneer on T24 MDF / wood veneer on T5 MDF / wood veneer on T24 MDF / wood veneer on T5 MDF / T1.2 stainless steel on T9 MDF / T1.2 stainless steel on T9 MDF 2 T1.2 stainless steel on T9 MDF 3 T18 wood on 20X40 metal square timber 4 App. color enamel painting on T5 flat steel bar 5 App. tile / customized glass drawer installed / app. tile / app. wood veneer on T9 MDF on 30X30 metal frame / app. wood veneer on T9 MDF on 30X30 metal frame / app. tile

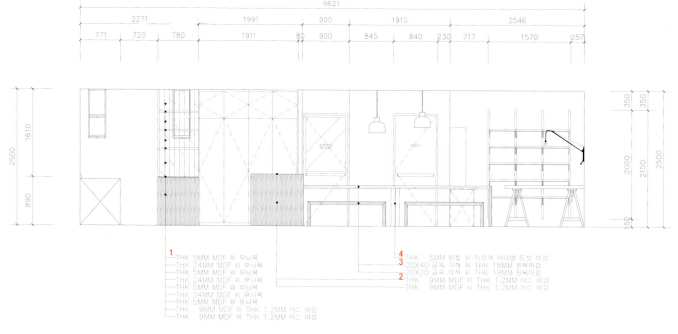

홀 입면 N / hall elevation N

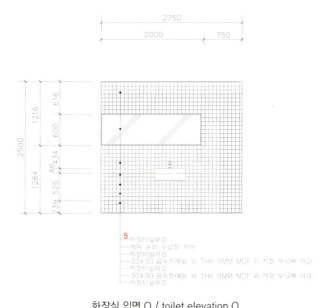

화장실 입면 O / toilet elevation O

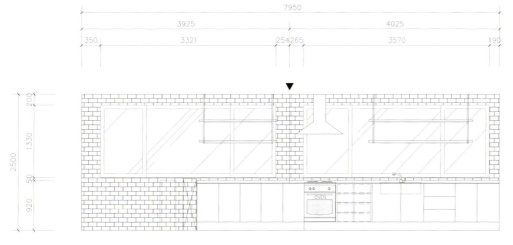

홀 입면 P / hall elevation P

JACQUELINE

DESIGN STUDIO | Kim Jong Ho, Baek Soo Heum, Shin Kwang Jin

재클린은 합리성과 개성을 추구한 프로젝트로, 도시적이고 세련된 이미지와 클래식의 조화를 통해 고급스러우면서도 개성 있는 공간으로 디자인되었다. 대기공간은 테라스에 면하도록 하여 옥외 테라스도 활용하도록 계획하였고, 헤어존은 유리창이 면한 밝은 공간에 배치하였다. 리셉션 공간은 엘리베이터 홀에 근접하게 배치하고 네일샵, 메이크업 룸과 연계하였다. 리셉션공간과 엘리베이터 홀 및 네일샵이 면하는 복도 부분은 클래식 몰딩으로 구성한 패널의 사각패턴으로 벽면과 천장을 마감하여 고급스럽고 우아한 분위기를 연출하였으며, 홀과 복도 부분의 바닥은 에폭시 마감으로 모던한 느낌의 대비를 주고자 하였다. 헤어존은 스테인리스 슈퍼미러 프레임 거울의 반복과 클래식한 느낌의 갓 형태의 스탠드 조명을 배치하였으며, 창과 면한 공간은 백색 커튼을 이용하여 자연채광을 가리는 동시에 우아한 느낌을 주고자 하였다.

A project that aimed for rationality and individuality, Jacqueline was designed to be a space that is classy and unique from the harmony of urbanely sophisticated images and the classic. The waiting area is planned adjacent to the terrace so that it can be used as an outdoor terrace as well; the hair zone is arranged in a bright space that faces the windows. The reception area is placed close to the elevator hall and is connected to the nail shop and the make-up room. In the hallway area, to where the reception area, the elevator hall, and the nail shop are faced, the walls and the ceiling are finished with the squared pattern from the panels composed of classic moldings, thus creating a classy and elegant ambience. The floor on the hallway, on the other hand, gives a contrasting modern effect with epoxy finish. The hair zone is arranged with mirrors framed with super-mirror-polished stainless steel along with stand lamps with shades that have a classical feel. White curtains are used in the space facing the windows to shield natural light and concurrently produce an elegant effect.

디자인 김종호, 백수흠, 신광진 / (주)디자인스튜디오
위치 서울특별시 청담2동 90-19
용도 미용실
면적 294.13m²
마감 바닥 - 에폭시 / 벽 - 패널 위 래커 / 천장 - 비닐 페인트
디자인팀 이은혜, 류제연
시공팀 정구일
사진 (주)디자인스튜디오 제공

Location 90-19, Cheongdam 2-dong, Seoul
Use Hair salon
Area 294.13m²
Finishing Floor - Epoxy / Wall - Lacquer on panel / Ceiling - Vinyl paint
Photos offer DESIGN STUDIO

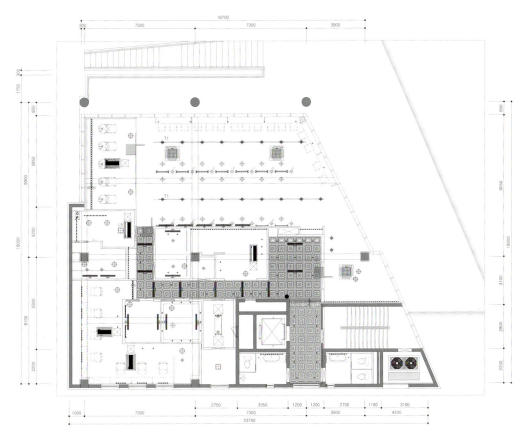

천장도 / ceiling plan

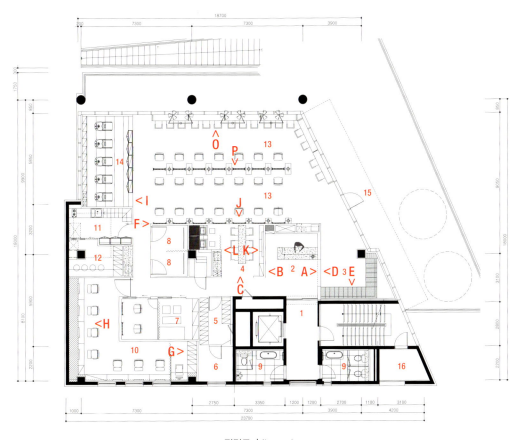

평면도 / floor plan

1 입구 **2** 리셉션 **3** 대기공간 **4** 네일바 **5** 락커룸 **6** 보일러실 **7** 상담실 / 원장실 **8** 탈의실 **9** 화장실 **10** 메이크업룸 **11** 탕비실 **12** 직원실 **13** 헤어존 **14** 샴푸실 **15** 테라스

1 Entrance **2** Reception **3** Waiting area **4** Nail bar **5** Locker room **6** Boiler room **7** Counseling room / director's room **8** Changing room **9** Toilet **10** Make-up room **11** Canteen **12** Staff room **13** Hair zone **14** Sampoo room **15** Terrace

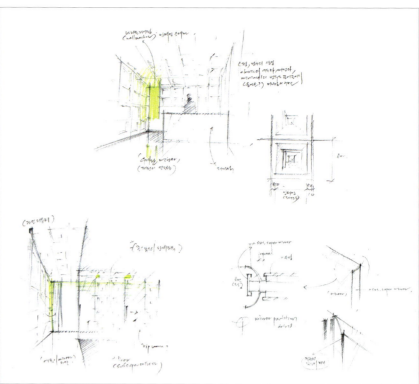

1 걸레받이 : 지정 메인 도장 2 지정 패널 위 도장 3 은경 위 라인에칭 4 지정 도장 5 후면 바리솔 마감(탈착식) / 선반 : 지정 도장 6 지정 대리석 7 선반 : 지정 도장 8 바리솔 9 거울 위 지정 시트 10 지정 사인 11 지정 시트 12 지정 패브릭 가구

1 Baseboard : app. main painting 2 App. painting on panel 3 Line etching on silver mirror 4 App. painting 5 Backside barrisol (separable) / shelf : app. painting 6 App. marble 7 Shelf : app. painting 8 Barrisol 9 App. sheet on mirror 10 App. sign 11 App. sheet 12 App. fabric furniture

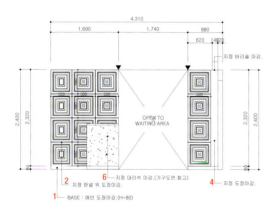

리셉션 입면 A / reception elevation A

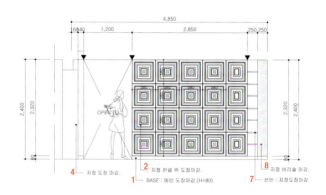

리셉션 입면 B / reception elevation B

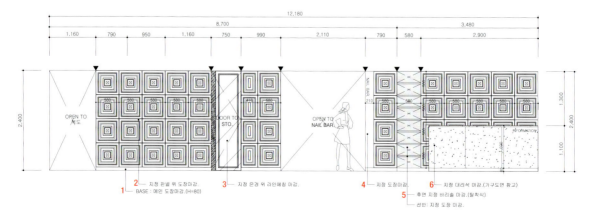

리셉션 입면 C / reception elevation C

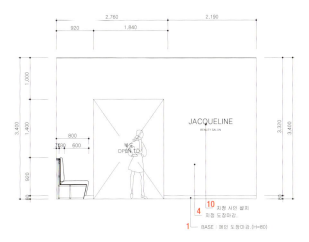

대기실 입면 D / waiting area elevation D

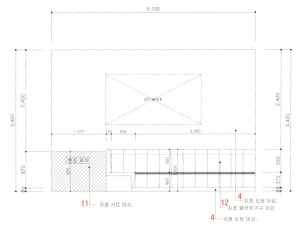

대기실 입면 E / waiting area elevation E

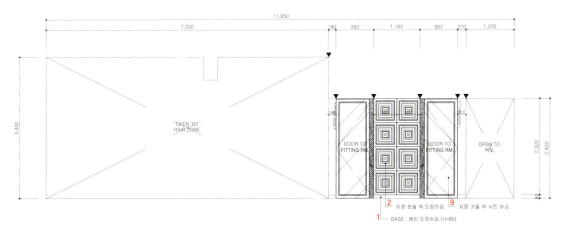

복도 입면 F / corridor elevation F

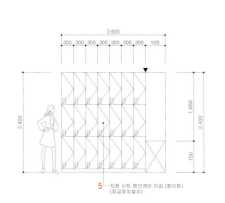

메이크업룸 입면 G / make-up room elevation G

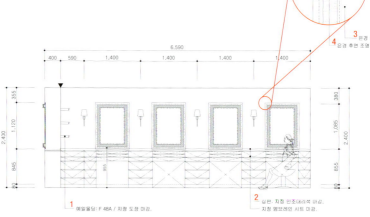

메이크업룸 입면 H / make-up room elevation H

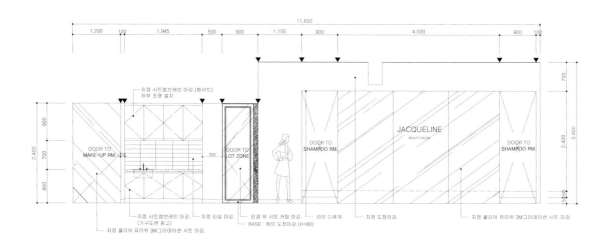

복도 입면 I / corridor elevation I

1 몰딩 : 지정 도장 2 상판 : 지정 인조대리석 / 지정 멤브레인 시트 3 은경 4 은경 후면 조명 설치 5 지정 흰색 멤브레인 시트 6 지정 몰딩 위 도장 7 지정 선반 설치 / 지정 도장 8 지정 도장 / 지정 패브릭 / 지정 인조 대리석 / 상판 : 인조 대리석 / 걸레받이 : 지정 스테인리스 스틸 9 상판 : 지정 인조 대리석 10 선반 현장설치

1 Moulding : app. painting 2 Tabletop : app. artificial marble 3 Silver mirror 4 Lighting embedded back side of silver mirror 5 App. white membrane sheet 6 Painting on app. moulding 7 App. shelf installed / app. painting 8 App. painting / app. fabric / app. mock marble / tabletop : mock marble / base : app. stainless steel 9 Tabletop : app. mock marble 10 Shelf installed

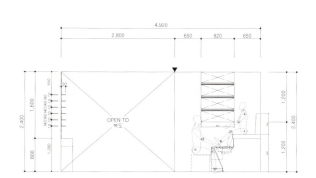

네일바 입면 J / nail bar elevation J

수납장 정면 M / shelf front view M

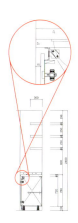

수납장 단면 N / shelf section N

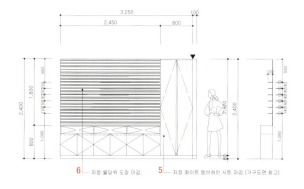

네일바 입면 K / nail bar elevation K

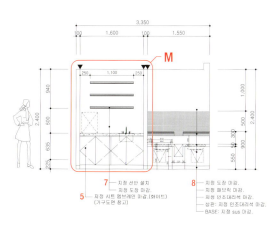

네일바 입면 L / nail bar elevation L

47

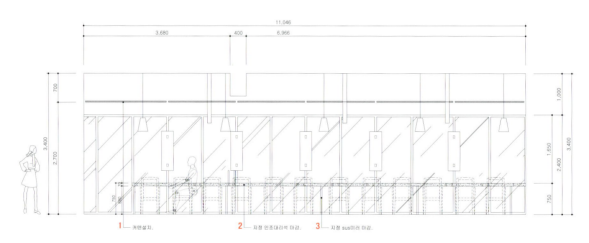

헤어존 입면 O / hair zone elevation O

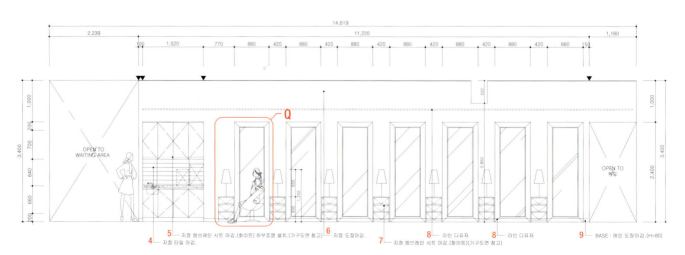

헤어존 입면 P / hair zone elevation P

1 커튼 설치 2 지정 인조 대리석 3 지정 스테인리스 스틸 4 지정 타일 5 지정 흰색 멤브레인 시트, 하부 조명 설치 6 지정 도장 7 지정 흰색 멤브레인 시트 8 라인 디퓨저 9 걸레받이 : 메인 도장 10 Ø30 상판 전선홀 타공 11 스탠드 매입

1 Curtain installed 2 App. mock marble 3 App. stainless steel 4 App. tile 5 App. white membrane sheet, lower lighting installed 6 App. painting 7 App. white membrane sheet 8 Line diffuser 9 Base : main painting 10 Ø30 tabletop wire hole perforated 11 Stand lamp embedded

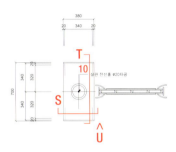

가구 평면 Q / furniture top view Q

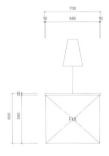

가구 측면 R / furniture side view R

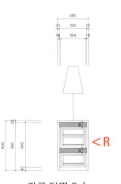

가구 단면 S / furniture section S

가구 단면 T / furniture section T

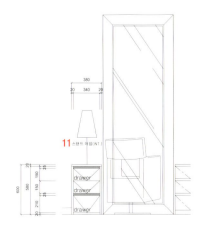

가구 정면 U / furniture front view U

HAIR MARUNI

MSAnD | Cha Myeong Soo

가로수길에 위치한 헤어 마루니는 기존의 미용실과는 차별화된 공간 구성으로 개인 스타일링 공간에서 시술을 받는 동안 다른 사람들의 시선에 구애 받지 않도록 독립적인 파티션을 배치하였다. 독립적인 파티션은 그래픽 이미지의 CNC 타공과 함께 강화유리와 패브릭으로 마감하였다. 복도에서 스타일링 부스로 들어가는 벽면은 아이보리색의 안티스투코 도장으로 마감하여 포근함을 주었다. 옛 원목가구들을 재가공하여 리셉션의 활용도를 높이고, 고풍스러운 느낌을 살렸다. 또한 VIP실과 손톱관리실을 별도로 마련하여 개인별 맞춤 서비스를 제공할 수 있도록 계획하였다.

Hair Maruni located on Garosu-gil has a distinct layout set apart from usual hair salons, providing an independent individual styling space away from other customers. The separating partition was perforated in CNC and finished in tempered glass and fabric. The walls leading into the styling booths from the hallway were finished in antistucco painting in ivory colors to give a cozy feeling. Old antique furniture was reformed to make the reception more useful and deliver an antique atmosphere. Also, rooms for VIP and nail care are established to provide individual, customized service.

디자인 차명수 / 엠에스에이엔디
위치 서울특별시 강남구 신사동 532-11
용도 미용실
면적 245.3㎡
마감 바닥 – 복합 대리석, 원목마루 / 벽 – 안티스투코, 원목, 흑경 / 천장 – 도장, 바리솔
완공 2013. 3
디자인팀 정명하
사진 고영도

Location 532-11, Sinsa-dong, Gangnam-gu, Seoul
Use Hair salon
Area 245.3㎡
Finishing Floor - Composite marble, Natural wooden floor / Wall - Anti stucco, Hardwood, Black mirror / Ceiling - Painting, Barrisol
Completion 2013. 3
Photographer Ko Young Do

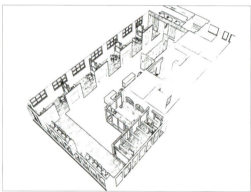

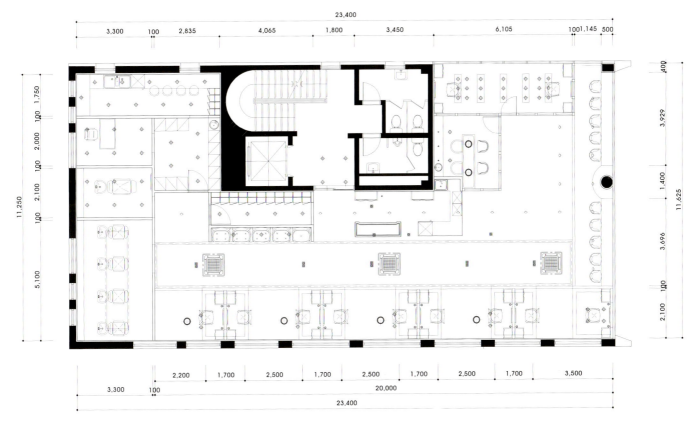

천장도 / ceiling plan

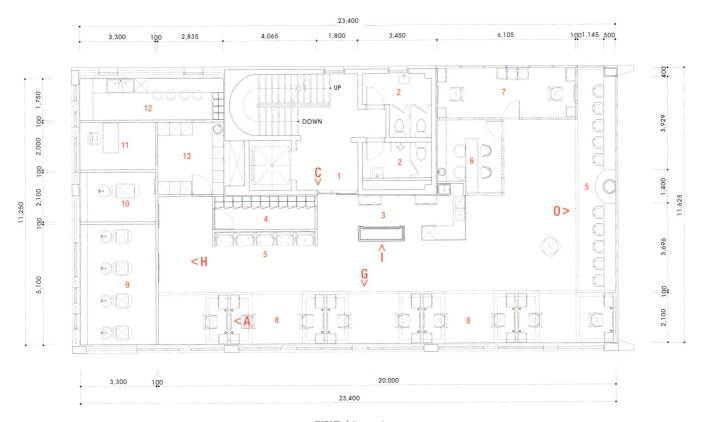

평면도 / floor plan

1 입구 2 화장실 3 리셉션 4 소지품 보관실 5 대기공간 6 손톱관리실 7 VIP실 8 스타일링 존 9 샴무실 10 헤어클리닉실 11 사무실 12 직원실 13 연구실

1 Entrance 2 Toilet 3 Reception 4 Locker room 5 Waiting zone 6 Nailcare room 7 VIP room 8 Styling zone 9 Shampoo room 10 Hair clinic room 11 Office 12 Staff's room 13 Laboratory

1 지정 흑경 부착 / 지정 앤티크 프레임 은경 설치 / 걸레받이 : 지정색 목재 2 Ø100 원목 가공 후 지정색 도장 설치 3 소화전 / 지정색 도장 / 지정 몰딩 : 지정색 부식 도장 4 지정 금속 CNC 타공 후 지정색 부식 도장 / 지정 금속 CNC 타공 후 지정색 부식 도장 / 지정색 도장 5 CNC 타공 후 지정색 부식 도장 / 지정색 도장 / 지정색 시트 로고 부착 6 지정색 부식 도장 7 지정색 안티스투코 도장 / CNC 가공 후 지정색 안티스투코 도장 / T5 강화유리 부착(내부 지정 패브릭) / 걸레받이 : 지정색 목재 8 T5 강화유리 부착 / 지정 패브릭 부착 / CNC 가공 후 지정색 안티스투코 도장 9 CNC 가공 후 지정색 안티스투코 도장 10 지정 30X30 각재 부착 11 T5 강화유리 부착 / 지정 패브릭 부착 / T5 강화유리 부착 12 지정 목재 몰딩, T10 황동 몰딩 부착 / 지정색 안티스투코 도장 13 지정색 목재 / 지정색 안티스투코 도장 / 걸레받이 : 지정색 목재 14 T18 CNC 가공 후 지정색 안티스투코 도장 / T8 강화유리(내부 지정 패브릭) 15 지정 흑경

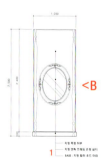

스타일링 존 정면 A / styling zone front view A

스타일링 존 측면 B / styling zone side view B

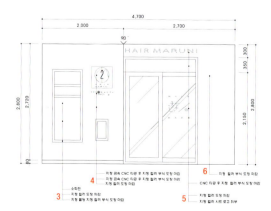

입구 파사드 C / entrance facade C

1 App. black mirror attached / app. antique frame silver mirror installed / baseboard : app. color wood   2 App. color painting installed after Ø100 hardwood processing   3 Fireplug / app. color painting / app. molding : app. color corrosion painting   4 App. color corrosion painting after app. metal CNC punching / app. color corrosion painting after app. metal CNC punching / app. color painting   5 App. color corrosion painting after CNC punching / app. color painting / app. color sheet logo attached   6 App. color corrosion painting   7 App. color antistucco painting / app. color antistucco painting after CNC processing / T5 tempered glass attached (app. fabric inside) / baseboard : app. color wood   8 T5 Tempered glass attached / app. fabric attached / app. color antistucco painting after CNC processing   9 App. color antistucco painting after CNC processing   10 App. 30X30 square timber attached   11 T5 Tempered glass attached / app. fabric attached / T5 tempered glass attached   12 App. wood molding, T10 brass molding attached / app. color antistucco painting   13 App. color wood / app. color antistucco painting / baseboard : app. color wood   14 App. color antistucco painting after T18 CNC processing / T8 tempered glass (app. fabric inside)   15 App. black mirror

스타일링 존 정면 D / styling zone front view D

스타일링 존 측면 E / styling zone side view E

스타일링 존 평면 F / styling zone top view F

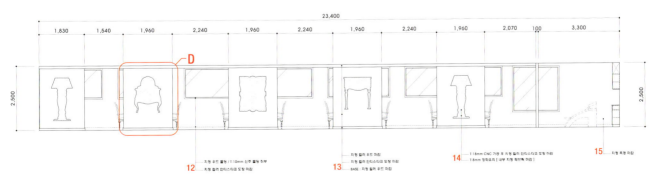

입면 G / elevation G

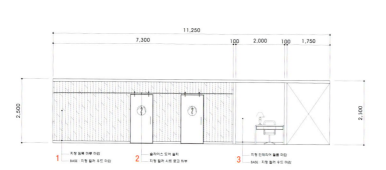

홀 입면 H / hall elevation H

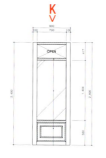

VIP실 벽 정면 J /
VIP room wall front view J

VIP실 벽 평면 K /
VIP room wall top view K

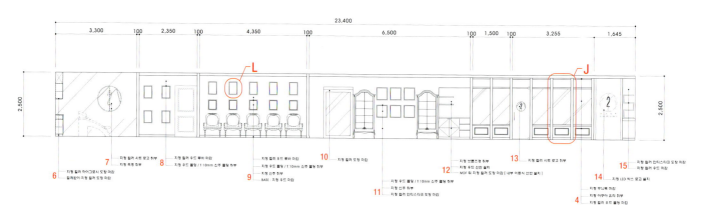

홀 입면 I / hall elevation I

1 지정 원목 마루 / 걸레받이 : 지정색 목재   2 미닫이문 설치 / 지정색 시트 로고 부착   3 지정 인테리어 필름 / 걸레받이 : 지정색 목재   4 지정 무늬목 / 지정 아쿠아 유리 부착 / 목재 몰딩 : 지정색   5 지정 무늬목 / 지정 에칭 무늬 유리 부착   6 지정색 하이글로시 도장 / 걸레받이 : 지정색 도장   7 지정색 시트 로고 부착   8 지정 흑경 부착   8 지정색 목재 루버 / 지정 목재 몰딩, T10 황동 몰딩 부착   9 지정색 목재 루버 / 지정 목재 몰딩, T10 황동 몰딩 부착 / 지정 황동 부착 / 걸레받이 : 지정 목재   10 지정색 도장   11 지정 목재 몰딩, T10 황동 몰딩 부착 / 지정 황동 부착 / 지정색 안티스투코 도장   12 지정 청동 거울 부착 / 지정 목재 선반 설치 / MDF 위 지정색 도장(내부 이동식 선반 설치)   13 지정색 시트 로고 부착   14 지정 LED 박스 로고 설치   15 지정색 안티스투코 도장 / 지정색 목재   16 T10 황동 몰딩 부착, 내부 황동 부착 / 목재 몰딩 : 지정색   17 목재 몰딩 : 지정색 / T10 황동 몰딩 부착 / 지정 황동 부착   18 목재 몰딩 : 지정색 / T10 황동 몰딩 부착, 내부 황동 부착   19 지정색 안티스투코 도장   20 지정 모자이크 타일   21 Ø100 목재 가공 : 지정색   22 지정 흑경 설치 / 지정 앤티크 프레임 경대 설치 / 걸레받이 : 지정 목재

1 App. hardwood floor / baseboard : app. color wood 2 Slide door installed / app. color sheet logo attached 3 App. interior film / baseboard : app. color wood 4 App. wood veneer / app. aqua glass attached / wood molding : app. color 5 App. wood veneer / app. etching patterned glass attached 6 App. color highglossy painting / baseboard : app. color painting 7 App. color sheet logo attached 8 App. black mirror attached 8 App. color wooden louver / app. wood molding, T10 brass molding attached 9 App. color wooden louver / app. wood molding, T10 brass molding attached / app. brass attached / baseboard : app. wood 10 App. color painting 11 App. wood molding, T10 brass molding attached / app. brass attached / app. color antistucco painting 12 App. bronze mirror attached / app. wood shelf installed / app. color painting on MDF (inner movable shelf installed) 13 App. color sheet logo attached 14 App. LED box logo installed 15 App. color antistucco painting / app. color wood 16 T10 brass molding attached, molding attached inside / wood molding : app. color 17 Wood molding : app. color / T10 Brass molding attached / app. brass attached 18 Wood molding : app. color / T10 Brass molding attached, brass attached inside 19 App. color antistucco painting 20 App. mosaic tile 21 Ø100 wood processing : app. color 22 App. black mirror installed / app. antique frame mirror stand installed / baseboard : app. wood

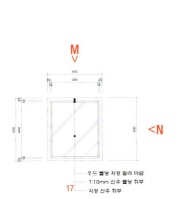
대기실 창 정면 L /
waiting zone window front view L

대기실 창 평면 M /
waiting zone window top view M

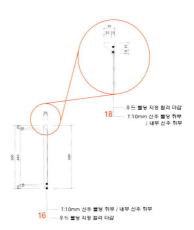
대기실 창 측면 N /
waiting zone window side view N

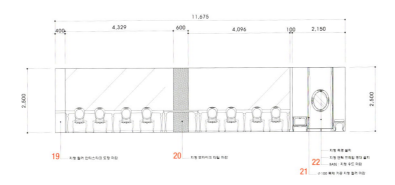
대기실 입면 O / waiting zone elevation O

IL LAGO BAKERY & WINE SHOP IN MVL HOTEL

DAEMYUNG RESORT + DESIGN BONO

엠블호텔의 로비에 자리잡은 베이커리 & 와인숍 일라고는 주출입구를 등지고 숨겨져 있는 위치상의 한계를 극복하고자 로비의 벽면을 마주보며 숨겨져 있던 축을 최대한 이동시켜 입구에서의 인지성을 향상하는데 주력하였다. 외관을 아우르는 아치형태의 구조물과 배경을 이루는 겹겹이 쌓아올린 클래식한 몰딩의 오브제 월로 중세 아치형태의 와이너리를 현대적으로 재해석하고, 아치의 중첩되는 형태적 깊이감과 자연채광을 실내로 유입시키어 생동감을 주는 건축적 기법을 활용하였다. 특히 공간적요소로써 자연스러운 아치구조를 선과 면으로 풀어내고 그 면적인 요소에 입체감있는 기둥의 오브제와 몰딩을 쌓아올려 디테일을 최대한 강조하였다. 또한 곡선과 직선, 선과 면을 누르는 입체감있는 오브제의 요소가 어울려 생동감있고 다이내믹한 공간을 연출함으로써 독특하면서 품위있는 공간과 상징적 요소를 가진 공간을 기획하고자 하였다.

This project located at the lobby of MVL hotel, and the space designed for bakery and wine shop. The designer tried to overcome the limit of the location which is located at back of the main entrance. In addition, they created sculptural structure to develop the lobby design and then the sculptures are connected from the shop to the entrance area, and it could make the shop to be perceived well from the entrance. Arch shape structure and classical layered molding which is harmonized with facade reinterpet an arch of old winery in the middle age as modern, and the arch, that could be seen frequently through a space having historical background in Europe, has been used as architectural skill for deep of repeated shape and daylight into the space. Especially, as factor of space, arch structure has been designed by line and face and column object and molding which are layered on the element of the face extremely emphasize the detail. In addition, it makes an independent structure by resisting and adapting the curve of the arch and the harmony of the massive object, curved line, horizontal line and faces, makes dynamic and live space.

기획설계 배연준 / (주)대명레저산업
기본실시설계 장성진 / (주)디자인 本晉
위치 경기도 고양시 일산동구 장항동 1248, 엠블호텔
용도 베이커리 & 와인숍
면적 150㎡
설계기간 2013. 1 ~ 2013. 3
공사기간 2013. 3 ~ 2013. 4
마감 바닥 - 폴리싱 타일 / 벽 - 우레탄 도장, 몰딩 월, 부식 도장 / 천장 - 노출천장 위 수성 도장
PM 심한주 / (주)디자인 本晉
시공 오경래, 추성민 / (주)디자인 本晉
사진 이표준

Location MVL Hotel, 1248, Janghang-dong, Ilsandong-gu, Goyang, Gyeonggi-do
Use Bakery & Wine shop
Area 150㎡
Design period 2013. 1 ~ 2013. 3
Construction period 2013. 3 ~ 2013. 4
Finishing Floor - Polishing tile / Wall - Urethane painting, Moulding wall, Corrosion painting / Ceiling - Water painting on exposed ceiling
Photographer Lee Pyo Jun

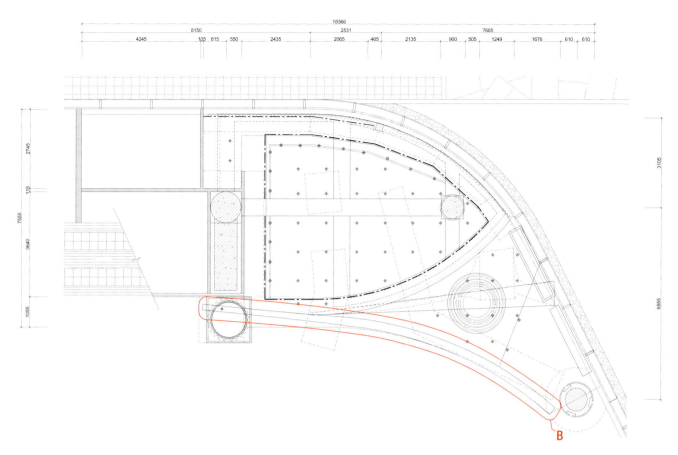

천장도 / ceiling plan

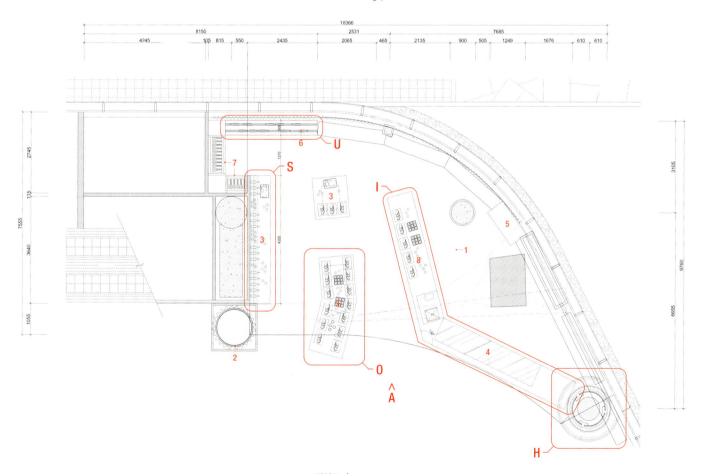

평면도 / floor plan

1 지정 대리석 2 디스플레이 오브제 3 디스플레이 테이블 4 쇼케이스 5 선반 6 와인 랙 7 와인 저장실 8 디스플레이 테이블 & 카운터

1 App. marble 2 Display object 3 Display table 4 Show case 5 Shelf 6 Wine rack 7 Wine cellar 8 Display table & counter

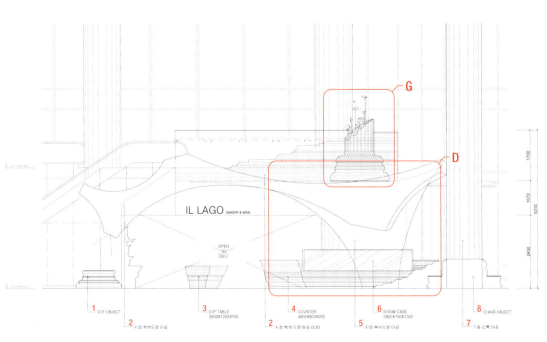

매장 입면 A / store elevation A

IL LAGO BAKERY & WINE SHOP IN MVL HOTEL | 헬름호텔 일라고 베이커리 & 와인숍

1 디스플레이 오브제   2 지정 백색 도장   3 3600X1200X750 디스플레이 테이블   4 4800X900X950 카운터   5 지정 부식도장   6 3800X700X1300 쇼케이스   7 기존 건축마감   8 의자 오브제   9 갈바륨 절곡 위 지정 도장   10 아크릴 환봉 고정   11 유리섬유강화플라스틱 성형 위 지정 백색 도장   12 베이지 가죽 방석   13 유리섬유강화플라스틱 성형 위 지정 백색 도장 / 걸레받이 : 스테인리스 스틸 미러   14 매시 형성

1 Display object   2 App. white painting   3 3600X1200X750 display table   4 4800X900X950 counter   5 App. corrosion painting   6 3800X700X1300 showcase   7 Existing architectural finishing   8 Chair object   9 App. painting on galvalume bent   10 Acryl pipe fixed   11 App. white painting on FRP moulded   12 Beige leather sitting cushion   13 App. white painting on FRP moulded / base : stainless steel mirror

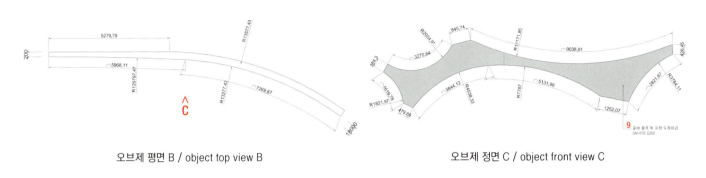

오브제 평면 B / object top view B

오브제 정면 C / object front view C

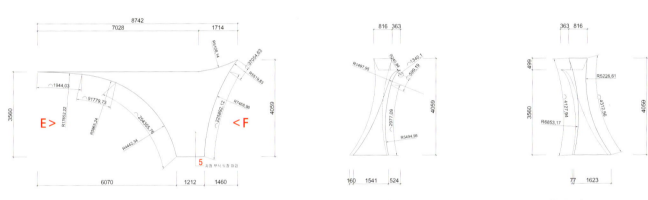

오브제 정면 D / object front view D

오브제 좌측면 E / object left side E

오브제 우측면 F / object right side F

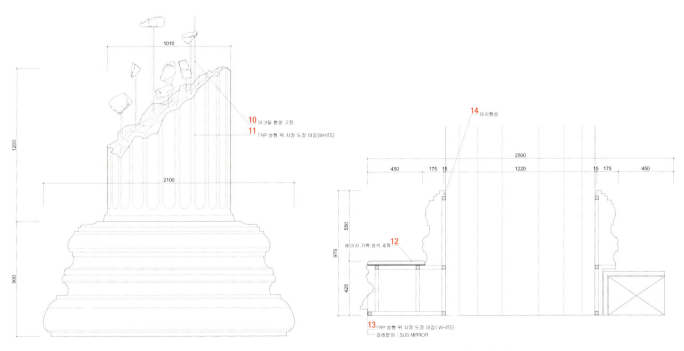

오브제 정면 G / object front view G

오브제 단면 H / object section H

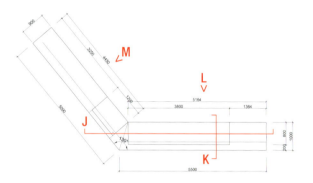

가구 평면 I / furniture top view I

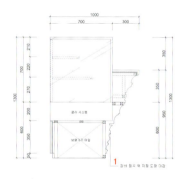

가구 단면 K / furniture section K

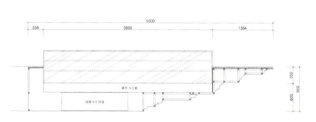

가구 단면 J / furniture section J

가구 단면 N / furniture section N

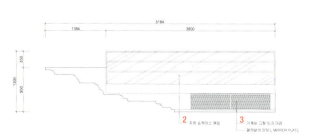

가구 입면 L / furniture elevation L

가구 입면 M / furniture elevation M

1 갈바륨 절곡 위 지정 도장 2 지정 쇼케이스 매입 3 기계실 그릴 스테인리스 스틸 마감 / 걸레받이 : 스테인리스 스틸 미러 4 지정 대리석 5 걸레받이 : 스테인리스 스틸 미러 6 지정 도장 7 상판 : 지정 대리석
8 LED 조명 9 지정 대리석 / 각파이프 보강 10 갈바륨 절곡 위 지정 도장 / 걸레받이 : 스테인리스 스틸 미러

1 App. painting on galvalume bent 2 App. showcase embedded 3 Electric grill : stainless steel / base : stainless steel mirror 4 App. marble 5 Base : stainless steel mirror 6 App. painting 7 Tabletop : app. marble 8 LED lighting 9 App. marble / square pipe reinforced 10 App. painting on galvalume bent / base : stainless steel mirror

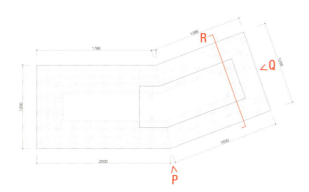

가구 평면 O / furniture top view O

가구 단면 R / furniture section R

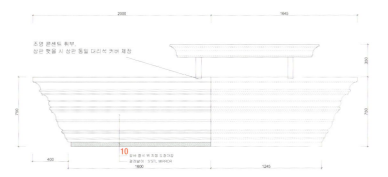

가구 정면 P / furniture front view P

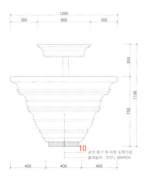

가구 측면 Q / furniture side view Q

1 걸레받이 : 스테인리스 스틸 미러 2 지정 대리석 3 상부 몰딩 : 지정 백색 도장 4 스테인리스 스틸 헤어라인 파이프 5 지정 백색 도장 6 LED 조명 설치, 아크릴 커버 타입 7 LED 조명 설치 8 몰딩 위 지정 백색 도장

1 Base : stainless steel mirror 2 App. marble 3 Upper moulding : app. white painting 4 Stainless steel hairline pipe 5 App. white painting 6 LED lighting installed, acryl cover type 7 LED lighting installed 8 App. white painting on moulding

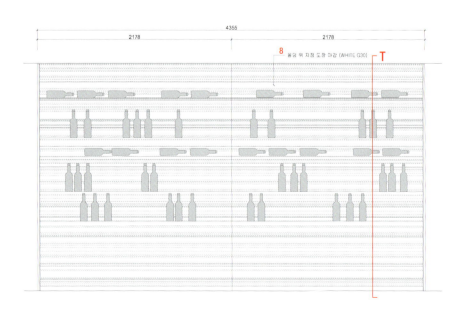

가구 정면 S / furniture front view S

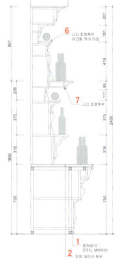

가구 단면 T / furniture section T

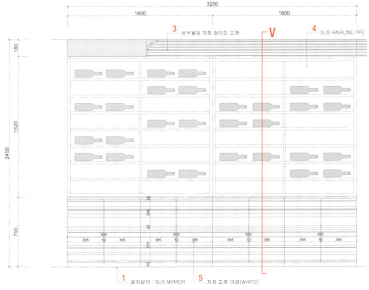

가구 정면 U / furniture front view U

가구 단면 V / furniture section V

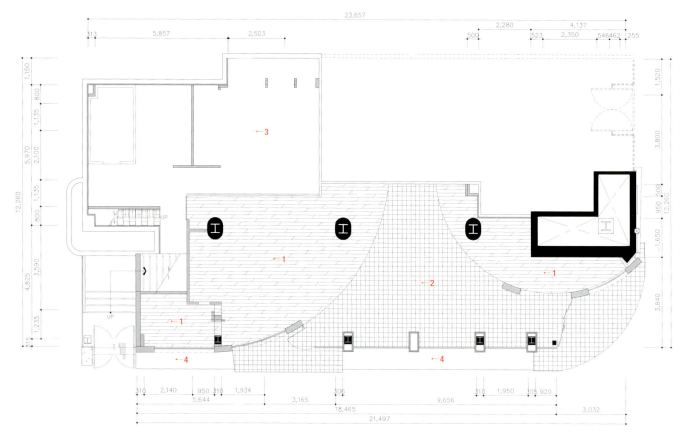

평면 패턴도 / floor pattern plan

1 지정 우드 플로링 2 200X200 지정 테라조 타일 3 150X150 지정 타일 4 기존 고흥석 활용 5 고흥석 잔다듬 6 갈바륨 위 백색 도장, 드로잉(스크래치) / 갈바륨 위 백색 도장, 드로잉(일러스트 기법) 7 지정 테라조 타일 8 아연강판 / 시멘트 모노 타일 9 차양 / T12 투명 강화유리 10 시멘트 모노 타일 11 간판 12 철망 겹치기 / 갈바륨 위 백색 도장, 드로잉(일러스트기법)

1 App. wood flooring 2 200X200 app. terrazzo tile 3 150X150 app. tile 4 Existing granite applied 5 Granite dabbed finish 6 White painting on galvalume, drawing (scratch) / white painting on galvalume, drawing (illustrating) 7 App. terrazzo tile 8 Galvanized steel sheet / cement mono tile 9 Awning / T12 clear tempered glass 10 Cement mono tile 11 Sign 12 Wire mesh layered / white painting on galvalume, drawing (illustrating)

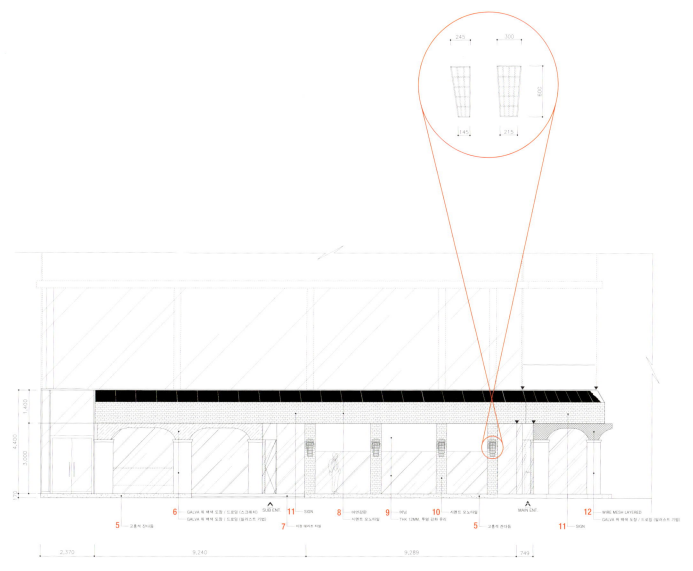

파사드 A / facade A

1 철망 겹치기 / 갈바륨 위 백색 도장, 드로잉(일러스트기법) 2 가구 3 지정 시멘트 타일 4 갈바륨 위 백색 도장, 드로잉(스크래치) / 갈바륨 위 백색 도장, 드로잉(일러스트 기법) 5 T12 투명 유리 6 지정 도장 / 금속 몰딩, 유광 검은색 도장 / 지정 시멘트 타일 7 백색 안티스투코 8 골함석 위 지정 오렌지색 도장 9 고재 부착 10 2X4 나왕 각재 11 T9 나왕 12 대리석(비안코 카라라) 13 T12 합판 위 투명 도장 14 H=300 유리 칸막이 설치

1 Wire mesh layered / white painting on galvalume, drawing (illustrating) 2 Furniture 3 App. cement tile 4 White painting on galvalume, drawing (scratch) / white painting on galvalume, drawing (illustrating) 5 T12 clear glass 6 App. painting / metal molding, glossy black painting / app. cement tile 7 White antistucco 8 App. orange painting on corrugated sheet iron 9 Old wood attached 10 2X4 lauan square timber 11 T9 lauan 12 Marble (Bianco carara) 13 Clear painting on T12 plywood 14 H=300 glass partition installed

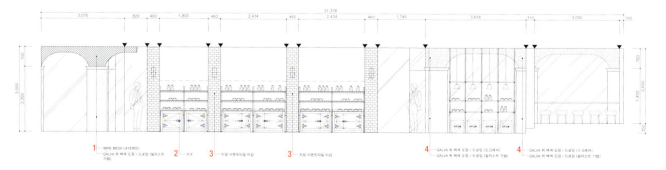

홀 입면 B / hall elevation B

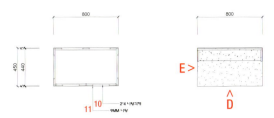

서비스 테이블 평면 C / service table top view C

서비스 테이블 정면 D / service table front view D   서비스 테이블 좌측면 E / service table left side view E

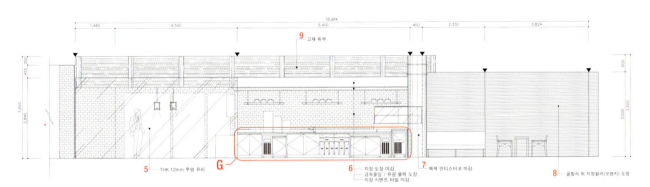

홀 입면 F / hall elevation F

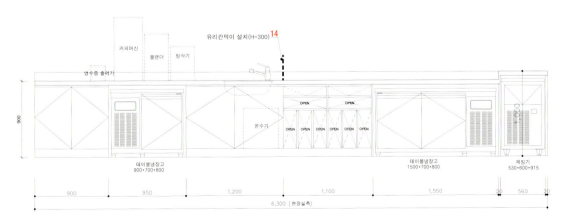

케익 진열장 후면장 G / cake showcase back storage closet G

1 지정 시멘트 타일 2 지정 내화 벽돌 3 아연 판재 위 부식 도장 4 장식 선반 제작 / 지정 시멘트 타일 5 지정 도장 / 금속 몰딩, 유광 검은색 도장 6 고재 7 2X4 나왕 각재 8 T9 나왕 9 T3 열연강판

1 App. cement tile 2 App. fire brick 3 Corrosion painting on zinc board 4 Making decoration shelf / app. cement tile 5 App. painting / metal molding, glossy black painting 6 Old wood 7 2X4 lauan square timber 8 T9 lauan 9 T3 hot rolled steel sheet

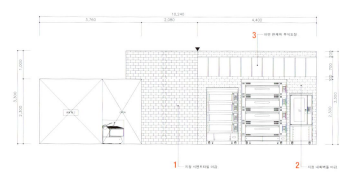

제빵 공간 입면 H / baking area elevation H

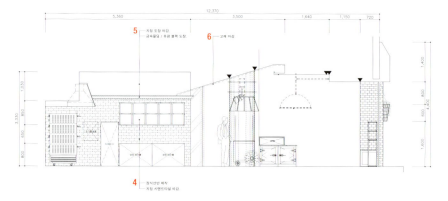

제빵 공간 입면 I / baking area elevation I

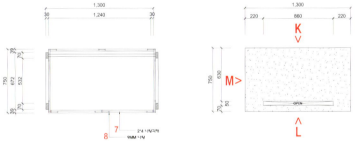

커팅대 평면 J / cutting stand top view J

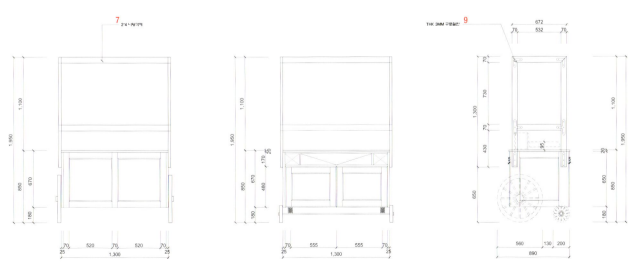

커팅대 후면 K / cutting stand rear view K   커팅대 정면 L / cutting stand front view L   커팅대 좌측면 M / cutting stand left side view M

1 지정 오렌지색 도장 2 계산대 : 지정 도장 3 빵 진열대 : 지정 도장 4 케익 진열장 : 지정 도장 5 고재 루버 6 철망 겹치기 / 갈바륨 위 백색 도장, 드로잉(일러스트 기법) 7 T20 티크목 패널 8 스테인리스 스틸 거울 9 T20 대리석(비안코 카라라) 10 지정 경첩 11 지정 밀폐손잡이 12 지정 손잡이 13 지정 진회색 도장

1 App. orange painting 2 Counter : app. painting 3 Bread display stand : app. painting 4 Cake showcase : app. painting 5 Old wood louver 6 Wire mesh layered / white painting on galvalume, drawing (illustrating) 7 T20 teak wood panel 8 Stainless steel mirror 9 T20 marble (Bianco carara) 10 App. hinge 11 App. sealed handle 12 App. handle 13 App. dark gray painting

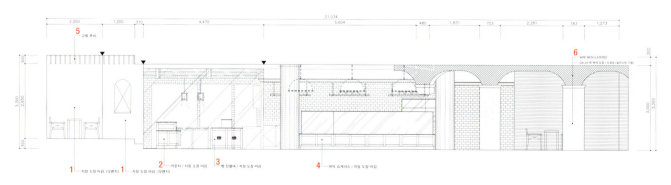

홀 입면 N / hall elevation N

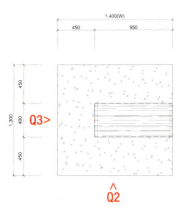
중앙 진열대 A 평면 O1 / main display table A top view O1

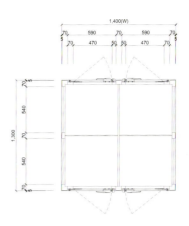
중앙 진열대 A 평단면 O1 / main display table A top section O1

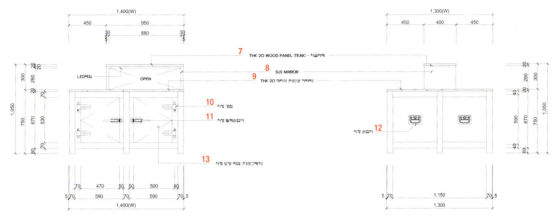
중앙 진열대 A 정면 O2 / main display table A front view O2

중앙 진열대 A 측면 O3 / main display table A side view O3

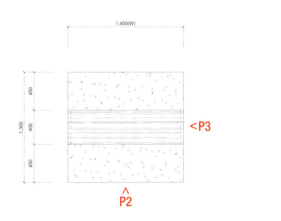
중앙 진열대 B 평면 P1 / main display table B top view P1

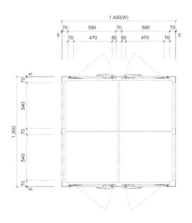
중앙 진열대 B 평단면 P1 / main display table A top section P1

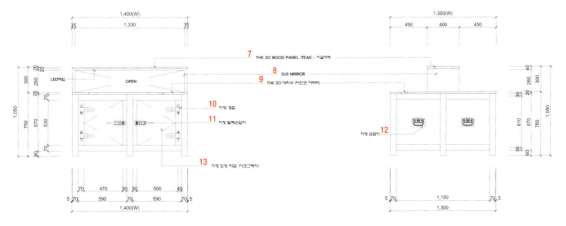
중앙 진열대 B 정면 P2 / main display table B front view P2

중앙 진열대 B 평단면 P3 / main display table B side view P3

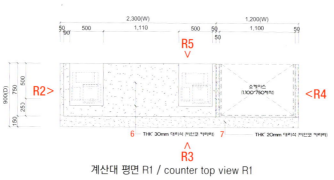

계산대 평면 R1 / counter top view R1

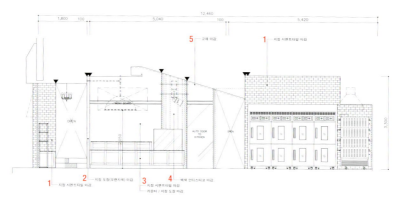

홀 입면 Q / hall elevation Q

1 지정 시멘트 타일 2 지정 오렌지색 도장 3 지정 시멘트 타일 / 계산대 : 지정 도장 4 백색 안티스투코 5 고재 6 T30 대리석(비안코 카라라) 7 T20 대리석(비안코 카라라) 8 스테인리스 스틸 헤어라인 9 지정 진회색 도장

1 App. cement tile 2 App. orange painting 3 App. cement tile / counter : app. painting 4 White antistucco 5 Old wood 6 T30 marble (Bianco carara) 7 T20 marble (Bianco carara) 8 Stainless steel hairline 9 App. dark gray painting

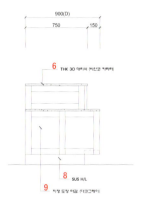

계산대 좌측면 R2 / counter left side view R2

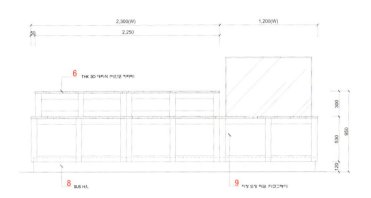

계산대 정면 R3 / counter rear front view R3

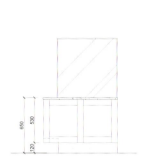

계산대 우측면 R4 / counter right side view R4

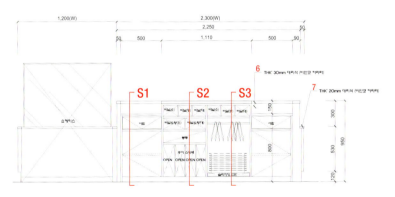

계산대 후면 R5 / counter rear side view R5

계산대 단면 S1 / counter section S1

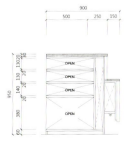

계산대 단면 S2 / counter section S2

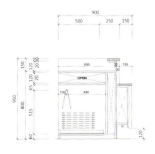

계산대 단면 S3 / counter section S3

1 T20 티크 목재 패널 2 □40X60 파이프, 지정색 분체도장 3 T20 대리석(비안코 카라라) 4 T5 열연강판 5 지정 진회색 도장 6 지정 밀폐 손잡이 7 지정 경첩 8 높이 조절굽 9 □40X60 파이프, 티크 무늬목 10 이동식 하부장 11 LED 매입 12 Ø36 타공 13 Ø15 타공 14 T20 티크목 선반 15 20X20 스테인리스 스틸 거울 파이프 16 Ø30 스테인리스 스틸 거울 파이프 17 캡

1 T20 teak wood panel 2 □40X60 pipe, app. color powder painting 3 T20 marble (Bianco carara) 4 T5 hot rolled steel sheet 5 App. dark gray painting 6 App. sealed handle 7 App. hinge 8 Height control heel 9 □40X60 pipe, teak wood veneer 10 Movable lower storage closet 11 LED embedded 12 Ø36 perforating 13 Ø15 perforating 14 T20 teak wood shelf 15 20X20 stainless steel mirror pipe 16 Ø30 stainless steel mirror pipe 17 Cap

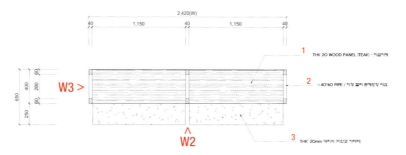

창문 진열대 B 평면 W1 / window display stand B top view W1

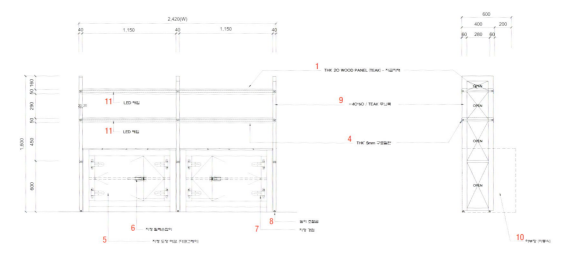

창문 진열대 B 정면 W2 / window display stand B front view W2

창문 진열대 B 측면 W3 / window display stand B side view W3

MAINZ DOM

마인츠돔

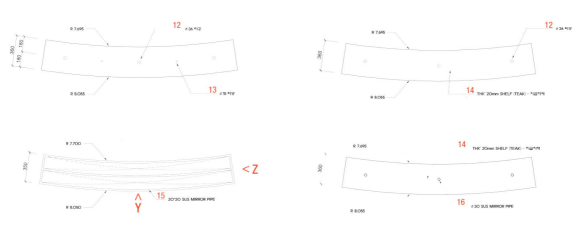

창문 진열대 A 평면 X / window display stand A top view X

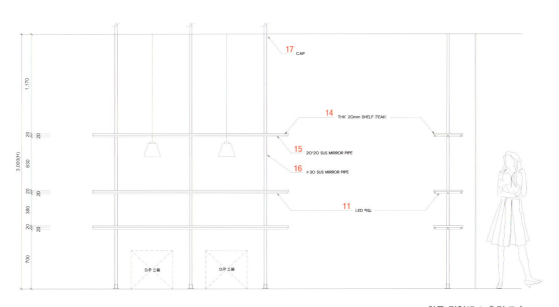

창문 진열대 A 정면 Y / window display stand A front view Y

창문 진열대 A 측면 Z / window display stand A side view Z

ANGSEE HAIR SHOP

RAUMDESIGN. Co., Ltd. | Jin Hee Won

앙시 헤어숍은 두 개의 층에 각각 다른 컨셉의 디자인을 적용한 프로젝트이다. 젊은 층을 대상으로 한 2층은 가공하지 않은 천연 재료들의 물성을 살려 빈티지하면서도 따뜻한 느낌의 공간이다. 특히, 입구부터 내부까지의 공간을 가로지르는 사선 형태의 복도는 각재를 수직, 수평으로 이어 붙여 만든 울퉁불퉁한 벽으로 리듬감을 살려 자연스럽게 고객들을 내부로 인도한다. 복도 끝자락에 위치한 대기공간은 원목기둥으로 공간을 분리하고 있는데, 드문드문 설치된 기둥들 사이로 외부와 소통할 수 있는 개방적인 공간이 만들어진다. 3층은 어두운 색상의 원목과 타일을 사용하여 중후한 느낌을 주며 클래식하게 디자인되었다. 특히 파마존의 천장에는 흑경을 사용하여 클래식하면서도 모던한 형태의 구조물을 계획하였다. 반대편의 커팅존은 독립적인 형태의 원목 경대를 배치하고 곳곳에 서랍장을 두어 편리함을 극대화하였다. 이외에 공간마다 마감재들을 달리함으로써 공간들이 기능에 따라 자연스럽게 분리되어 통일성과 기능성을 동시에 만족시켰다.

Angsee Hair Shop is a project that adopted mutually different design concepts for each floor of the two-story business. The 2nd floor targeting the young clients is designed to give a vintage and warm look by taking advantage of the properties of unprocessed natural materials. The hallway, in particular, which cuts through the space from the entrance to the interior in a diagonal line, creates a sense of rhythm with the bumpy wall built with lumbers joggled vertically and horizontally, and leads the clients into the shop in a natural manner. The waiting area, located at the end of the hallway, is separated from the rest of the space with hard wood pillars, which in turn create open spaces that communicate with the outside area through spaces in between sparsely standing pillars. The 3rd floor is designed in a classical manner and delivers a stately atmosphere from using dark color hard wood and tiles. The perm zone, in particular, displays a structure combined with classical sensibility and modern touch using a tinted mirror on the ceiling. The cutting zone at the opposite side is arranged with independent-style hard wood mirrors. It is also equipped with drawers in multiple places to maximize convenience. In addition, each space is decorated with different finishing materials that naturally divide the space according to function, thereby satisfying unity and functionality at the same time.

디자인 진희원 / (주)라움디자인
위치 부산광역시 해운대구 중동 1378-77, 2~3층
용도 미용실
면적 2층 - 149㎡ / 3층 - 158㎡
마감 바닥 - 타일, 우드 플로링, 공자갈, 에폭시 / 벽 - 우드 플로링, 에쉬 원목, 타일, 적삼목, 티크원목, 골드 미러, 스톤 슬라이스 / 천장 - 노출천장, 비닐 페인트, 가문비나무 목재
설계 김명섭
설계기간 2012. 12 ~ 2013. 1
공사기간 2013. 1 ~ 2013. 3
사진 김명섭

Design Kim Myeong Seop / RAUMDESIGN. Co., Ltd.
Location 2-3F, 1378-77, Jung-dong, Haeundae-gu, Busan
Use Hair salon
Area 2F - 149㎡ / 3F - 158㎡
Design period 2012. 12 ~ 2013. 1
Construction period 2013. 1 ~ 2013. 3
Finishing Floor - Tile, Wood flooring, Gravel, Epoxy / Wall - Wood flooring, Ash wood, Tile, Red cedar, Teak wood. Gold mirrror, Stone slice / Ceiling - Exposed ceiling, Vinyl paint, Spruce wood
Photographer Kim Myeong Seop

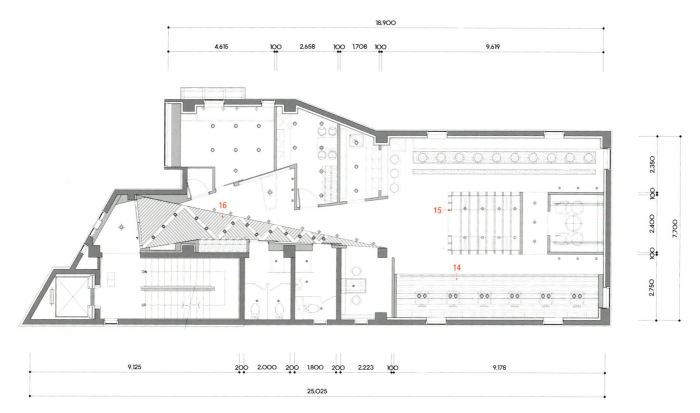

2층 천장도 / 2nd ceiling plan

2층 평면도 / 2nd floor plan

1 리셉션 2 메이크업룸 3 직원실 4 제품실 5 파마존 6 커팅존 7 바 테이블 8 대기실 9 샴푸존 10 네일 바 11 화장실 12 지정 600X600 커팅 타일 13 지정 콩자갈 + 투명 에폭시 14 지정 자작나무 15 지정 티크 원목 16 지정 가문비나무 원목

1 Reception 2 Make up room 3 Staff room 4 Product room 5 Permanent zone 6 Cutting zone 7 Bar table 8 Waiting zone 9 Shampoo zone 10 Nail bar 11 Toilet 12 App. 600X600 cutting tile 13 App. gravel + clear epoxy 14 App. birch wood 15 App. teak wood 16 App. spruce wood

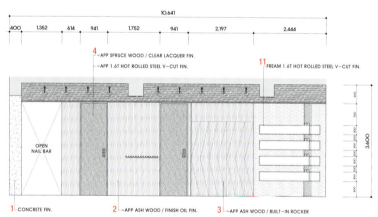

리셉션 입면 A / reception elevation A

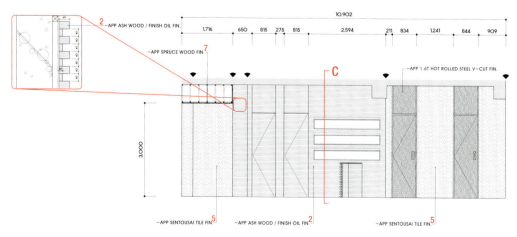

리셉션 입면 B / reception elevation B

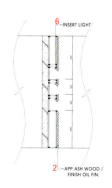

벽 단면 C / wall section C

1 콘크리트   2 지정 애쉬 목재 + 오일 마감   3 지정 애쉬 목재 + 붙박이 락커   4 지정 가문비나무 목재 + 투명 래커 / 지정 T1.6 열연강판 V커팅   5 지정 센토자이 타일   6 조명 삽입   7 지정 유리 에칭, LED조명 삽입   8 지정 모르타르 + 투명 에폭시   9 T5 거울 / 지정 T1.6 열연강판 V 커팅   10 T20 보티치노 석재 / □30X30 철재 사각 파이프, 가문비나무 목재   11 지정 열연강판 V커팅

1 Concrete   2 App. ash wood + finish oil   3 App. ash wood + built in locker   4 App. spruce wood + clear lacquer / app. T1.6 hot rolled steel sheet V-cut   5 App. sentousai tile   6 Lighting inserted   7 App. etching glass, LED lighting inserted   8 App. mortar + clear epoxy   9 T5 mirror / app. T1.6 hot rolled steel sheet V-cut   10 T20 botticino stone / □30X30 steel square pipe, spruce wood   11 App. hot rolled steel sheet V-cut

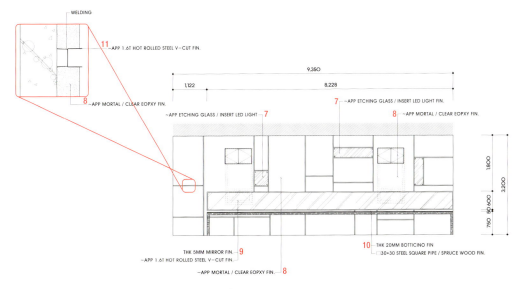

파마존 입면 D / permanent zone elevation D

RAKU IZAKAYA & SAKE PUB

MSAnD | Cha Myeong Soo

'라쿠'는 편안함, 안락함을 뜻하는 일본어로 어느 공간에서든지 편안함을 주는 선술집을 계획하고자 하였다. 매장으로 들어서면 일본식 포장마차인 '야타이'를 단순화한 메뉴판이 손님들을 내부로 안내한다. 여러 공간의 동선을 간소화하고 천장의 채널과 원목마루, 현수막으로 야타이 거리 같은 느낌을 주고자 하였다. 또한 개방형 주방에서의 쇼를 홀에서도 만끽할 수 있도록 계획하였다. 내부공간은 다다미와 방으로 구성하여 모던하면서도 안락한 공간으로 계획하였다.

'Raku' means comfort and convenience in Japanese and the space was designed to give comfort as a bar. A menu in a simpler form of 'Yatai (やたい)', a Japanese cart bar, greets the customers as they enter the store leading the way. The routes to different places were streamlined and the channels on the ceiling, wooden floor, and banners were used to resemble a street of Yatai. Additionally, the open kitchen allows customers in the hall to view the shows they put on in the kitchen. The interior space is made up of Japanese floor mat and rooms providing a modern and comfortable space.

디자인 차명수 / 엠에스에이엔디
위치 서울특별시 강남구 역삼동 824-25
용도 상업
면적 218㎡
마감 바닥 – 시멘트 모르타르, 투명 에폭시 / 벽 – 도장, 대나무, 노출콘크리트 타일 / 천장 – 채널, 노출콘크리트
완공 2013. 10
디자인팀 정명하
사진 고영도

Location 824-25, Yeoksam-dong, Gangnam-gu, Seoul
Use Commerce
Area 218㎡
Finishing Floor - Cement mortar, Clear epoxy / Wall - Painting, Bamboo, Exposed concrete tile / Ceiling - Channel, Exposed concrete
Completion 2013. 10
Photographer Ko Young Do

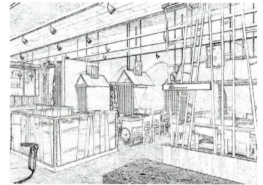

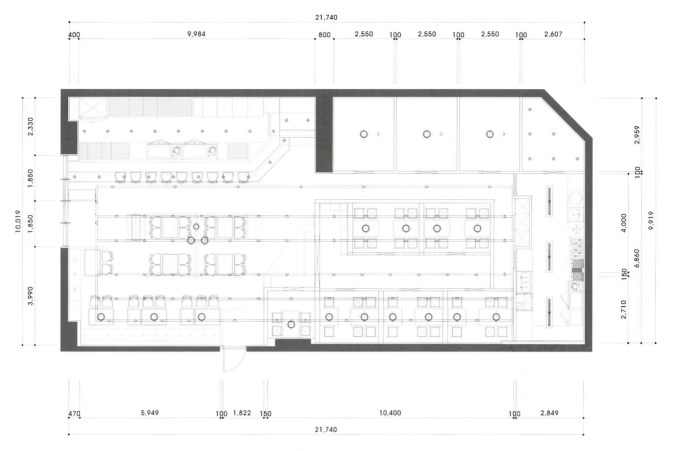

천장도 / ceiling plan

평면도 / floor plan

1 입구 2 홀 3 파티션 좌석 4 붙박이 좌석 5 주방 6 보조주방 7 실 8 창고 9 다다미실 10 다다미홀

1 Entrance 2 Hall 3 Partition seats 4 Built-in seats 5 Kitchen 6 Sub kitchen 7 Room 8 Storage 9 Japanese floor mat room 10 Japanese floor mat hall

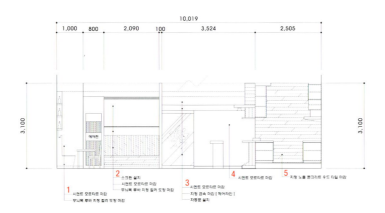

입구 입면 A / entrance elevation A

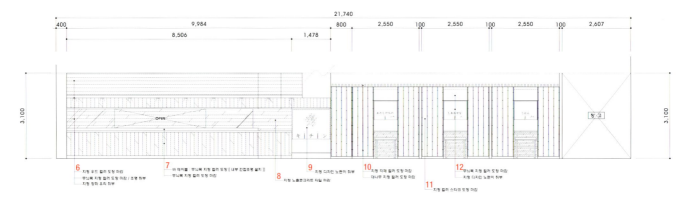

주방 입면 B / kitchen elevation B

1 시멘트 모르타르 / 무늬목 루버 : 지정색 도장 2 스크린 / 시멘트 모르타르 / 무늬목 루버 : 지정색 도장 3 시멘트 모르타르 / 지정 금속 헤어라인 / 자동문 4 시멘트 모르타르 5 지정 노출콘크리트 목재 타일 6 목재 : 지정색 도장 / 지정색 도장 무늬목, 조명 부착 / 지정 강화유리 부착 7 바 테이블 : 지정색 도장 무늬목(내부 간접조명 설치) / 지정색 도장 무늬목 8 지정 노출콘크리트 타일 9 지정 디자인 주렴 부착 10 지정색 도장 각재 / 지정색 도장 대나무 11 지정색 스투코 도장 12 지정색 도장 무늬목 / 지정 디자인 주렴 부착 13 목재 : 지정색 도장 / 목재 : 지정색 도장 14 목재 : 지정색 도장 / 루버 : 지정색 도장(내부 조명 설치) / 흑보드 도장 / 목재 : 지정색 도장 / 14인치 자전거 바퀴 : 지정색 도장 / 지정 슬레이트 부착 15 목재 : 지정색 도장 16 LED 채널(지정색 시트) / T5 강화유리 부착 / 목재 : 지정색 도장 / 목재 : 지정색 부식 도장 17 T5 강화유리 부착 18 목재 : 지정색 도장 / 목재 : 지정색 부식 도장

1 Cement mortar / wood veneer louver : app. color painting 2 Screen / cement mortar / wood veneer louver : app. color painting 3 Cement mortar / app. metal hairline / automatic door 4 Cement mortar 5 App. exposed concrete wood tile 6 Wood : app. color painting / app. color painting wood veneer, lighting attached / app. tempered glass attached 7 Bar table : app. color painting wood veneer (interior indirect lighting installed) / app. color painting wood veneer 8 App. exposed concrete tile 9 App. design hanging screen attached 10 App. color painting square timber / app. color painting bamboo 11 App. color stucco painting 12 App. color painting wood veneer / app. design hanging screen attached 13 Wood : app. color painting / wood : app. color painting 14 Wood : app. color painting / louver : app. color painting (interior lighting installed) / blackboard painting / wood : app. color painting / 14 inch bicycle wheel : app. color painting / app. slate attached 15 Wood : app. color painting 16 LED Channel (app. color sheet) / T5 tempered glass attached / wood : app. color painting / wood : app. color corrosion painting 17 T5 tempered glass attached 18 Wood : app. color painting / wood : app. color corrosion painting

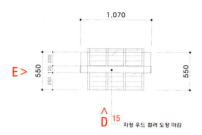

가구 평면 C / furniture top view C

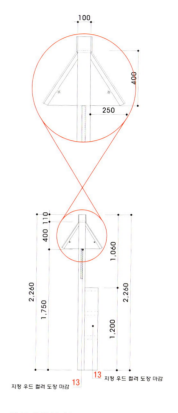

가구 측면 E / furniture side view E

가구 정면 D / furniture front view D

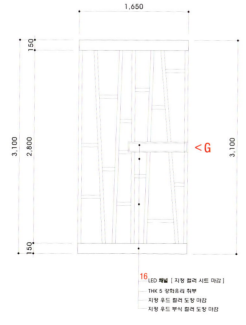

입구 파티션 정면 F / entrance partition front view F

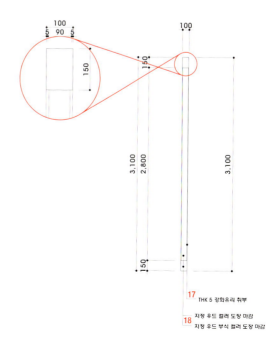

입구 파티션 측면 G / entrance partition side view G

SALON DE H

MIDAS DESIGN | Lee Sung Min

살롱 드 에이치는 과감한 색채와 철, 콘크리트, 유리 등 냉철한 도시 이미지를 일깨우는 소재를 활용하여 군더더기 없는 모던 스타일로 완성하여, 그 속에 깃든 일말의 따스함으로 아름다움을 향한 인간의 감성을 보듬는 것을 콘셉트로 하였다. 내부는 잿빛의 노출콘크리트로 마감하고, 낮은 채도의 검은색 열연강판을 사용하여 차가운 느낌을 강조하였으며, 빨강, 파랑 등의 원색을 디자인 포인트로 활용하여 강렬한 인상을 형성하였다. 여기에 고객 동선을 따라 원목을 적절히 섞어 배치하여 도시적 분위기의 완급을 조절하도록 하였다. 또한 헤어숍 특성상 펌, 염색 등의 시술과정에서 빈번한 자리이동과, 거울 속에 비치는 고객의 모습에 집중할 수 있도록 전체적으로 단순하게 구성하였다. 또한 직원들의 서비스 동선과 분리된 주동선도 단순하게 구성하여 개방감을 선사하고, 기능에 따라 공간을 구분하였다.

Salon de H uses bold colors, steel, concrete, and glass to transfer images of a cold city and to create a simple modern style. It also adds a hint of warmth to embrace people's longing for beauty. The interior was finished in grey, exposed concrete and used black hot rolled steel plate of low-chrome level to accentuate a cold feeling. Bright colors were also used as design points to give a strong impression. Hardwood was put in appropriate places along the route of customers to control the sense of being in a city. A frequent change of seats, during a perm and coloring at hair salons, was taken into consideration, allowing the flow of movement to be simplified, giving an open feeling. Customers can also concentrate on their own images in the mirror as the space is divided according to its function.

디자인 이성민 / 미다스 디자인
위치 경기도 성남시 분당구 백현동 557번지 로데오 프라자 2층
용도 미용실
면적 495㎡
마감 바닥 - 노출콘크리트 위 에폭시 도장 / 벽 - 노출콘크리트, 열연강판, 색유리 / 천장 - 노출배관 위 검은색 도장
완공 2013.10
디자인팀 이성민
시공 이성민
사진 홍인근

Location 2F, Rodeo Plaza, 557, Baekhyeon-dong, Bundang-gu, Seongnam, Gyeonggi-do
Use Beauty parlor
Area 495㎡
Finishing Floor - Epoxy painting on exposed concrete / Wall - Exposed concrete, Hot rolled steel sheet, Color glass / Ceiling - Black painting on exposed pipe
Completion 2013.10
Photographer Hong In Geun

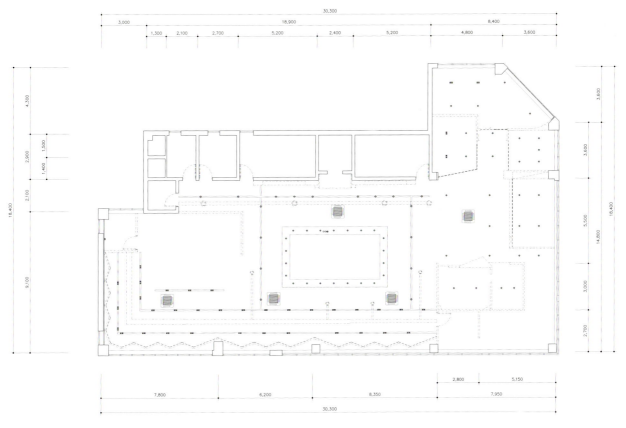

천장도 / ceiling plan

평면도 / floor plan

1 입구 2 계단 3 화장실 4 계산대 5 바 6 샴푸존 7 창고 8 중화존 9 헤어 스타일링존 10 메이크업실 11 직원실 12 원장실 13 대기공간 및 중화존 14 VIP실 15 두피 케어실

1 Entrance 2 Stairs 3 Toilet 4 Counter 5 Bar 6 Shampoo zone 7 Storage 8 Neutralization zone 9 Hairstyling zone 10 Makeup room 11 Staff room 12 Director's room 13 Waiting area & neutralization zone 14 VIP room 15 Scalp caring room

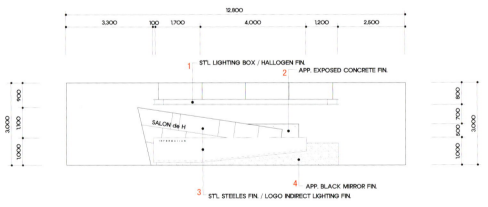

계산대 입면 A / counter elevation A

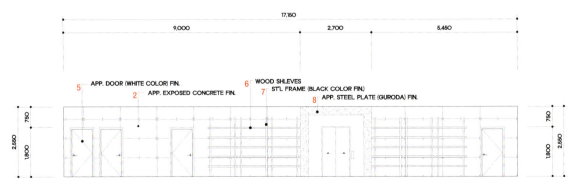

입구 입면 B / entrance elevation B

1 철제 조명박스, 할로겐 램프 2 지정 노출콘크리트 3 스테인리스 스틸, 로고 간접조명 4 지정 검은색 거울 5 지정 백색 문 6 목재 선반 7 검은색 철제 프레임 8 지정 열연강판 9 스테인리스 스틸 10 지정 소나무 럼버 11 지정 자동문 12 지정 시트 13 지정 주황색 유리 14 지정 유리, 시트 15 지정 래커 16 지정 적색 유리

1 Steel lighting box, hallogen lamp 2 App. exposed concrete 3 Stainless steel, logo indirect lighting 4 App. black mirror 5 App. white door 6 Wooden shelves 7 Black steel frame 8 App. hot rolled steel plate 9 Stainless steel 10 App. pine lumber 11 App. automatic door 12 App. sheet 13 App. orange glass 14 App. glass, sheet 15 App. laquer 16 App. red glass

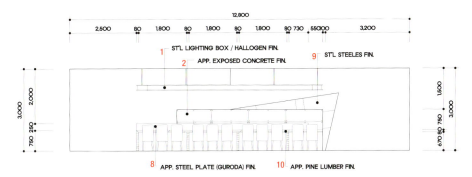

바 입면 C / bar elevation C

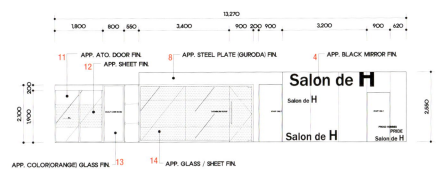

대기공간 및 중화존 입면 D / waiting area & neutralization zone elevation D

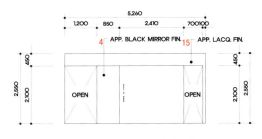

대기공간 및 중화존 입면 E / waiting area & neutralization zone elevation E

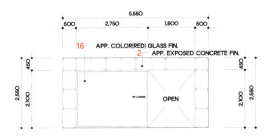

대기공간 및 중화존 입면 F / waiting area & neutralization zone elevation F

1 지정 도장 / 지정 거울, 간접조명 2 지정 소나무 럼버 3 지정 검은색 거울 4 지정 패브릭 보드 5 간접조명 6 지정 노출콘크리트 7 지정 열연강판 8 지정 거울 9 지정 수납장 10 철제 조명 박스, 할로겐 램프 11 스테인리스 스틸 12 지정 적색 도장 13 수납장 : 검은색 거울, 간접조명 14 칸막이 : 검은색 거울 15 수납장 : 검은색 거울 16 지정 적색 도장, 지정 레일 조명 17 지정 검은색 문

1 App. painting / app. mirror, indirect lighting 2 App. pine lumber 3 App. black mirror 4 App. fabric board 5 Indirect lighting 6 App. exposed concrete 7 App. hot rolled steel plate 8 App. mirror 9 App. storage closet 10 Steel lighting box, hallogen lamp 11 Stainless steel 12 App. red painting 13 Storage closet : black mirror, indirect lighting 14 Partition : black mirror 15 Storage closet : black mirror 16 App. red painting, app. rail lighting 17 App. black door

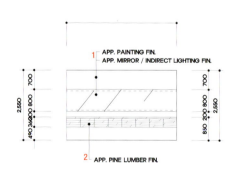

VIP실 입면 G / VIP room elevation G

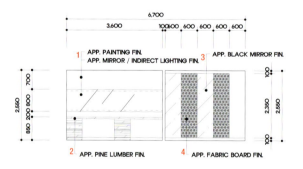

VIP실 입면 H / VIP room elevation H

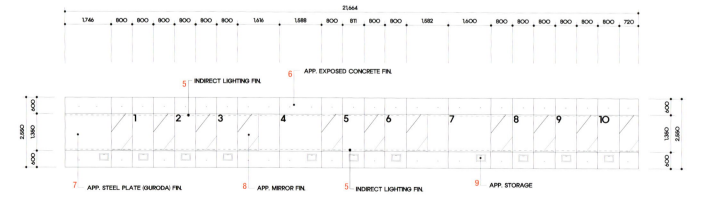

헤어 스타일링존 입면 I / hairstyling zone elevation I

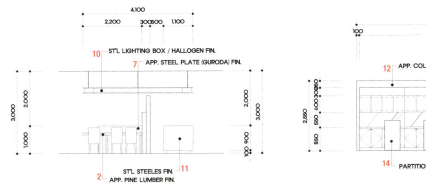

바 입면 J / bar elevation J

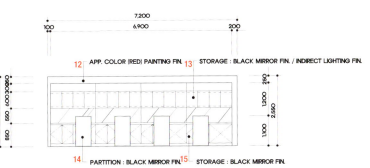

샴푸존 입면 K / shampoo zone elevation K

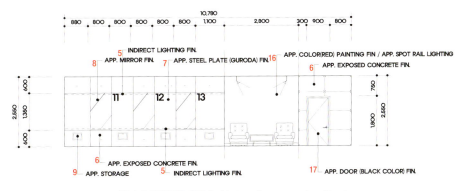

헤어 스타일링존 입면 L / hairstyling zone elevation L

1 30X30 나왕 각재 / T9.5 석고보드 2겹   2 T2 EG / 50X50 각파이프 / T100 우레탄폼 / 100X100 각파이프   3 방수턱   4 최소 T80 모르타르 위 하드너 / 기초 콘크리트 타설

1 30X30 Lauan square timber / T9.5 gypsum board 2ply   2 T2 EG / 50X50 square timber / T100 urethane form / 100X100 square timber   3 Waterproof hummock   4 Hardner on minimum T80 mortar / base concrete cast-in-piece

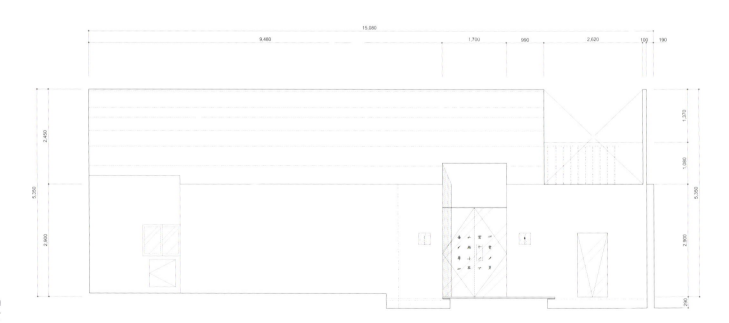

파사드 B / facade B

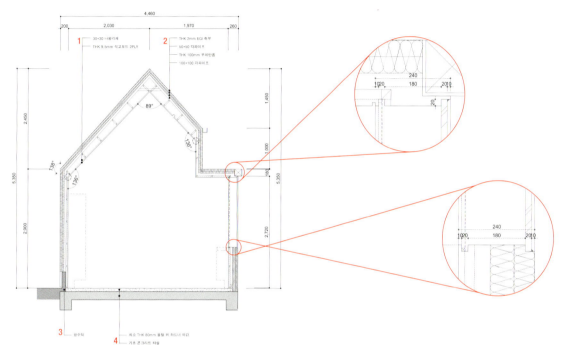

골조 단면 C / frame section C

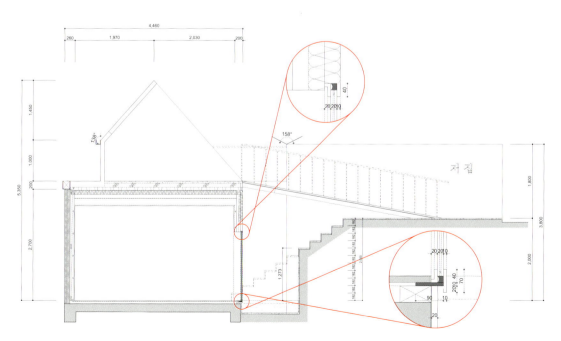

골조 단면 D / frame section D

1 트랙조명 설치 **2** 지정 도장 **3** T24 복층유리 위 지정시트 / 목재 위 지정 도장 / T1.2 청동 **4** 지정 한지 위 먹물 염색

1 Track lighting installed **2** App. painting **3** App. sheet on T24 paired glass / app. painting on wood / T1.2 bronze **4** Ink dying on app. Korean paper

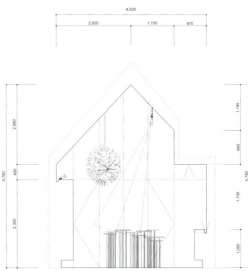

부엌 입면 F / kitchen elevation F

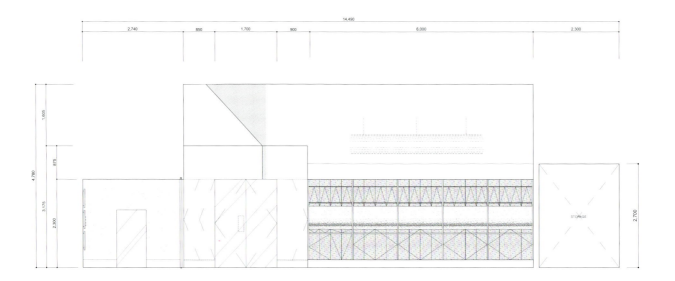

부엌 입면 E / kitchen elevation E

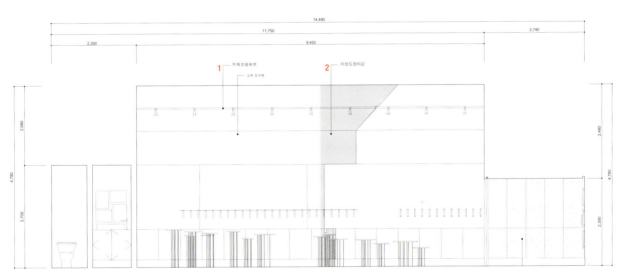

부엌 입면 G / kitchen elevation G

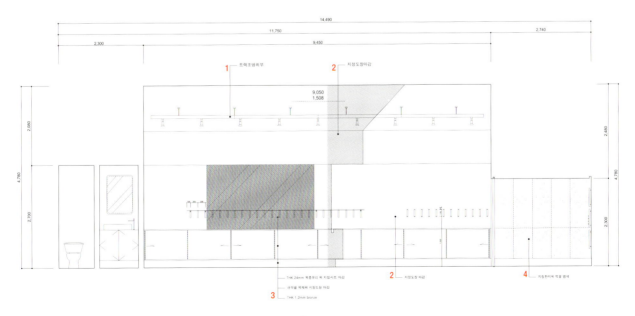

부엌 입면 H / kitchen elevation H

VB DIET LAB

PARASCOPE | Ha Jin Young

VB 다이어트 랩은 산업적인 느낌의 콘셉트로 VB의 제품과 다이어트 프로그램을 연결시켜 전문성과 최신 트렌드를 갖추도록 디자인한 공간이다. 1층에는 VB 브랜드를 체험해 볼 수 있는 카페와 편집 매장을 배치하였다. 매장 곳곳에 다이어트에 대한 문구들을 전략적으로 배치하여 이용자들의 공감을 유도하고자 하였다. 2층과 3층은 본격적인 다이어트 해결책을 제공하고 프로그램을 진행하는 전문 트레이닝 공간으로 계획하였다. 또한 체형분석 및 상담을 2층으로 유도하여 프로그램에 대한 방문객의 관심도가 높아지도록 하였다. 2층의 일부와 3층 프라이빗 존은 회원 전용 공간으로 계획하여 사적인 성격의 프로그램과 어울리도록 소음이나 조명, 마감재의 질감 및 촉감을 고려하여 계획 하였다. 또한 회원의 프로그램 진행 경로를 고려하여 다이어트에 대한 자극과 동기부여가 될 수 있도록 긍정적고 활기 넘치는 브랜드 이미지를 구축하였다.

VB DIET LAB is a space designed with the concept of industrial touch connecting VB products and its diet program to have speciality and the lastest trends. A cafeteria and a select store where people can experience VB brand is located on the 1st floor. Diet phrases are strategically placed in the store here and there to draw sympathy from the users. The 2nd and the 3rd floor spaces are planned as professional training space where full-scale diet solutions are provided and programs are carried out. Also body-type analysis and consulting are carried out on the 2nd floor to heighten visitors' interest for the program. One part of the 2nd floor and the 3rd floor private zone are planned as membership exclusive spaces, for which details such as noise, lighting, the texture and touch of the finishing materials were carefully chosen to match the private nature of the program. Also, a positive and lively brand image is constructed to stimulate and motivate the members considering the direction of their program progress.

디자인 하진영 / 파라스코프
위치 서울특별시 강남구 압구정로8길 26
용도 카페
면적 947.58㎡
마감 테라조 타일, 우드 플로링, 시멘트 블록타일, 애쉬 각재, 무늬목, 판도모, 열연강판, 목모보드
설계기간 2012. 8 ~ 2012. 12
공사기간 2012. 12 ~ 2013. 4
디자인팀 양경미, 라윤지, 황보강범, 김다은, 신영경
시공 박영환, 박충구, 전희원 / (주)모티브
사진 김재윤

Location 26, Apgujung-ro 8-gil, Gangnam-gu, Seoul
Use Cafe
Area 947.58㎡
Finishing Terazzo tile, Wood flooring, Cement block tile, Ash timber, Wood veneer, Pandomo, Hot rolled steel plate, Wood fiber board
Design period 2012. 8 ~ 2012. 12
Construction period 2012. 12 ~ 2013. 4
Photographer Kim Jae Yoon

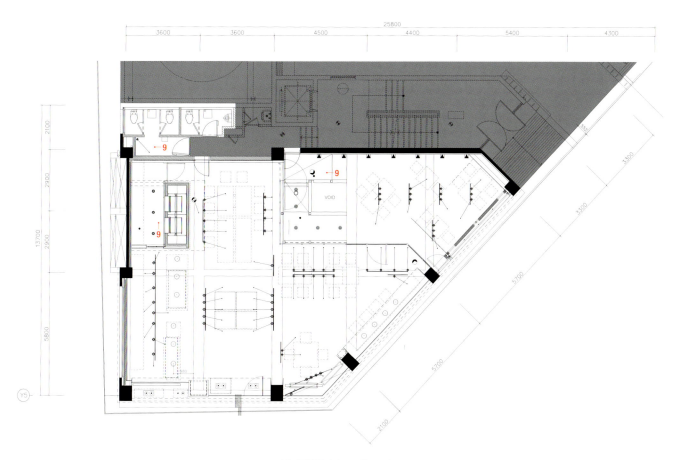

1층 천장도 / 1st ceiling plan

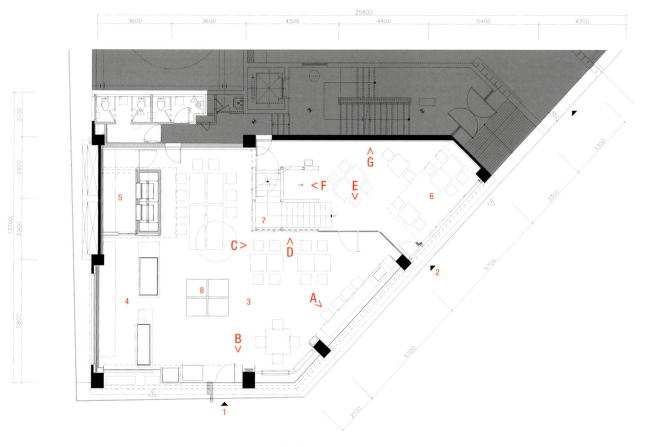

1층 평면도 / 1st floor plan

1 주출입구 2 보조출입구 3 카페 4 계산 및 픽업대 5 식음료 저장실 6 VB 카페 7 계단 하부창고 8 제품 진열대 9 지정 백색 페인트

1 Main entrance 2 Sub entrance 3 Cafe 4 Counter & pick-up table 5 Food & beverage pantry 6 VB cafe 7 Storage under stairs 8 Product display table 9 App. white paint

1 기존 건축 마감   2 T12 투명유리, T3 결로방지 필름   3 지정 회색 시멘트 페인트   4 지정 백색 페인트   5 애쉬 우드 각재(백색 페인트 마감)   6 T0.5 골강판(백색 페인트 마감)   7 T12 투명유리   8 지정 진회색 페인트   9 T8 투명 바둑판 망입유리   10 애쉬 무늬목(백색 페인트 마감)

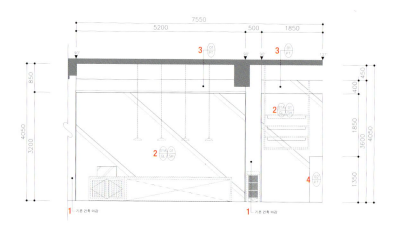

카페 입면 A / cafe elevation A

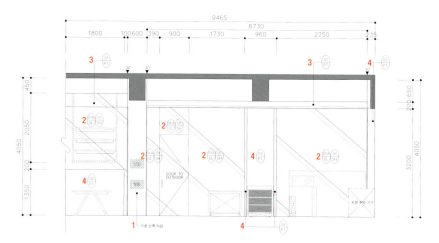

카페 입면 B / cafe elevation B

1 Existing architectural finish 2 T12 clear glass, T3 dew proofing film 3 App. gray cement paint 4 App. white paint 5 Ash wood square timber (white paint finish) 6 T0.5 corrurated steel sheet (white paint finish) 7 T12 clear glass 8 App. dark gray paint 9 T8 grid patterned wire sheet glass 10 Ash wood veneer (white paint finish)

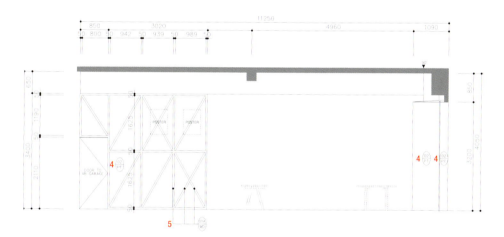

카페 입면 C / cafe elevation C

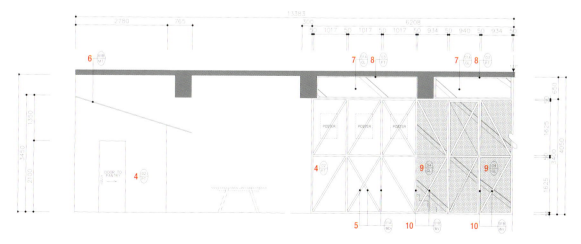

카페 입면 D / cafe elevation D

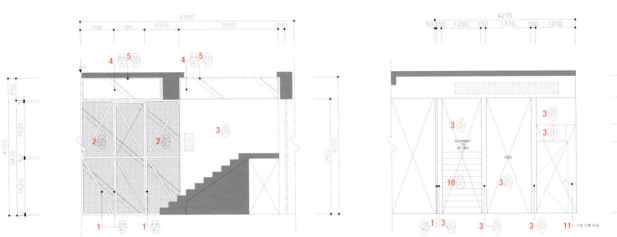

VB 카페 입면 E / VB cafe elevation E

VB 카페 입면 F / VB cafe elevation F

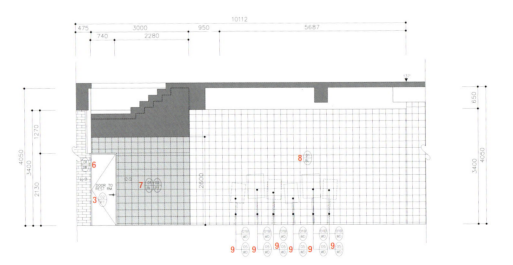

VB 카페 입면 G / VB cafe elevation G

1 애쉬 무늬목(백색 페인트 마감) 2 T8 투명 바둑판 망입유리 3 지정 백색 페인트 4 T12 투명유리 5 지정 진회색 페인트 6 190X90X57 시멘트 벽돌(수퍼 화이트 페인트 마감) 7 시멘트 블록 모노타일, 지정 백색 페인트 8 시멘트 블록 모노타일 9 애쉬 우드 각재(투명 우레탄 마감) / T24 미송합판 10 투명 에폭시 셀프 레벨링 11 기존 건축 마감 12 500X500X22 지정 타일(3X22 @1,500 황동 줄눈 시공) 13 회색 핸드 크래프트 타일 14 핑크색 수퍼 하이글로시 에나멜 도장 15 재료 분리(T3 평철)

1 Ash wood veneer (white paint finish) 2 T8 grid patterned wire sheet glass 3 App. white paint 4 T12 clear glass 5 App. dark gray paint 6 190X90X57 cement brick (super white paint finish) 7 Cement block monotile, app. white paint 8 Cement block monotile 9 Ash wood square timber (clear urethane finish) / T24 douglas fir plywood 10 Clear epoxy self-leveling 11 Existing architectural finish 12 500X500X22 app. tile (3X22 @1,500 brass masonry joint construction) 13 Gray handcraft tile 14 Pink super high glossy enamel painting 15 Material division (T3 flat steel)

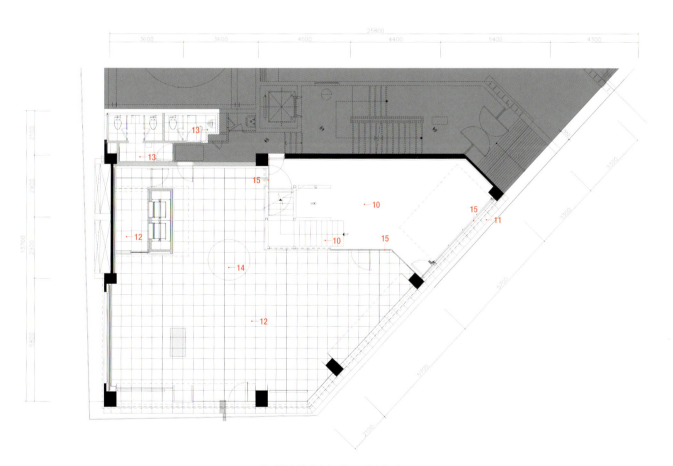

1층 바닥 마감 / 1st floor finish plan

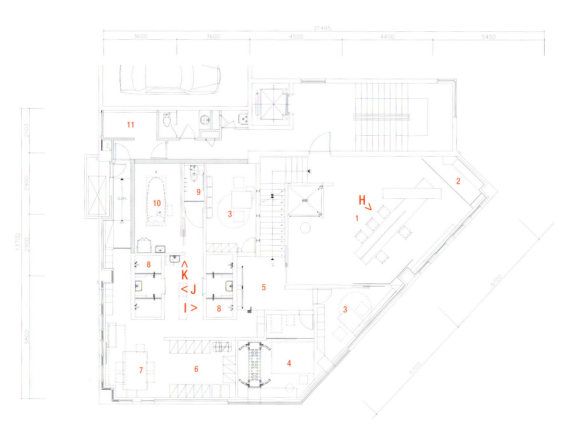

2층 평면도 / 2nd floor plan

1 리셉션 2 안쪽 사무실 3 상담실 4 측정실 5 로비 6 소지품 보관실 7 파우더룸
8 샤워실 9 화장실 10 디톡스 라이트 존 11 기계실 12 T5 열연강판 13 애쉬 무늬목
(투명 우레탄 마감) 14 200X200X8 H-빔(백색 페인트 마감) 15 지정 회색 시멘트 페인트
16 T8 투명 바둑판 망입유리, 유백색 시트 17 지정 회색 페인트 18 T3 스테인리스 스틸
19 지정 웜그레이 페인트 20 T1.2 스테인리스 스틸 21 T6 거울

1 Reception 2 Back room 3 Counselling room 4 Measurement room 5 Foyer 6 Locker room 7 Powder room 8 Shower room 9 Restroom 10 Detox lite zone 11 Machinery room 12 T5 hot rolled steel sheet 13 Ash wood veneer (clear urethane finish) 14 200X200X8 H-beam (white paint finish) 15 App. gray cement paint 16 T8 grid patterned wire sheet glass, milky white sheet 17 App. gray paint 18 T3 stainless steel 19 App. warm gray paint 20 T1.2 stainless steel 21 T6 mirror

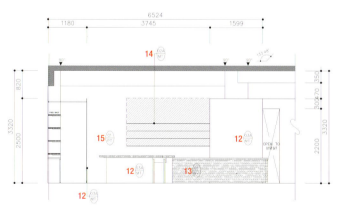

리셉션 입면 H / reception elevation H

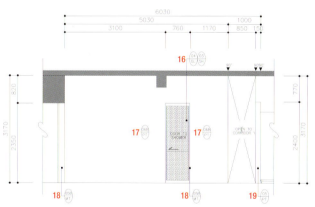

복도 입면 I / corridor elevation I

복도 입면 J / corridor elevation J

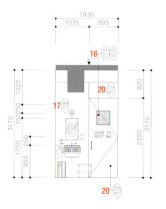

복도 입면 K / corridor elevation K

3층 천장도 / 3rd ceiling plan

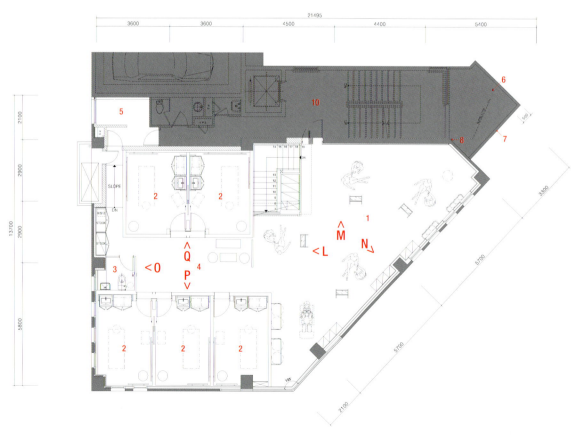

3층 평면도 / 3rd floor plan

1 바디핏 운동 공간   2 라인셋 테라피실   3 화장실   4 홀   5 기계실   6 지붕 배수구   7 캐노피   8 □120X60 스테인리스 스틸 선홈통 설치   9 지정 백색 페인트   10 엘리베이터 홀   11 목재 트러스   12 지정 녹회색 페인트   13 지정 회색 시멘트 페인트   14 지정 벽돌   15 T1.6 황동 유광 골드 금속   16 T1.6 황동 유광 골드 금속 / T2 체인연결 울타리 철망(백색 분체도장 마감)   17 지정 백색 도장 방화셔터 레일

1 Body fit training zone   2 Line set therapy room   3 Restroom   4 Hall   5 Machinery room   6 Roof drain   7 Canopy   8 □120X60 stainless steel downpipe installed   9 App. white paint   10 Elevator hall   11 Wooden truss   12 App. greenish gray paint   13 App. gray cement paint   14 App. brick   15 T1.6 brass glossy gold metal   16 T1.6 brass glossy gold metal / T2 fence mesh chain-connected (white powder painting finish)   17 App. white painting fire shutter rail

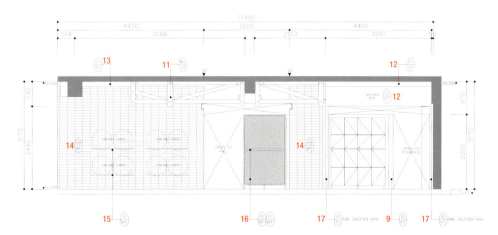

운동 공간 입면 L / training zone elevation L

115

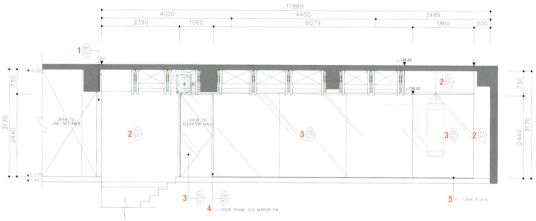

운동 공간 입면 M / training zone elevation M

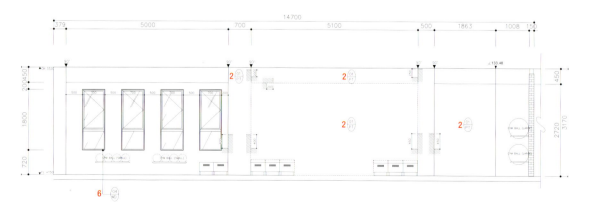

운동 공간 입면 N / training zone elevation N

1 지정 벽돌 2 지정 회색 시멘트 페인트 3 T6 거울 4 T1.6 스테인리스 스틸 거울, 문 프레임 : 스테인리스 스틸 거울 5 10mm 리빌 6 T9 미송합판 7 T0.5 골강판(백색 페인트 마감) 8 지정 백색 페인트 9 지정 금색 도장 10 T1.2 스테인리스 스틸 11 T3 스테인리스 스틸 12 150X75X9 ㄷ형강(지정 백색 도장) 13 T1.6 황동 유광 골드 금속 14 유백색 시트, 투명유리 15 지정 목재 16 방화셔터 레일 17 T1.6 황동 유광 골드 금속, T2 체인 연결 울타리 철망(백색 분체도장 마감)

1 App. brick 2 App. gray cement paint 3 T6 mirror 4 T1.6 stainless steel mirror, door frame : stainless steel mirror 5 10mm reveal 6 T9 douglas fir plywood 7 T0.5 corrugated steel sheet (white paint finish) 8 App. white paint 9 App. gold painting 10 T1.2 stainless steel 11 T3 stainless steel 12 150X75X9 C-steel (app. white paint) 13 T1.6 brass glossy gold metal 14 Milky white sheet, clear glass 15 App. wood 16 Fire shutter rail 17 T1.6 brass glossy gold metal, T2 fence mesh chain-connected (white powder painting finish)

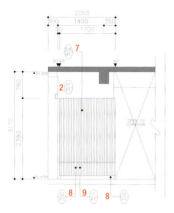

라인셋 테라피실 입면 O / line set therapy room elevation O

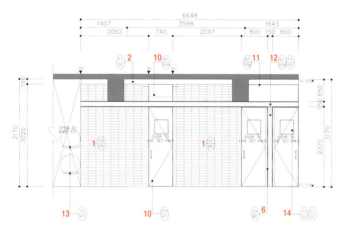

라인셋 테라피실 입면 P / line set therapy room elevation P

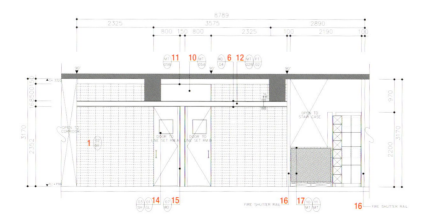

라인셋 테라피실 입면 Q / line set therapy room elevation Q

9 TOPAZ

CORE ID | Lim Eun Sik

나인 토파즈는 넘쳐나는 상점들 사이에서 정체성을 드러낼 수 있는 차별화된 디자인을 필요로 하였다. '연결'을 주제로 외관과 내부를 아우르는 디자인에 조형적 요소를 더하고 시선을 유도할 수 있도록 하였다. 또한 기하학적인 매스들이 연결되어 만들어진 독특한 형태의 창이 내부를 담아내며 공간에 깊이감을 준다. 내부에는 전체적으로 노출콘크리트에 목재와 검은색을 사용하여 모던하면서도 빈티지한 분위기를 담았다. 자칫 단조롭고 무게감이 느껴질 수 있는 공간에 간접조명을 사용하여 따뜻하고 감성적인 공간을 연출하였다. 특히, 스타일을 완성하는 공간은 검은색으로 마감하여 다른 공간과의 차별성을 주었다. 그 밖에 다양하게 연결된 간결한 구조체들을 이용하여 1층에는 오브제를 통한 공간의 연속성과 깊이감을 전달하고, 2층에는 선형 요소로써 공간 전체를 연결하여 자연스럽고 간결한 공간을 조성하였다.

9 TOPAZ required a differentiated design to highlight its identity in the midst of overflowing surrounding stores. Based on the theme of 'connection,' formative elements were added to the design that brings together the interior and the exterior in order to draw people's attention. Also, distinctively shaped windows built from the connection of geographic mass, embrace the interior giving a sense of depth to the space. Using exposed concrete, wood, and black fishing in general, the interior presents a modern look which also creates a vintage atmosphere. In a space which could have almost felt simple and heavy, indirect lighting contributed warmth and sensibility. In particular, the space where the final styling is carried out is differentiated from other spaces with black finishing. Using simple structures that are connected in various ways, the 1st floor presents continuity and depth of the space through objet, and the 2nd floor forms a natural and simple space from connecting the overall space with a linear element.

디자인 임은식 / 코어 아이디
위치 서울특별시 서대문구 대현동 90-40
용도 미용실
면적 160㎡
마감 바닥 - 노출콘크리트, 투명 에폭시 / 벽 - 모르타르, 도장, 목재 / 천장 - 모르타르, 도장, 바리솔
완공 2012. 10
사진 임은식

Location 90-40, Daehyeon-dong, Seodaemun-gu, Seoul
Use Hair salon
Area 160㎡
Finishing Floor - Exposed concrete, Clear epoxy / Wall - Mortar, Painting, Wood / Ceiling - Mortar, Painting, Barrisol
Completion 2012. 10
Photographer Lim Eun Sik

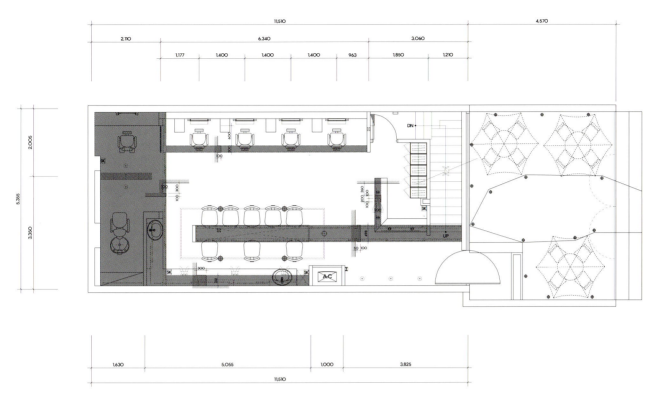

1층 천장도 / 1st ceiling plan

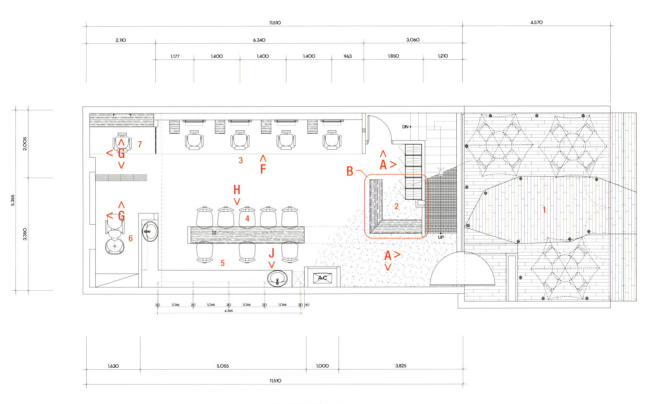

1층 평면도 / 1st floor plan

1 데크 공간   2 안내데스크   3 스타일링 공간   4 중화 및 대기공간   5 음료 공간   6 샴푸실   7 메이크업 공간

1 Deck area   2 Information desk   3 Styling area   4 Neutralization & waiting area   5 Drinking area   6 Shampoo room   7 Makeup room

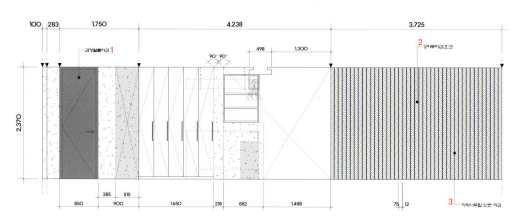

안내데스크 입면 A / information desk elevation A

1 검은색 필름   2 오크 강마루   3 자작나무 합판 단면   4 낙엽송 마감 위 래커   1 Black film   2 Oak HPL flooring   3 Birch plywood section   4 Lacquer on larch wood finish

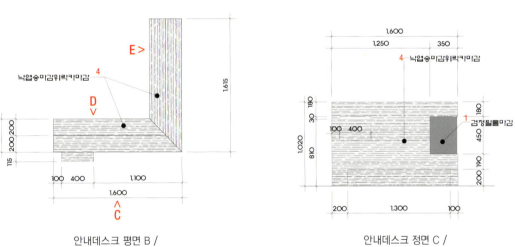

안내데스크 평면 B /
information desk top view B

안내데스크 정면 C /
information desk front view C

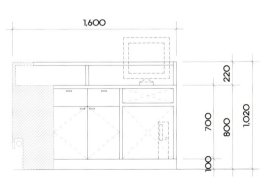

안내데스크 배면 D /
information desk rear view D

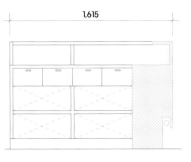

안내데스크 배면 E /
information desk rear view E

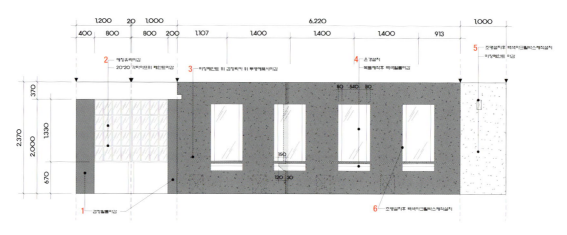

스타일링 공간 입면 F / styling area elevation F

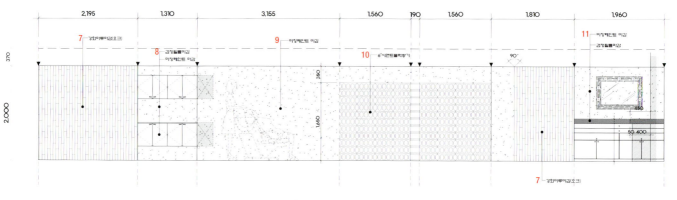

샴푸실, 메이크업실 입면 G / shampoo room, makeup room elevation G

1 검은색 필름 2 에칭 유리 / 20X20 각파이프 위 페인트 3 미장 페인트 위 검은색 래커 위 투명 에폭시 4 은경 설치 / 목틀 제작 후 백색 필름 5 조명 설치 후 백색 아크릴 박스 제작 및 설치 / 미장 페인트 6 조명 설치 후 백색 아크릴 박스 제작 및 설치 7 오크 강화마루 8 검은색 필름 / 미장 페인트 9 미장 페인트 10 6인치 시멘트 블럭 쌓기 11 미장 페인트 / 검은색 필름 12 간판 제작(조명 설치) 13 낙엽송 마감 위 래커 / 목틀 14 디퓨저 위 검은색 래커 15 낙엽송 마감 위 래커

1 Black film 2 Etching glass / paint on 20X20 square pipe 3 Clear epoxy on black lacquer on plastering paint 4 Silver mirror installed / white film after wooden frame making 5 White acrylic box making and installed after light installed / plastering paint 6 White acrylic box making and installed after light installed 7 Oak laminate floor 8 Black film / plastering paint 9 Plastering paint 10 6 inches cement block piling 11 Plastering paint / black film 12 Sign making (light installed) 13 Lacquer on larch wood finish / wooden frame 14 Black lacquer on diffuser 15 Lacquer on larch wood finish

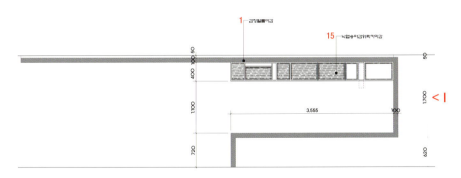

대기 공간 가구 정면 H / waiting area furniture front view H

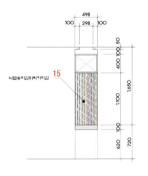

대기 공간 가구 측면 I / waiting area furniture side view I

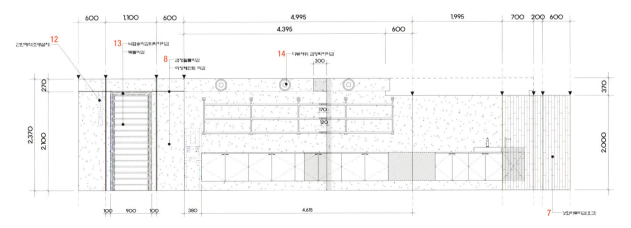

음료 공간 입면 J / drinking area elevation J

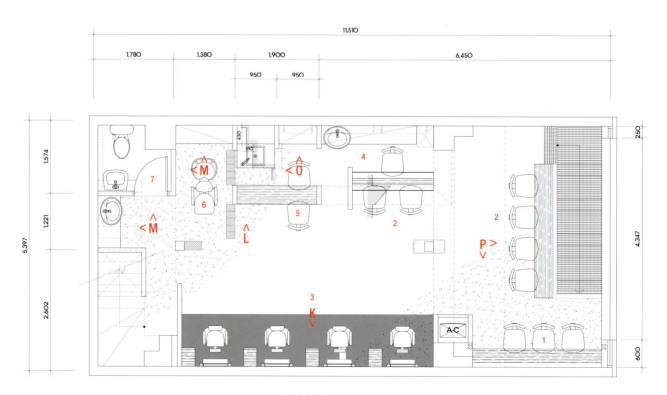

2층 평면도 / 2nd floor plan

1 중화 공간　2 대기 공간　3 스타일링 공간　4 음료 공간　5 네일 공간　6 샴푸실　7 화장실　8 검은색 필름 / 미장 페인트　9 검은색 필름

1 Neutralization area　2 Waiting area　3 Styling area　4 Drinking area　5 Nail area　6 Shampoo room　7 Restroom　8 Black film / plastering paint　9 Black film

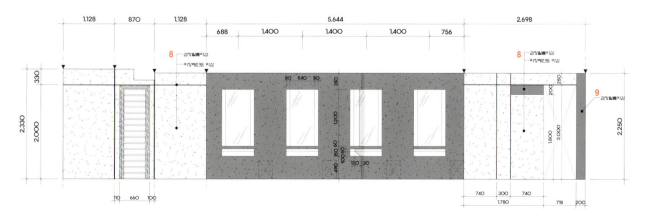

스타일링 공간 입면 K / styling area elevation K

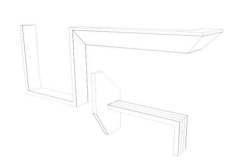

네일 공간 가구 투시도 / nail area furniture perspective

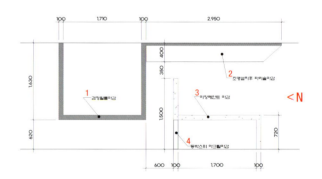

네일 공간 가구 정면 L / nail area furniture front view L

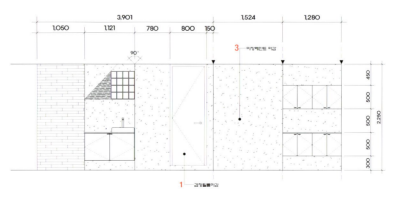

화장실 및 샴푸실 입면 M / restroom & shampoo room elevation M

1 검은색 필름 2 조명 설치 후 바리솔 3 미장 페인트 4 등 박스 위 아크릴 5 등 박스 위 에칭 유리 6 낙엽송 마감 위 래커 7 6인치 시멘트 블럭 쌓기 8 미장 페인트 / 주문 소파 제작 / 낙엽송 마감 위 래커 9 검은색 필름 / 은경 설치 / 미장 페인트

1 Black film 2 Barrisol after light installed 3 Plastering paint 4 Acrylic on light box 5 Etching glass on light box 6 Lacquer on larch wood finish 7 6 inches cement block piling 8 Plastering paint / order-made sofa / lacquer on larch wood finish 9 Black film / silver mirror / plastering paint

네일 공간 가구 측면 N / nail area furniture side view N

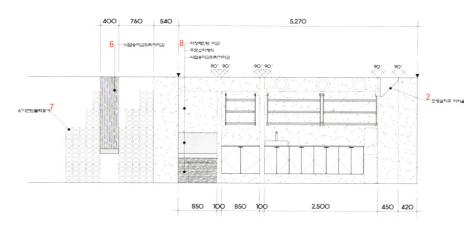

네일 공간 및 음료 공간 입면 O / nail area & drinking area elevation O

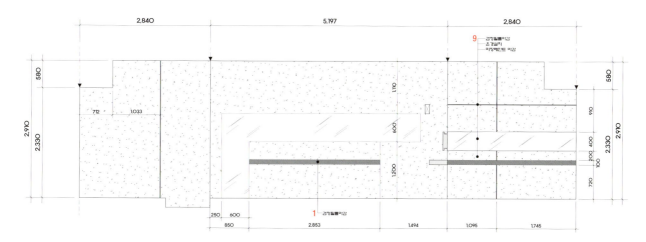

중화 공간 및 대기 공간 입면 P / neutralization area & waiting area elevation P

2014 ANNUAL INTERIOR DETAIL

CLINIC

130 MIRAE MEDICAL FOUNDATION HEALTH IMPROVEMENT CENTER
미래의료재단 건강증진센터

138 OLIVE PLASTIC SURGERY
올리브성형외과

148 GOOD FLOWER DERMATOLOGY CLINIC
굿플라워 피부과

154 E.EUM ANIMAL MEDICAL CLINIC
이음동물병원

162 INURI ORIENTAL MEDICAL CLINIC
아이누리 한의원

176 HOSAN HOSPITAL POSTNATAL CARE CENTER
호산병원 산후조리원

184 PYUNKANG ORIENTAL CLINIC_SEOMYUN
편강한의원_서면

194 SUUM SLEEP CLINIC
숨 수면클리닉

200 AGAON FERTILITY CLINIC
아가온 여성의원

206 SEOUL BEST DENTAL CLINIC
서울 베스트 치과

214 DREAM DENTAL CLINIC
드림 치과

226 KOWON PLASTIC SURGERY
코원 성형외과

232 SHINSEGAE DENTAL CLINIC
신세계 치과

242 S PEDIATRICS (HOUSE IN HOUSE)
S 소아과(집 속의 집)

MIRAE MEDICAL FOUNDATION HEALTH IMPROVEMENT CENTER

jay is working. | Jang Soon Gak

미래의료재단 건강검진센터는 뇌에 특화된 검진과 앞서가는 검진기술의 집약적인 공간이다. 이러한 연구소적 검진센터의 이미지는 주로 백색을 사용하여 생명공학적 공간으로 표현하였고, 오전에 몰리는 검진센터의 성격을 고려하여 압축적 순환동선으로 설계하였다. 각종 검진의 순서에 따라 가다, 서다를 반복하는 건강검진센터의 흐름이 생체학적 순환과 매우 유사하다는 결론과 함께, 생태모방의 공간기법을 적용시켰다. 동물의 근간을 이루는 '갈비뼈'를 활용하여 계단구조와 틀을 구성하였다. 공간 전체에 반복되는 '갈비뼈'에 의한 비정형성과 리듬감을 통해 센터의 공간적 정체성을 형성하였다. 움직임에 대한 공간언어를 유지시키는 또 다른 시각적 요소로서, 원과 정사각형으로 만들어진 새로운 로고를 디자인하였다. 움직이는 공간 사이사이에 정적인 형태의 원을 이미지월로 배치함으로써 시선을 집중시키고 멈추는 지점을 암시하며, 전체적으로는 공간의 균형을 유지시켰다.

The Mirae Medical Foundation Health Examination Center, through its space, intended to convey that it is an epitome of specialized examinations for brains and advanced examination technologies. This laboratory-like examination center's image expresses the shape of a biotechnological space by mainly using the color white, and its compressive circulation flow, being the unique feature of the examination center where everyone gathers in the morning time, had to be considered in the design. With the conclusion of the health examination center spatial flow of stop-and-go by the sequence of various examinations, it was very similar to that of a biological circulation, where the designer decided to apply the space technique of biometrics to this space. Utilizing the 'ribs', whose structural shape consists in the basis of animals, the designer made the structure and frame of the staircase. These atypical characteristics and rhythmic sense of the ribs which are repeated atypically was applied and used in the entire space sequentially so that it forms the space identity of this center. Another visual point which will maintain the 'space language' regarding the flow is the center's new static logo, made based on circles and squares. Image walls, which are static circles, are arranged within the space, thus provide a focal point and suggest locations where to stop while maintaining a balance within the entirety of the space.

디자인 장순각 / (주)제이이즈워킹
위치 서울특별시 강남구 삼성동 158-23 K타워 9-10층
용도 병원
면적 1,340.92㎡
마감 안티스투코, 원목 바닥, 타일, 무늬목, 인조대리석
완공 2012. 11
디자인팀 채원우, 이현주, 김은경, 안효정, 이진국
C.I & 사인디자인팀 송종현, 김경환, 이윤희
시공 (주)명성인토피아
사진 (주)제이이즈워킹 제공

Location 9-10F, K Tower, 158-23 Samseong 1-dong, Gangnam-gu, Seoul
Use Hospital
Area 1,340.92m²
Finishing Antistucco, Wood flooring, Tile, Wood veneer, Mock marble
Completion 2012. 11
Photos offer jay is working.

10층 평면도 / 10th floor plan

9층 평면도 / 9th floor plan

1 안내데스크 2 라운지 3 소지품 보관실 4 상담데스크 5 진료실 6 초음파실 7 구강 검사실 8 스트레스 검사실 9 골밀도 측정실 10 기초검사실 11 인바디 측정실 12 안과 검사실 13 VIP 소지품 보관실 14 VIP 회의실 15 지정 타일 16 지정 원목마루 17 대기공간 18 CT 촬영실 19 MRI 촬영실 20 X-ray 실 21 채혈실 22 폐기능 검사실 23 내시경실 24 내시경 회복실 25 심전도실 26 VIP 내시경 회복실 27 VIP 초음파실 28 홀 29 PET/CT 촬영실

1 Information desk 2 Lounge 3 Locker room 4 Counseling room 5 Consulting room 6 Ultrasound room 7 Dental care room 8 Stress testing room 9 Bone density measurement room 10 Basic testing room 11 Inbody measurement room 12 Ophthalmology inspection room 13 VIP locker room 14 VIP conference room 15 App. tile 16 App. hardwood floor 17 Waiting area 18 CT scan room 19 MRI scan room 20 X-ray room 21 Blood collecting room 22 Pulmonary function testing room 23 Endoscope room 24 Recovery room for endoscope 25 Electrocardiogram room 26 VIP recovery room for endoscope 27 VIP ultrasound room 28 Hall 29 PET/CT scan room

1 문 : 지정 무늬목 알판   2 벽면 : 백색 안티스투코   3 벽면 : 지정 무늬목 알판   4 강화유리 위 지정 그라데이션 시트   5 상부 : 간접조명 매입   6 문   7 문 손잡이   8 매입 벽면 : 지정 무늬목 알판   9 RFID 시스템 17인치 모니터 매입   10 고정 의자   11 걸레받이 : 지정 필름   12 강화유리 문   13 강화유리 위 지정 그라데이션 시트   14 무늬목 알판

1 Door : app. wood veneer board   2 Wall : white antistucco   3 Wall : app. wood veneer board   4 App. gradation sheet on tempered glass   5 Top : indirect lighting embedded   6 Door   7 Door handle   8 Embedded wall : app. wood veneer board   9 RFID system 17" monitor embedded   10 Fixed bench   11 Baseboard : app. film   12 Tempered glass door   13 App. gradation sheet on tempered glass   14 Wood veneer board

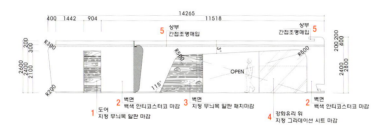

9층 라운지 입면 A / 9th floor lounge elevation A

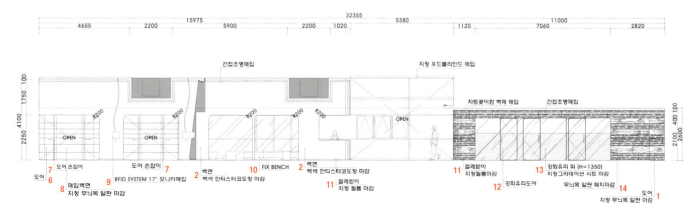

9층 입면 B / 9th floor elevation B

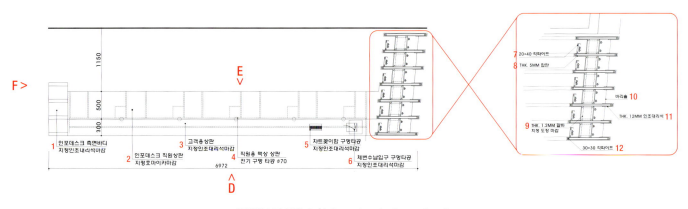

안내데스크 평면 C / information desk top view C

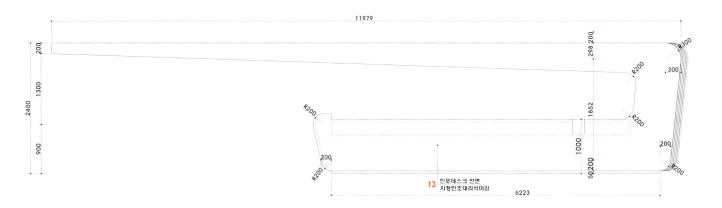

안내데스크 정면 D / information desk view D

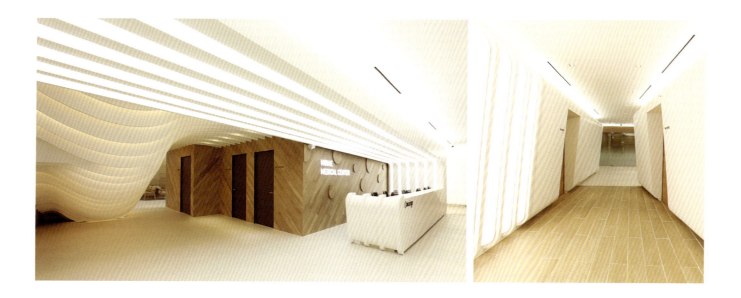

1 안내데스크 측면 : 지정 인조대리석 2 안내데스크 직원용 상판 : 지정 포마이카 3 고객용 상판 : 지정 인조대리석 4 직원용 책상 상판 : Ø70 전기구멍 타공 5 차트꽂이함 구멍 타공 : 지정 인조대리석 6 채변수납 입구 구멍 타공 : 지정 인조대리석 7 20X40 각파이프 8 T5 합판 9 T1.2 갈바륨 : 지정 도장 10 바리솔 11 T12 인조대리석 12 30X30 각파이프 13 안내데스크 전면 : 지정 인조대리석 14 카운터 내부 : 지정색 도장 15 카운터 전면 : 지정 인조대리석 16 수납함 : 지정색 도장 17 잠금장치 : 상하 수납함 일체형 18 책상 후면 : 지정색 도장 19 차트꽂이함 : 지정색 도장 20 쿠폰함 : 지정색 도장

1 Information desk side : app. mock marble 2 Information desk top board for staff : app. formica 3 Top board for customer : app. mock marble 4 Desk top board for staff : Ø70 hole perforated for electricity 5 Chart holder hole perforated : app. mock marble 6 Feces sample storage entry hole perforated : app. mock marble 7 20X40 square pipe 8 T5 plywood 9 T1.2 galvalume : app. painting 10 Barrisol 11 T12 mock marble 12 30X30 square pipe 13 Information desk front : app. mock marble 14 Counter interior : app. color painting 15 Counter front : app. mock marble 16 Storage tray : app. color painting 17 Locking device : upper and lower trays, integral type 18 Desk back : app. color painting 19 Chart holder : app. color painting 20 Coupon tray : app. color painting

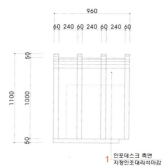

안내데스크 좌측면 F / information desk left side view F

안내데스크 단면 G / information desk section G

안내데스크 좌측면 H / information desk left side view H

안내데스크 단면 I / information desk section I

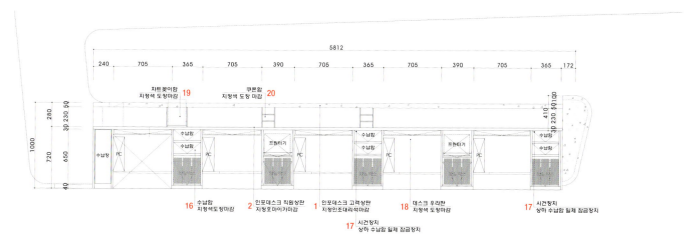

안내데스크 후면 E / information desk rear view E

계단 루버 전개도 / stairs louver extended elevation

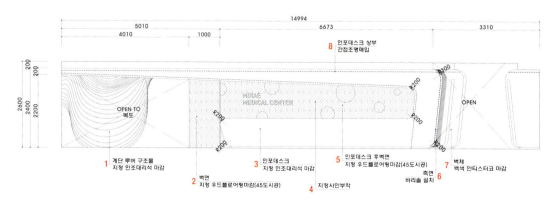

1 계단 루버 구조물 지정 인조대리석 마감
2 벽면 지정 우드플로어링마감(45도시공)
3 인포데스크 지정 인조대리석 마감
4 지정사인부착
5 인포데스크 후벽면 지정 우드플로어링마감(45도시공)
6 측면 바리솔 설치
7 벽체 백색 안티스터코 마감
8 인포데스크 상부 간접조명매입

9층 입면 J / 9th floor elevation J

1 계단 루버 구조물 : 지정 인조대리석 2 벽면 : 지정 우드 플로링 (45° 시공) 3 안내데스크 : 지정 인조대리석 4 지정 사인 부착 5 안내데스크 후벽면 : 지정 우드 플로링(45° 시공) 6 측면 : 바리솔 설치 7 벽체 : 백색 안티스투코 8 안내데스크 상부 : 간접조명 매입 9 걸레받이 : 지정 필름 10 벽체 하부 : 간접조명 설치 11 벽체 : 지정 안티스투코 12 벽체 상부 : 간접조명 설치 13 벽체 : 지정색 유리 14 RFID 시스템 17인치 모니터 매입 15 간이 데스크 : 지정 인조대리석 16 문 : 지정 필름 17 천장 : 바리솔 설치 18 RFID 모니터 통풍구 설치 19 벽면 : 사인 디자인월 설치 20 미닫이문 : 지정 필름

1 Stair louver strcture : app. mock marble 2 Wall : app. wood flooring (45° construction) 3 Information desk : app. mock marble 4 App. sign attached 5 Information desk back wall : app. wood flooring (45° construction) 6 Side : barrisol installed 7 Wall : white antistucco 8 Information desk top : indirect lighting embedded 9 Baseboard : app. film 10 Wall bottom : indirect lighting installed 11 Wall : app. antistucco 12 Wall top : indirect lighting installed 13 Wall : app. color glass 14 RFID system 17" monitor embedded 15 Station desk : app. mock marble 16 Door : app. film 17 Ceiling : barrisol installed 18 RFID monitor vent installed 19 Wall : sign design wall installed 20 Sliding door : app. film

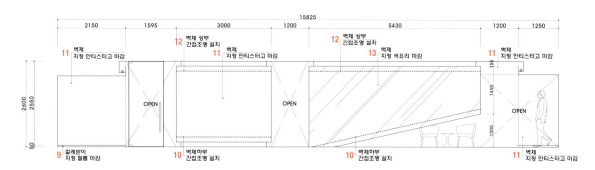

10층 입면 K / 10th floor elevation K

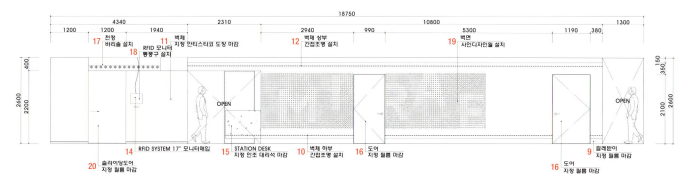

10층 입면 L / 10th floor elevation L

OLIVE PLASTIC SURGERY

BALSANG Inc. | Lee Kyu Hyuk, Park Ji Yoon

성형을 결정하는 사람은 그것을 자신의 스타일에 대한 시작 혹은 완성의 개념으로 인식하고 외형에 대한 사회적 대우를 의식한다. 이러한 점에서 성형외과 공간의 주체자인 그들은 다른 의료 공간의 사용자와 뚜렷이 구분되는 지향점을 갖고 있고, 그들과 공감할 수 있는 패션을 테마로 공간을 해석하고자 하였다. 자연스러운 인체선을 살리는 디자인에서 좀 더 과장되고 기하학적인 에지(edge)를 포인트로 강조하는 패션 트렌드의 재해석은 이 공간을 좌우하는 개념으로 탄생하였다. 공간은 벽과 천장, 창틀에 이르기까지 강렬하고 기하학적인 느낌을 담아 유쾌한 감성으로 연출되었으며, 블랙&화이트의 일관된 톤과 유광의 자재들이 결합되고 부딪히며 독특한 카오스적 미를 형성하였다. 이는 절제미를 약화시키고 과장과 혼돈을 강화시킨 공간 개념으로 스타일링된 하나의 패션 장르와 같이, 외형에 민감한 사용자에게 공간미에 대한 새로운 관심과 흥미를 불러일으키며 신선한 감성을 체험하게 한다.

People who decide to have plastic surgery perceive the procedure as the beginning or completion of their style and are conscious of the social treatment of their appearance. In this regard, these people, being the main bodies of the surgery space, share an orientation that is distinct from that of users of other medical service space. Accordingly, the design for Olive Plastic Surgery attempted to interpret the space with the theme of fashion with which these people can identify. Thus, the reinterpretation of fashion trend, from designs that point out the natural curve of the body to designs that emphasize exaggerated and geometric edge as points, was born as the concept that determines this space. Hence, the space is presented with pleasant sensibility delivering strong and geometric impressions throughout the wall and ceiling and even the window ledge. A unique and chaotic beauty is formed as the consistent tone of black and white is combined with or clashed against glossy materials. Like a fashion genre that has been styled with a space concept that undermines restrained beauty but reinforces exaggeration and chaos, the place evokes new interest for beauty of space from the people who are sensitive to appearance and lets them experience fresh sensibility.

디자인 이규혁, 박지윤 / (주)발상
위치 서울특별시 강남구 역삼동 825-5 8층
용도 병원
면적 650㎡
마감 바닥 – 타일, 카페트 / 벽– 래커, 페인팅 유리, 스테인리스 스틸, 그래픽 시트 / 천장 – 비닐 페인트, 래커
완공 2012. 10
시공팀 임진수
사진 (주)발상 제공

Location 8F, 825-5, Yeoksam-dong, Gangnam-gu, Seoul
Use Hospital
Area 650㎡
Finishing Floor - Tile, Carpet / Wall - Lacquer, Painting glass, Stainless steel, Graphic sheet / Ceiling - Vinyl paint, Lacquer
Completion 2012. 10
Photos offer BALSANG Inc.

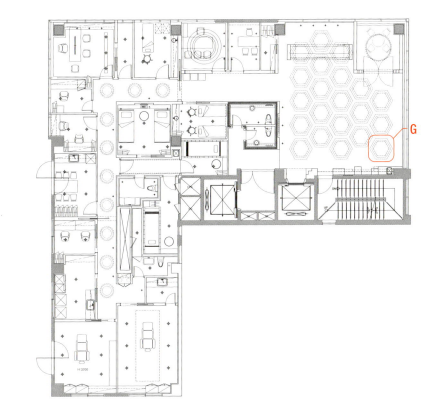

천장도 / ceiling plan

평면도 / floor plan

1 대기공간 2 안내데스크 3 상담실 4 VIP 상담실 5 치료실 6 촬영실 7 진료실 8 원장실 9 홍보실 10 직원실 11 의국 12 창고, 소독, 세탁실 13 수술실 14 회복실 15 관리실

1 Waiting area 2 Information desk 3 Counseling room 4 VIP counseling room 5 Treatment room 6 Photo room 7 Consulting room 8 Director's room 9 PR department 10 Staff room 11 Medical office 12 Storage, disinfecting, laundry room 13 Surgery room 14 Recovery room 15 Care room

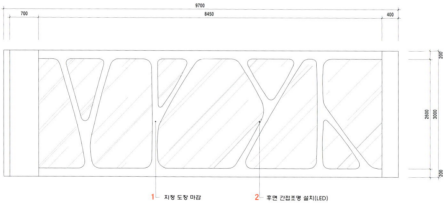

1 지정 도장 마감   2 후면 간접조명 설치(LED)

대기공간 입면 A / waiting area elevation A

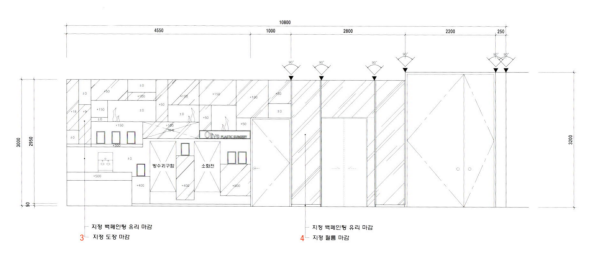

지정 백페인팅 유리 마감   지정 백페인팅 유리 마감
3 지정 도장 마감   4 지정 필름 마감

대기공간 입면 B / waiting area elevation B

1 지정 도장 2 후면 LED 간접조명 설치 3 지정 백페인트 글래스 / 지정 도장 4 지정 백페인트 글래스 / 지정 필름 5 지정 도장 / 지정 백페인트 글래스 / 지정 도장 6 지정색 하이글로시 문 7 지정 인조대리석 / 지정 백페인트 글래스 / 지정 인조대리석 / 간접조명 위 투명유리, 지정 그래픽 시트 8 지정 도장 / 투명 강화유리 위 지정 그래픽 시트

1 App. painting 2 Back side LED indirect lighting installed 3 App. back painted glass / app. painting 4 App. back painted glass / app. film 5 App. painting / app. back painted glass / app. painting 6 App. color high glossy door 7 App. mock marble / app. back painted glass / app. mock marble / clear glass on indirect lighting, app. graphic sheet 8 App. painting / app. graphic sheet on clear tempered glass

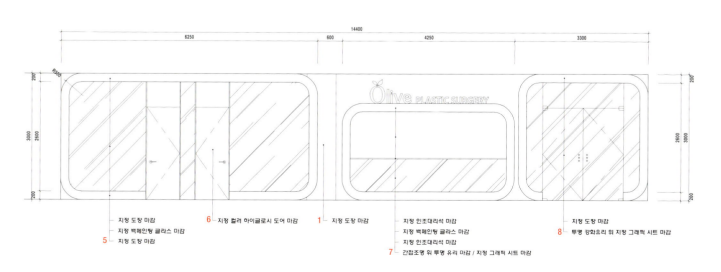

안내데스크 & 상담실 입면 C / information desk & courseling room elevation C

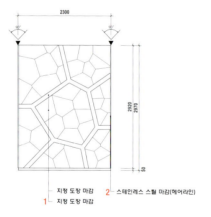

화장실 입면 D / toilet elevation D

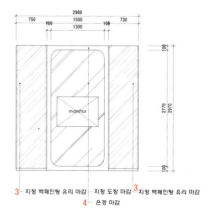

화장실 입면 E / toilet elevation E

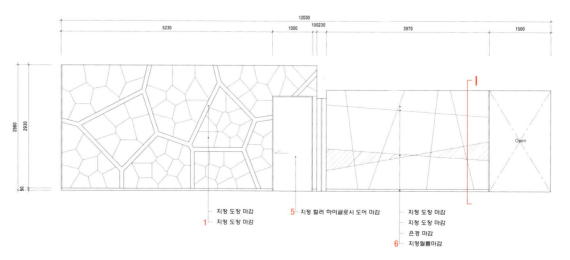

복도 입면 F / corridor elevation F

천장 조명박스 평면 G / ceiling light box top view G

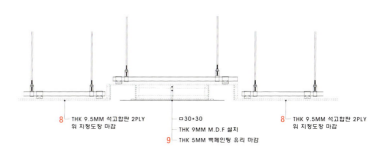

천장 조명박스 단면 H / ceiling light box section H

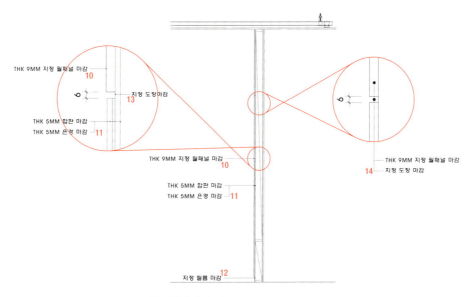

복도 벽체 단면 I / corridor wall section I

1 지정 도장 / 지정 도장 2 스테인리스 스틸 헤어라인 3 지정 백페인트 글래스 4 지정 도장 / 은경 5 지정색 하이글로시 문 6 지정 도장 / 지정 도장 / 은경 / 지정 필름 7 LED 간접조명 설치 8 T9.5 석고 합판 2겹 위 지정 도장 9 □30X30 / T9 MDF 설치 / T5 백페인트 글래스 10 T9 지정 벽패널 11 T5 합판 / T5 은경 12 지정 필름 13 지정 도장 14 T9 지정 벽패널 / 지정 도장

1 App. painting / app. painting 2 Stainless steel hairline 3 App. back painted glass 4 App. painting / silver mirror 5 App. color high glossy door 6 App. painting / app. painting / silver mirror / app. film 7 LED indirect lighting installed 8 App. painting on T9.5 gypsum plywood 2 ply 9 □30X30 / T9 MDF installed / T5 back painted glass 10 T9 app. wall panel 11 T5 plywood / T5 silver mirror 12 App. film 13 App. painting 14 T9 app. wall panel / app. painting

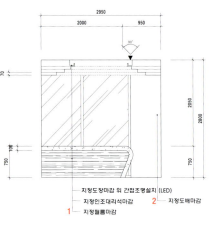

VIP 상담실 입면 J /
VIP counseling room elevation J

VIP 상담실 입면 K /
VIP counseling room elevation K

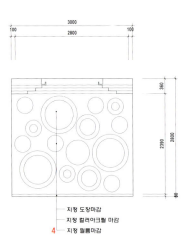

VIP 상담실 입면 L /
VIP counseling room elevation L

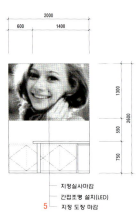

상담실 입면 M /
counseling room elevation M

상담실 입면 N /
counseling room elevation N

1 지정 도장 위 LED 간접조명 설치 / 지정 인조대리석 / 지정 필름 2 지정 도배 3 지정 실사 / LED 간접조명 설치 / 지정 도장 / 지정 실사 / 지정 실사 / 지정 도장 4 지정 도장 / 지정색 아크릴 / 지정 필름 5 지정 실사 / LED 간접조명 설치 / 지정 도장 6 지정 도배 / 지정 필름 7 지정 템바 보드 / 지정 금속 / 지정 도장 / 지정 도장 8 템바 보드 9 지정 도장 10 템바 보드 / 지정 도배 / 지정 필름

1 LED indirect lighting installed on app. painting / app. mock marble / app. film 2 App. wallpaper 3 App. actual image / LED indirect lighting installed / app. painting / app. actual image / app. actual image / app. painting 4 App. painting / app. color acrylic 5 App. actual image / LED indirect lighting installed / app. painting 6 App. wallpaper / app. film 7 App. tembar board / app. metal / app. painting / app. painting 8 Tembar board 9 App. painting 10 Tembar board / app. wallpaper / app. film

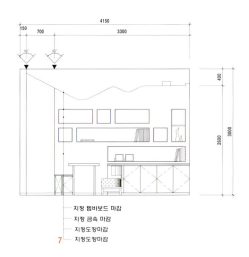

진료실 입면 O / consulting room elevation O

진료실 입면 P / consulting room elevation P

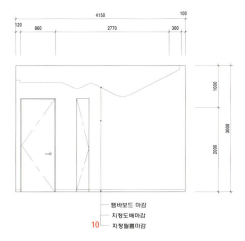

진료실 입면 Q / consulting room elevation Q

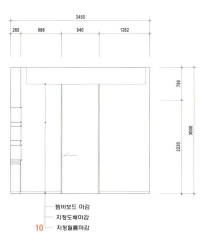

진료실 입면 R / consulting room elevation R

1 지정 도장 / 지정 도장 / 은경 / 지정 필름 2 지정색 하이글로시 문 3 지정 그래픽 실사 4 지정 인조대리석 5 지정 도장 / LED 간접조명 설치 / 지정 인조대리석 / 지정 그래픽 실사 / LED 간접조명 설치 6 은경 / 지정 인조대리석 7 지정 하이글로시 문 8 지정 도배 9 LED 간접조명 설치 10 지정 도배 / 지정 필름

1 App. painting / app. painting / silver mirror / app. film 2 App. color high glossy door 3 App. graphic actual image 4 App. mock marble 5 App. painting / LED indirect lighting installed / app. mock marble / app. graphic actual image / LED indirect lighting installed 6 Silver miror / app. mock marble 7 App. high glossy door 8 App. wallpaper 9 LED indirect lighting installed 10 App. wallpaper / app. film

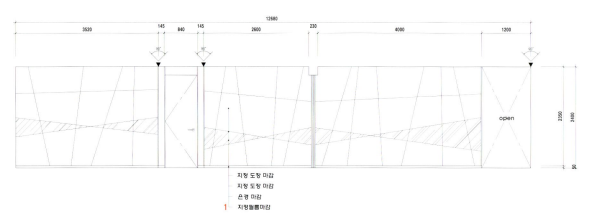

복도 입면 S / corridor elevation S

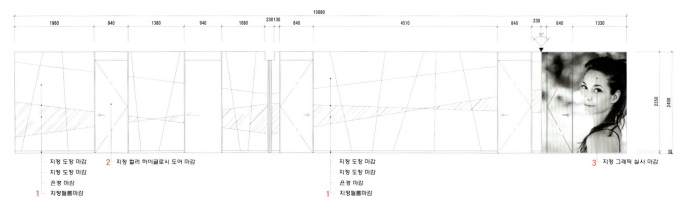

복도 입면 T / corridor elevation T

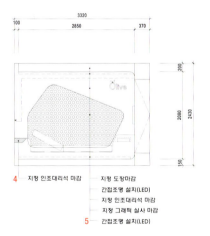

회복실 입면 U / recovery room elevation U

회복실 입면 V / recovery room elevation V

회복실 입면 W / recovery room elevation W

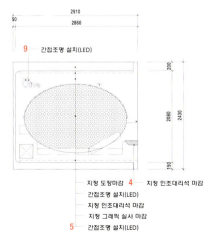

회복실 입면 X / recovery room elevation X

회복실 입면 Y / recovery room elevation Y

회복실 입면 Z / recovery room elevation Z

GOOD FLOWER DERMATOLOGY CLINIC

Limtaehee design studio | Lim Tae Hee

굿플라워 피부과는 비교적 작은 규모의 공간에 다기능의 많은 실을 필요로 하여 내부의 매스와 볼륨에 대해 고민한 프로젝트였다. 작은 단위의 방들을 배열하면서 질서를 만들고, 공간감을 상실하지 않기 위해 요구된 기능과 규모에 따라 무작위로 공간을 구성하여 큰 볼륨감과 매스감을 제공하였다. 결과적으로 방들은 들쑥날쑥한 공간 덕분에 넓고 자유로운 느낌을 가지게 되었다. 사용자가 이러한 공간구성에 친밀함을 느낄 수 있도록 매스와 일체화된 그래픽을 사용하여 공간 안에서 사람과 상호작용 할 수 있도록 계획하였다. 도트라는 작은 단위를 모아 숫자와 글자를 만들고, 각기 다른 크기와 위치에 그래픽을 덧붙였다. 공간과 다양한 그래픽들이 때로는 과장되게, 때로는 잔잔하게 조율되면서 그 자체가 공간과 볼륨, 그리고 매스의 역할을 할 수 있도록 유도하였다.

Good Flower Dermatology Clinic was a project that involved work on the interior mass and volume since the clinic required many multifunctional rooms in a relatively small space. In order to arrange rooms of small units and create order, while keeping a sense of spaciousness, the space is randomly organized according to function and scale to provide a sense of volume and mass. Consequently, the rooms come to emit a sense of freedom thanks to the potholed space. Using graphics that are integrated with the mass, the space is planned out so that these elements can interact with the users within the space and help the users feel familiar with the space arrangement. Small units called dots are put together to create numbers and letters, and graphics of various sizes are attached at different spots. The space arrangement and various graphics are designed to serve the role of space, volume, and mass as they are tuned to the extreme at times or tuned softly at different times.

디자인 임태희 / 임태희디자인스튜디오
위치 서울특별시 강동구 천호동 427-3
용도 피부과
면적 112.4㎡
마감 도장, 안티스투코, 벽지, 바리솔
설계기간 2013. 4 ~ 2013. 5
공사기간 2013. 6 ~ 2013. 7
디자인팀 박동은, 신은혜
사진 박영채

Location 427-3, Cheonho-dong, Gangdong-gu, Seoul
Use Dermatology
Area 112.4㎡
Finishing Painting, Anti stucco, Wallpaper, Barrisol
Design period 2013. 4 ~ 2013. 5
Construction period 2013. 6 ~ 2013. 7
Photographer Park Young Chae

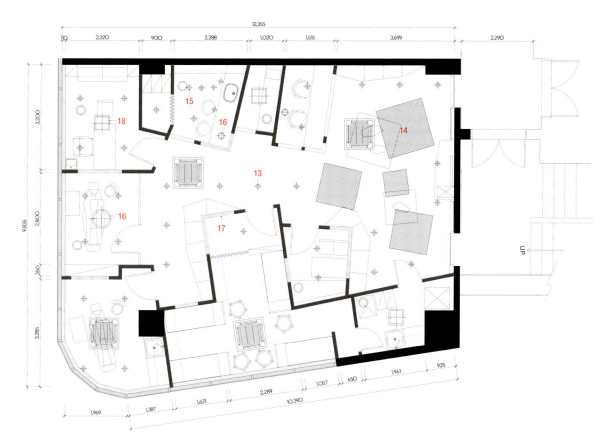

천장도 / ceiling plan

평면도 / floor plan

1 입구 2 로비 3 리셉션 4 상담실 5 준비실 / 간호사실 6 주사실 7 세면실 / 파우더룸 8 피부관리실 9 대기공간 10 탈의실 11 검사실 12 레이저실 13 U 램프 14 바리솔(백색 무광) 15 스포트라이트 16 팬던트 17 간접조명 18 매입등

1 Entrance 2 Lobby 3 Reception 4 Counseling room 5 Preparation / Nurse's room 6 Injection room 7 Wash room / Powder room 8 Skin care room 9 Waiting area 10 Changing room 11 Examination room 12 Laser room 13 U-lamp 14 Barrisol (matt white) 15 Spot light 16 Pendant 17 Indirect lighting 18 Down light

리셉션 입면 A / reception elevation A

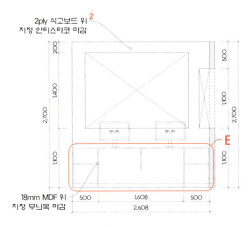

리셉션 입면 B / reception elevation B

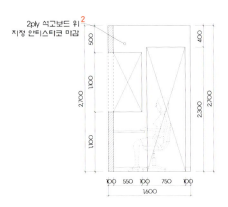

리셉션 입면 C / reception elevation C

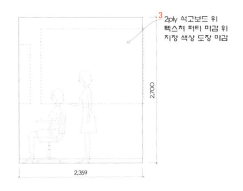

리셉션 입면 D / reception elevation D

1 지정색 도장 2 석고보드 2겹 위 지정 안티스투코 3 석고보드 2겹 위 퍼티 마감 위 지정색 도장 4 상판 타공 + 전선캡 5 T18 MDF 위 지정 무늬목 6 다보 선반 7 석고보드 2겹 8 45mm 금속 스터드, 석고보드 2겹 9 5mm 컬러유리 10 45mm 금속 스터드, 석고보드 2겹 위 지정 벽지 11 석고보드 2겹 위 지정 도배 12 지정 벽지

1 App. color painting 2 App. anti stucco on gypsum board 2ply 3 App. color painting on putty on gypsum board 2ply 4 Tabletop perforated + wire cap 5 App. wood veneer on T18 MDF 6 Bolted shelf 7 Gypsum board 2ply 8 45mm metal stud, gypsum board 2ply 9 T5 color glass 10 45mm metal stud, app. wallpaper on gypsum board 2ply 11 App. wallpaper on gypsum board 2ply 12 App. wallpaper

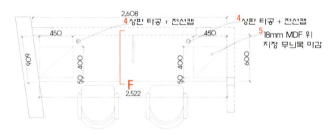

리셉션 데스크 평면 E / reception desk top view E

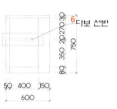

리셉션 데스크 단면 F / reception desk section F

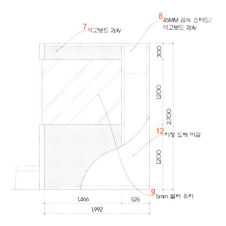

상담실 입면 G / counseling room elevation G

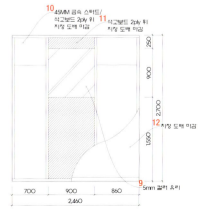

상담실 입면 H / counseling room elevation H

1 석고보드 2겹 위 지정 안티스투코 2 간접등 매입 3 T12 MDF 위 T5 거울 시공 4 T5 컬러유리 5 T18 MDF 위 지정 무늬목 6 카운터 밑 세면대 7 T5 거울 8 패브릭 소파 9 Ø29 금속 행거 10 지정색 도장
11 석고보드 2겹 위 지정 벽지 12 제작 목재 도어 위 지정 안티스투코 13 창문 프레임 : MDF 위 지정 안티스투코 14 열연강판 절곡 위 지정 도장

1 App. anti stucco on gypsum board 2ply 2 Indirect lighting embedded 3 T5 mirror installed on T12 MDF 4 T5 color glass 5 App. wood veneer on T18 MDF 6 Basin under counter 7 T5 mirror 8 Fabric sofa 9 Ø29 metal hanger 10 App. color painting 11 App. wallpaper on gypsum board 2ply 12 App. anti stucco on wooden door 13 Window frame : app. anti stucco on MDF 14 App. painting on hot rolled steel sheet bent

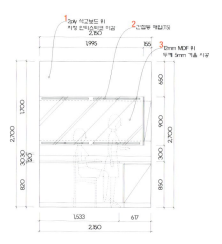

파우더 룸 입면 I / powder room elevation I

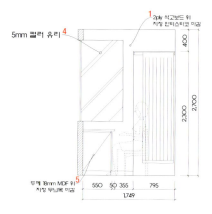

파우더 룸 입면 J / powder room elevation J

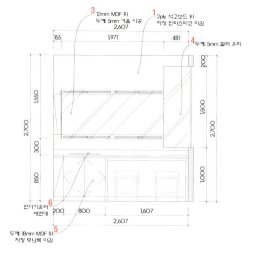

파우더 룸 입면 K / powder room elevation K

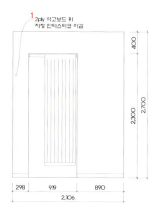

파우더 룸 입면 L / powder room elevation L

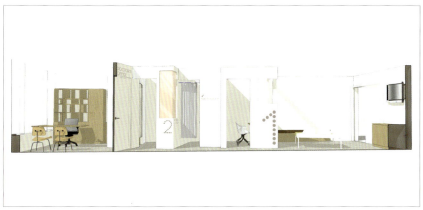

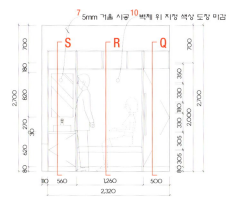

진료실 입면 M / examination room elevation M

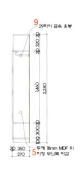

가구 단면 Q / furniture section Q

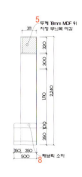

가구 단면 R / furniture section R

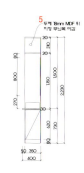

가구 단면 S / furniture section S

진료실 입면 N / examination room elevation N

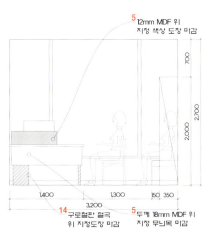

진료실 입면 O / examination room elevation O

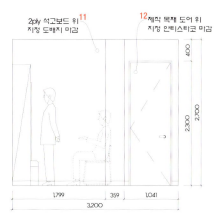

진료실 입면 P / examination room elevation P

E.EUM ANIMAL MEDICAL CLINIC

melloncolie fantastic space LITA | Kim Jae Hwa

이음동물병원은 반려동물을 위한 공간으로 클라이언트는 동물들이 본능적으로 느끼는 위협감을 없애고 아늑하고 친근한 느낌의 공간을 원했다. 전반적인 소재는 목재를 사용하여 따뜻한 느낌이 연출될 수 있도록 하였으며 기능적으로 용이한 타일소재를 사용하였다. 동물병원의 특성상 많은 개별공간이 많은 상황을 고려하여 공간감있고 아늑한 집모양으로 매스감을 연출하였다. 또한 공간감이 잘 부각될 수 있도록 간접 조명을 연출하여서 아늑한 조도를 유지하였다. 크기가 다양한 많은 종류의 용품들이 깔끔하게 디스플레이 될 수 있도록 전면에 타일로 가구를 제작하였고, 중앙에는 눈높이에 맞는 집기를 제작하여 작은 소품들을 정리할 수 있도록 하였다. 반려동물을 처음 만나게 되는 분양함도 답답한 박스형태에서 벗어나 전반적인 콘셉트에 맞도록 제작되었다. 반려동물이 이동할 수 있는 계단이나 사다리를 공간에 반복적으로 배치하여서 재미있는 공간을 경험할 수 있도록 계획하였다.

E.Eum Animal Medical Clinic, a space for animal companions, is planned out to eliminate threatening aspects animals instinctively feel and to create a space that is warm and friendly. Wood is used in general to deliver a warm impression and tiles are used for functional convenience. Considering the characteristics of an animal hospital, the clinic presents a sense of mass with the shape of a cozy house and by having many individual spaces generate diverse situations with spatial sensibility. Furniture made of tile is installed at the front of the clinic to neatly display various pet goods in difference sizes and a display rack is placed at the center to the eye level to organize small articles. Carriers for introducing animal companions are built according to the overall concept breaking away from the stifling box-shaped cages. The space is planned with repeated arrangements of stairs and ladders through which animals can move about allowing the customers to have a fun experience.

디자인 김재화 / 멜랑콜리 판타스틱 스페이스 리타
위치 경기도 용인시 기흥구 영덕동 989-6, 1층
용도 동물병원
면적 116㎡
마감 바닥 - 타일 / 벽 - 비닐 페인트 / 천장 - 비닐 페인트
시공 임병철
설계기간 2013. 2 ~ 2013. 3
완공 2013. 4
사진 김주원

Location 1F, 989-6, Yeongdeok-dong, Giheung-gu, Yongin, Gyeonggi-do
Use Animal clinic
Area 116㎡
Finishing Floor - Tile / Wall - Vinyl paint / Ceiling - Vinyl paint
Design period 2013. 2 ~ 2013. 3
Completion 2013. 4
Photographer Kim Ju Won

파사드 / facade

평면도 / floor plan

1 입구 2 홀 3 수술실 4 검사실 5 애견 미용실 6 애견 호텔 7 직원실 8 회복실 9 X-ray 실

1 Entrance 2 Hall 3 Opeating room 4 Examination room 5 Grooming room 6 Hotel 7 Staff room 8 Treatment room 9 X-ray room

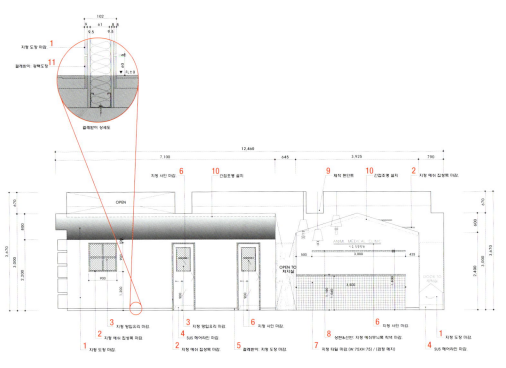

홀 입면 A / hall elevation A

1 지정 도장 2 지정 애쉬 집성목 3 지정 망입유리 4 스테인리스 스틸 헤어라인 5 걸레받이 : 지정 도장 6 지정 사인 7 지정 타일 8 상판 & 선반 : 지정 애쉬 무늬목 착색 9 제작 펜던트 10 간접조명 11 문 손잡이 : C 채널 숨은 손잡이 12 선반 : 지정 애쉬 집성목 13 LED 조명 매입 14 매입 할로겐 조명 15 도어 : 지정 도장 16 리셉션 상판 : 지정 애쉬 무늬목 착색 17 걸레받이 : 광택 도장 18 사다리 : 지정 애쉬 집성목

1 App. painting 2 App. ash laminated wood 3 App. wired glass 4 Stainless steel hairline 5 Base : app. painting 6 App. sign 7 App. tile 8 Table top & shelf : app. ash wood veneer coloring 9 Customized pendant 10 Indirect lighting 11 Door handle : C channel hiding handle 12 Shelf : app. ash laminated wood 13 LED lighting embedded 14 Halogen lighting embedded 15 Door : app. painting 16 Reception tabletop : app. ash wood veneer coloring 17 Base : glossy painting 18 Ladder : app. ash laminated wood

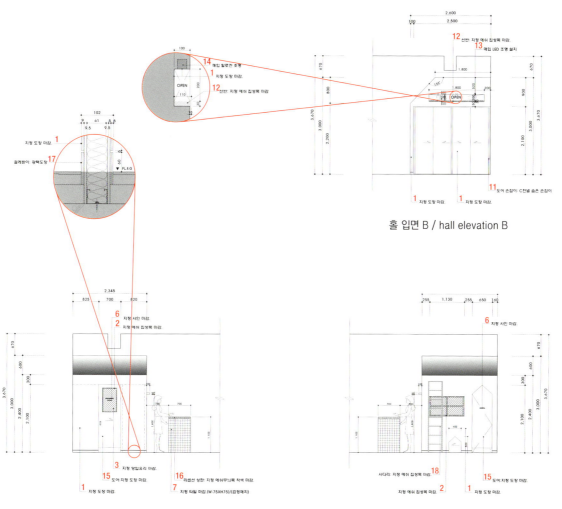

홀 입면 B / hall elevation B

홀 입면 C / hall elevation C

홀 입면 D / hall elevation D

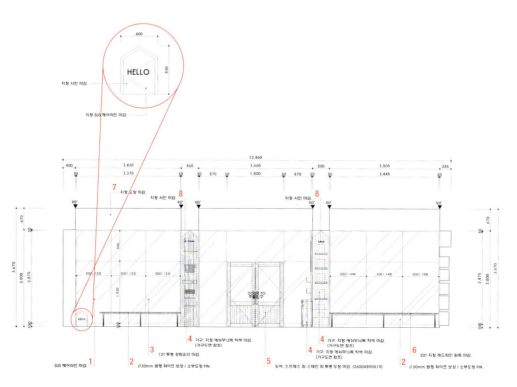

홀 입면 E / hall elevation E

1 스테인리스 스틸 헤어라인   2 Ø30 원형 파이프 보강, 소부도장   3 T12 투명 강화유리   4 가구 : 지정 애쉬 무늬목 착색   5 문 : 사이프러스 위 스테인, 투명 도장   6 T30 지정 레드파인 원목   7 지정 도장   8 지정 사인   9 □25X25 각재 / T9 합판 / 지정 타일   10 지정 타일   11 선반 : T5 투명 유리   12 장식볼트 설치   13 모서리 모따기

1 Stainless steel hairline   2 Ø30 circular pipe reinforced, baked painting   3 T12 clear tempered glass   4 Furniture : app. ash wood veneer coloring   5 Door : stain, clear painting on cypress   6 T30 app. red pine   7 App. painting   8 App. sign   9 □25X25 square timber / T9 plywood / app. tile   10 App. tile   11 Shelf : T5 clear glass   12 Decorative bolt installed   13 Chamfering

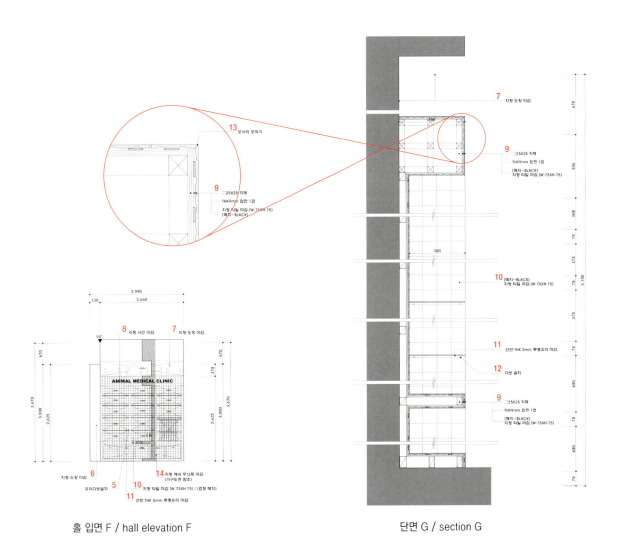

홀 입면 F / hall elevation F   단면 G / section G

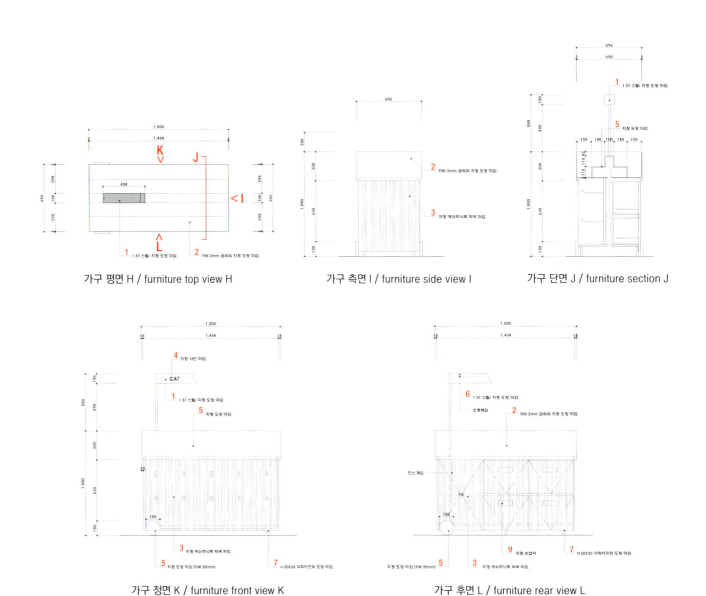

가구 평면 H / furniture top view H   가구 측면 I / furniture side view I   가구 단면 J / furniture section J

가구 정면 K / furniture front view K   가구 후면 L / furniture rear view L

1 T1.5 철제, 지정 도장 2 T3 금속 위 지정 도장 3 지정 애쉬 무늬목 착색 4 지정 사인 5 지정 도장 6 T1.5 철제, 지정 도장 / 조명 매입 7 □30X30 각 파이프 위 도장 8 □30X30 각 파이프 9 지정 매쉬 10 T5 투명 유리

1 T1.5 steel, app. painting 2 T3 app. painting on metal 3 App. ash wood veneer coloring 4 App. sign 5 App. painting 6 T1.5 steel, app. painting / lighting embedded 7 Painting on □30X30 square pipe 8 □30X30 square pipe 9 App. mash 10 T5 clear glass

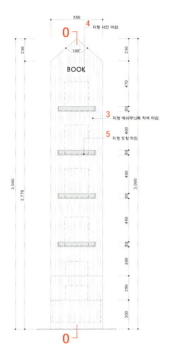

가구 정면 M / furniture front view M

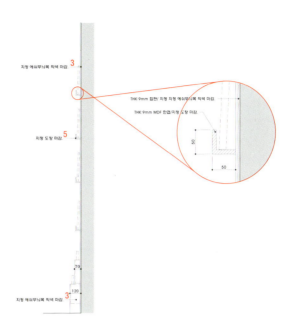

가구 단면 O / furniture section O

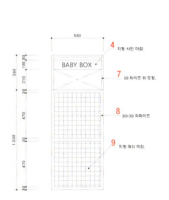

가구 정면 P / furniture front view P

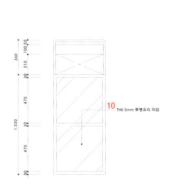

가구 후면 Q / furniture rear view Q

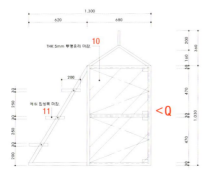

가구 측면 R / furniture side view R

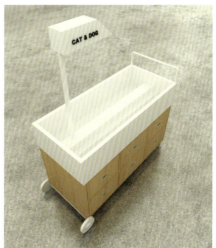

INURI ORIENTAL MEDICAL CLINIC

Friend's Design | Yang Jin Young, Kwon Il Kwon

아이누리 한의원은 아이들의 눈높이에 맞추어 소아과 인테리어의 새로운 방향을 제시하고자 하였다. 기존 병원과의 차별성을 위해 구름을 형상화한 입구에서부터 천장에 매달린 풍선 조명, 구름 형태의 접수대, 집 모양의 간이 부스 등 모든 디자인 요소들이 호기심과 동심을 자극하도록 하였다. '공간에 공간을 불어 넣는다.'는 개념으로, 집 모양의 부스들이 모여 하나의 마을로 보이도록 각 실을 연출하였다. 치료실에서 대기공간까지 이동하는 나무 기차는 아이들에게 친근하고 재미있는 병원의 이미지를 심어주는 동시에, 외부에서도 아이누리만의 색깔을 보여준다. 한약 제조 과정을 투명하게 보여주는 조제실은 병원에 대한 신뢰감을 높이고, 호흡기 치료공간은 아이들이 놀면서 치료받을 수 있도록 별집 형태의 공간으로 계획하였다.

Inuri Oriental Medical Clinic attempted to present a new direction of interior design for pediatrics by planning out the space according to the children's height of eye. From the entrance shaped as a cloud, to the balloon lighting hanging on the ceiling, the reception desk shaped like a cloud, and the makeshift booth with a house shape, all the design elements were aimed for sparking the curiosity and sentiments of children in order to create a space that stands apart from existing children's clinic. Incorporating the concept of 'giving space within a space,' each room is styled to give the impression that the house-shaped booths are gathered to create a village. The wooden train that moves from the doctor's office to the waiting area presents a friendly and fun image of the clinic to the children, and concurrently displays the unique color of Inuri to outside viewers. The pharmacy room that clearly displays the manufacturing process of Chinese medicine were planned in to boost the clients' trust for the clinic. Also, the respiratory treatment space was designed into a honeycomb shape so that children can play while receiving treatment.

디자인 양진영, 권일권 / (주)프랜즈디자인
위치 경기도 파주시 동패동 1759 형성프라자 202호
용도 한의원
면적 242.7㎡
마감 바닥 - 타일 / 벽 - 목재, 철물, 도장, 유리, 도배 / 천장 - 도장, 도배
설계기간 2013. 5 ~ 2013. 6
공사기간 2013. 6 ~ 2013. 7
디자인팀 박안나, 노지은, 박소희
사진 최정복

Location 202, Hyeongseong Plaza, 1759, Dongpae-dong, Paju, Gyeonggi-do
Use Oriental medical clinic
Area 242.7㎡
Finishing Floor - Tile / Wall - Wood, Iron ware, Painting, Glass, Wallpaper / Ceiling - Painting, Wall pater
Design period 2013. 5 ~ 2013. 6
Construction period 2013. 6 ~ 2013. 7
Photographer Choi Jeong Bok

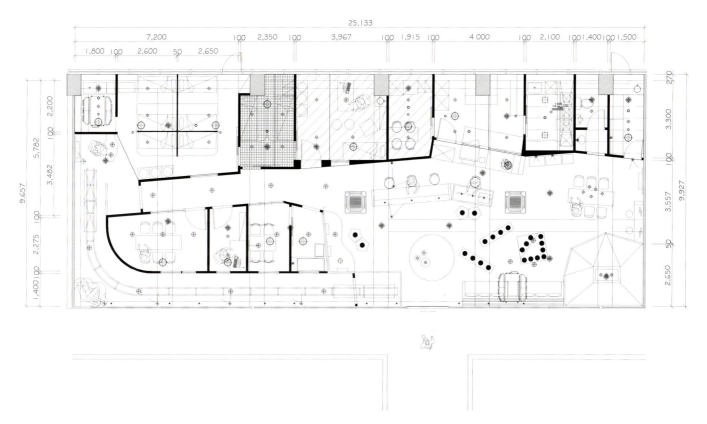

천장도 / ceiling plan

평면도 / floor plan

1 입구 2 접수대 3 대기공간 4 어린이공간 5 수유실 6 어린이화장실 7 탕전실 8 조제실 9 간호사실 10 진료실 11 성인치료실 12 어린이치료실 13 준비실 14 세미나실 15 상담실 16 검사실 17 호흡기 치료공간 18 블라인드 19 기찻길 20 이미지월

1 Entrance 2 Reception 3 Waiting area 4 Children's space 5 Nursing room 6 Children's toilet 7 Decoction room 8 Pharmacy room 9 Nurse's room 10 Consulting room 11 Cure room for adults 12 Cure room for children 13 Preparation room 14 Seminar room 15 Counseling room 16 Examination room 17 Respiratory treatment space 18 Blind 19 Railroad 20 Image wall

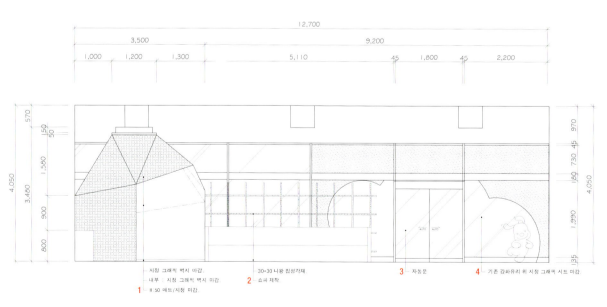

대기공간 입면 A / waiting area elevation A

1 지정 그래픽 벽지 / 내부 : 지정 그래픽 벽지 / H:50 매트, 지정 마감 2 30X30 나왕 집성각재 / 제작 소파 3 자동문 4 기존 강화유리 위 지정 그래픽 시트 5 T9 MDF, 지정 도장 / 선반(D:100) : T18 목구조 틀, T9 MDF, 지정 래커 / 걸레받이 : T9 MDF, 지정 필름 6 지정색 도장 / PC 케이블 7 H:50 매트, 지정 마감 8 지정 그래픽 벽지 / 내부 : 지정 그래픽 벽지 9 T9 MDF, 지정 래커

1 App. graphic wallpaper / inside : app. graphic wallpaper / H:50 mat, app. finish 2 30X30 lauan laminated square timber / making sofa 3 Automatic door 4 App. graphic sheet on existing tempered glass 5 T9 MDF, app. painting / shelf (D:100) : T18 wooden structure frame, T9 MDF, app. lacquer / baseboard : T9 MDF, app. film 6 App. color painting / PC cable 7 H:50 mat, app. finish 8 App. graphic wallpaper / inside : app. graphic wallpaper 9 T9 MDF, app. lacquer

 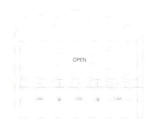

접수대 정면 C / reception front view C   접수대 측면 D / reception side view D   접수대 후면 E / reception rear view E

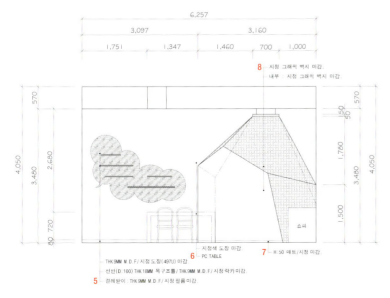 

어린이공간 입면 B / children's space elevation B   그래픽 선반 / graphic shelf

165

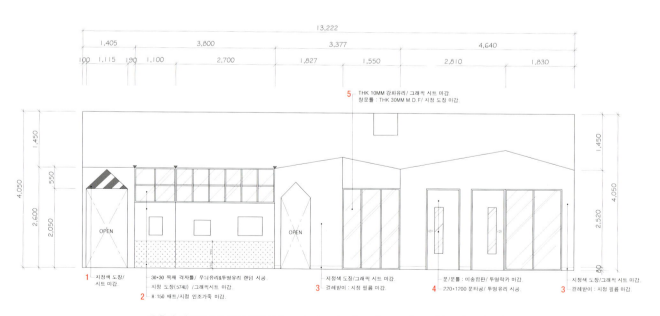

호흡기 치료공간 & 복도 입면 F / respiratory treatment room & corridor elevation F

1 지정색 도장, 시트   2 30X30 목재 격자틀, 무늬 유리 & 투명유리 / 지정 도장, 그래픽 시트 / H:150 매트, 지정 인조 가죽   3 지정색 도장, 그래픽 시트 / 걸레받이 : 지정 필름   4 문, 문틀 : 미송합판, 투명 래커 / 200X1,200 문 타공, 투명유리   5 T10 강화유리, 그래픽 시트 / 창문 틀 : T30 MDF, 지정 도장   6 400X400 타공, 투명유리 / 지정 실크 벽지   7 900X840XR450 타공, 투명유리 / 지정 실크 벽지   8 이미지 펜던트 / 걸레받이 : 지정 필름 / 지정 실크 벽지

1 App. color painting, sheet   2 30X30 wood grid frame, patterned glass & clear glass / app. painting, graphic sheet / H:150 mat, app. artificial leather   3 App. painting, graphic sheet / baseboard : app. film   4 Door, door frame : Douglas fir plywood, clear lacquer / 200X1,200 door perforated, clear glass   5 T10 tempered glass, graphic sheet / window frame : T30 MDF, app. painting   6 400X400 perforating, clear glass / app. silk wallpaper   7 900X840XR450 perforating, clear glass / app. silk wallpaper   8 Image pendant / baseboard : app. film / app. silk wallpaper

상담실 입면 G / counseling room elevation G

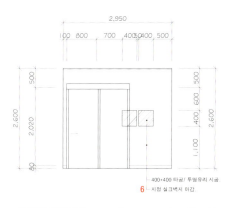

상담실 입면 H / counseling room elevation H

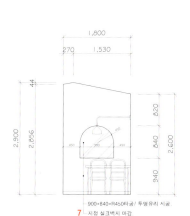

상담실 입면 I / counseling room elevation I

상담실 입면 J / counseling room elevation J

1 문, 문틀 : 미송합판, 투명 래커 / 200X1,200 문 타공, 투명유리 2 지정색 도장 / 창문 새시 3 가구 : T18 MDF, 지정 필름 4 지정색 도장 / 걸레받이 : 지정 필름 5 문, 문틀 : 미송합판, 투명 래커 6 지정색 도장 위 TV 모니터 부착 / 600X720 창문 타공, T5 투명유리, 창문틀 : T20 MDF 위 지정 필름 7 오픈 게이트 옆선 : 지정색 도장 8 격자 약재 진열장 9 상부장 / 포장대 10 지정 실크 벽지 / 작업대 : 지정 필름 11 뒷면 벽걸이 TV 보강, 전기 콘센트 12 지정 블라인드 / 싱크대, 인테리어 필름 & 인조대리석 상판 13 지정 벽지 / 지정 타일 / H:300 바닥 미장 14 상부장, 인테리어 필름 / H:300 바닥 미장

1 Door, door frame : Douglas fir plywood, clear lacquer / 200X1,200 door perforated, clear glass 2 App. color painting / window sash 3 Furniture : T18 MDF, app. film 4 App. color painting / baseboard : app. film 5 Door, door frame : douglas fir plywood, clear lacquer 6 TV monitor attached on app. color painting / 600X720 window perforated, T5 clear glass, window frame : app. film on T20 MDF 7 Open gate side line : app. color painting 8 Grid-type drug display stand 9 Upper storage closet / packing table 10 App. silk wallpaper / worktable : app. film 11 Back side reinforcement of wall mounted TV, electric outlet 12 App. blind / sink, interior film & mock marble top board 13 App. wallpaper / app. tile / H:300 floor plastering 14 Upper storage closet, interior film / H:300 floor plastering

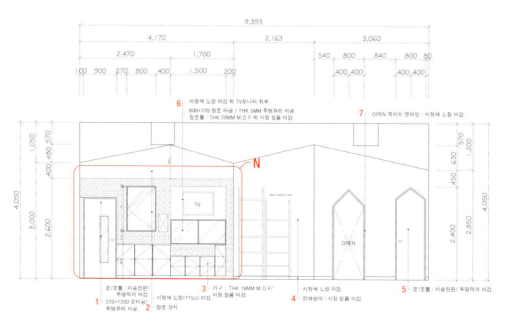

대기공간 입면 K / waiting area elevation K

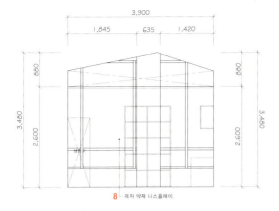

조제실 입면 O1 / pharmacy room elevation O1

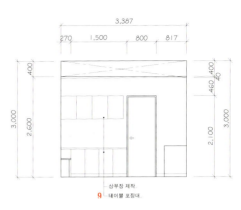

조제실 입면 O2 / pharmacy room elevation O2

조제실 입면 O3 / pharmacy room elevation O3

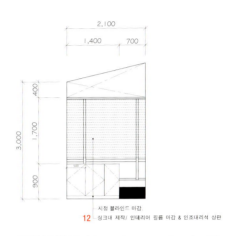

탕전실 입면 P1 / decoction room elevation P1

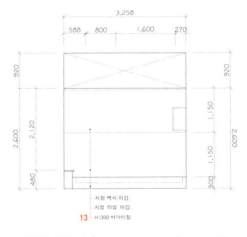

탕전실 입면 P2 / decoction room elevation P2

탕전실 입면 P3 / decoction room elevation P3

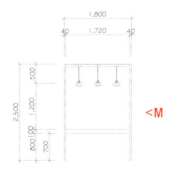

간이 상담데스크 정면 L /
ease couseling desk front view L

간이 상담데스크 측면 M /
ease couseling desk side view M

TV 모니터 장 투시도 N /
TV monitor furniture perspective N

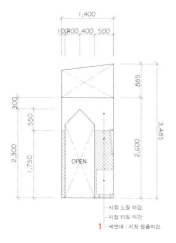

어린이화장실 입면 Q1 / children's toilet elevation Q1

어린이화장실 입면 Q2 / children's toilet elevation Q2

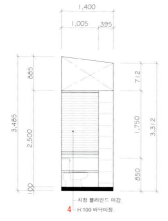

어린이화장실 입면 Q3 / children's toilet elevation Q3

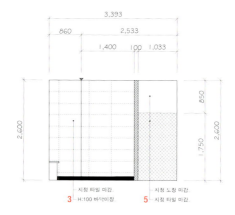

어린이화장실 입면 Q4 / children's toilet elevation Q4

1 지정 도장 / 지정 타일 / 세면대 : 지정 필름 2 지정 도장 / 지정 타일 / 상판 : 지정 인조대리석 / 세면대 : 지정 필름 3 지정 타일 / H:100 바닥 미장 4 지정 블라인드 / H:100 바닥 미장 5 지정 도장 / 지정 타일 6 지정색 도장, 시트 7 지정색 도장, 그래픽 시트 / 창문 타공(T5 투명유리), 창문틀(T24 MDF, 지정색 도장), 문살(T18 MDF, 지정색 도장) 8 지정 타일 9 220X1,200 문 타공, 투명유리 / 문, 문틀 : 오동나무 합판, 투명 래커 10 오동나무 패널(W:200), 투명 래커 / 800X600 타공, 투명유리 11 CNC 절삭 위 지정색 도장 / 전구 매입 디스플레이 12 220X1,200 문 타공, 투명유리 / 미닫이문, 문틀 : 미송합판, 투명 래커 13 T10 아크릴 문자 커팅, 지정색 래커

1 App. painting / app. tile / sink : app. film 2 App. painting / app. tile / top board : app. mock marble / sink : app. film 3 App. tile / H:100 floor plastering 4 App. blind / H:100 floor plastering 5 App. painting / app. tile 6 App. color painting, sheet 7 App. color painting, graphic sheet / window perforated (T5 clear glass), window frame (T24 MDF, app. color painting), lattice (T18 MDF, app. color paintng) 8 App. tile 9 200X1,200 door perforated, clear glass / door, door frame : Paulowniawood plywood, clear lacquer 10 Paulowniawood panel (W:200), clear lacquer / 800X600 perforating, clear glass 11 App. color painting on CNC cutting / lamp embedded display 12 200X1,200 door perforated, clear glass / sliding door, door frame : douglas fir plywood, clear lacquer 13 T10 acrylic letter cutting, app. color lacquer

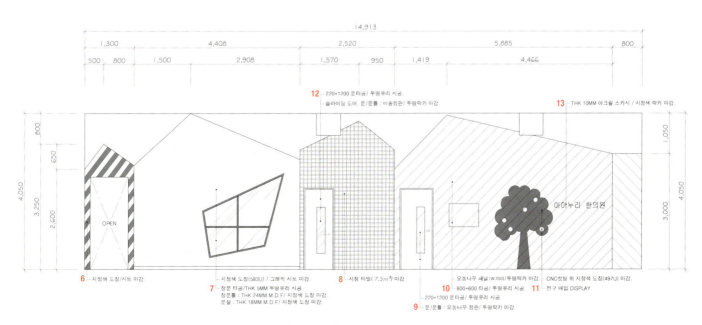

복도 입면 R / corridor elevation R

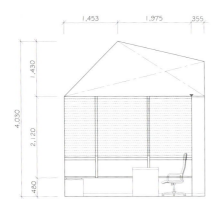

진료실 입면 W1 / consulting room elevation W1

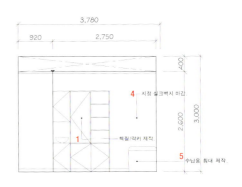

진료실 입면 W2 / consulting room elevation W2

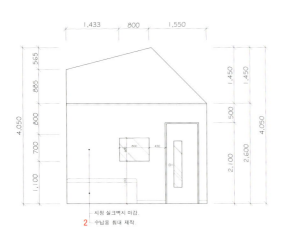

진료실 입면 X1 / consulting room elevation X1

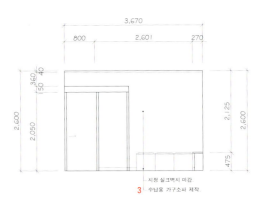

진료실 입면 X2 / consulting room elevation X2

1 책장, 소지품 보관함 제작   2 지정 실크 벽지 / 수납용 침대   3 지정 실크 벽지 / 수납용 가구 소파   4 지정 실크 벽지   5 수납용 침대   6 지정 도장 / 지정 도장 위 그래픽 시트   7 조형물 제작 위 지정 도장

1 Bookcase, making locker   2 App. silk wallpaper / bed for storage   3 App. silk wallpaper / sofa furniture for storage   4 App. silk wallpaper   5 Bed for storage   6 App. painting / graphic sheet on app. painting   7 App. painting on making sculpture

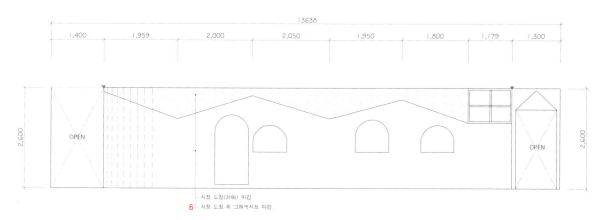

기찻길 입면 Y / railroad elevation Y

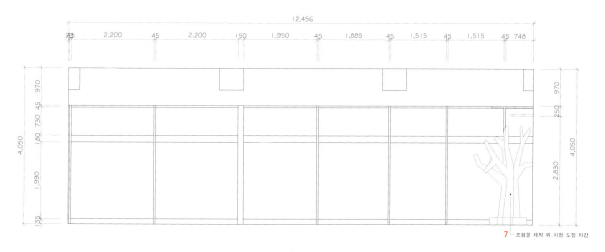

기찻길 입면 Z / railroad elevation Z

HOSAN HOSPITAL POSTNATAL CARE CENTER

Y SPACE | Yoon Seok Min

호산병원 산후조리원은 '새로운 생명과 함께하는 제2의 신혼여행지의 부티크 호텔'이라는 주제로 산모들이 최고급 대접을 받는 느낌을 주고자 하였다. 좁은 로비 공간의 한계를 극복하기 위해 천장을 미러 바리솔로 마감하여 공간의 확장감을 극대화하였다. 또한 천장의 조명을 없애고 벽에서 나오는 빛이 천장으로 퍼지도록 하여 충분한 조도와 함께 신비로운 분위기를 연출하였다. 직각으로 꺾인 무늬목의 로비 벽면은 복도의 천장으로 이어져 자연스럽게 공간이 전환된다. 한쪽에는 시원하게 뻗은 간접조명이 이 복도 공간 전체를 이끌고 있으며, 빛을 머금고 있는 사각 모듈이 바닥패턴과 한 쌍을 이루어 각 실로 안내한다. 무채색의 복도 바닥과 달리 대부분 실의 바닥은 색이 있는 스트라이프 볼론으로 마감하여 전체적으로 활기차면서도 신비로운 공간을 연출하였다. 반대로 벽과 천장은 차분한 느낌으로 마감하여 바닥과의 미묘한 대조와 함께 실 내부에 이완과 활기가 공존하도록 계획하였다.

Hosan Hospital Postnatal Care Center was designed to give the impression that the mothers are receiving the best treatment under the theme of 'a boutique hotel for the second honeymoon with a new life.' In order to overcome the limitation of a narrow lobby, the ceiling is finished with mirror barrisol maximizing the effect of space expansion. Also, overhead lights in the ceiling were eliminated and instead lighting on the wall, designed to spread light on the ceiling, created a mysterious ambiance along with ample intensity of illumination. The lobby wall surface finished with right-angled pattern wood veneer is extended to the ceiling producing the effect of a smooth transition of space. On one side, the indirect illumination stretched out along the wall leads this entire corridor space and the squared module swimming with light is paired up the with the floor pattern, thus guiding the way to the each room. Unlike the achromatic color of the corridor floor, the floor in each room is finished with the colorful striped Bolon for a presentation of an overall lively and mysterious space. On the contrary, the wall and the ceiling are finished in a calm tone to create a subtle contrast with the floor. In short, the interior of the room is planned out in such way that relaxation and vigor coexist.

디자인 윤석민 / 윤공간디자인
위치 서울특별시 강남구 신사동 617-5 8층
용도 산후조리원
면적 268.9㎡
마감 바닥 - 볼론, 타일 / 벽- 무늬목, 도배, 타일 / 천장 - 미러 바리솔, 무늬목, 도배, 유광 바리솔
완공 2013. 5
디자인팀 고유리, 윤은별
시공 권용석 / 페이즈아이디
사진 송기면 / 인디포스

Location 8F, 617-5, Sinsa-dong, Gangnam-gu, Seoul
Use Postnatal care center
Area 268.9㎡
Finishing Floor - Bolon, Tile / Wall - Wood veneer, Wallpaper, Tile / Ceiling - Mirror barrisol, Wood veneer, Wallpaper, Glossy barrisol
Completion 2013. 5
Photographer Song Gi Myoun / Indiphos

천장도 / ceiling plan

평면도 / floor plan

1 로비 2 복도 3 특실 4 좌욕실 5 피부관리실 6 VIP실 7 미러 바리솔 8 지정 천장지 9 지정 바리솔 10 지정 목재 11 지정 볼론 12 가구 위 조명 13 간접조명 매입

1 Lobby 2 Corridor 3 Executive room 4 Sitz bath room 5 Skin care room 6 VIP room 7 Mirror barrisol 8 App. ceiling paper 9 App. barrisol 10 App. wood 11 App. bolon 12 Lighting on furniture 13 Indirect lighting embedded

177

1 적색 LED 간접조명 2 내부 : 지정 백색 도장 3 지정 목재 4 보라색 LED 간접조명 5 LED 간접조명 6 후면 LED 간접조명 7 수납 : 지정 백색 도장 8 방화문 : 지정 백색 도장 9 검은색 금속 필름 시트 10 열연강판 11 지정 백색 도장 12 미닫이문 : 은경 13 지정 백색 벽지 / 걸레받이 : 지정 볼론 14 문 : 지정 백색 도장 15 시스템장 : 지정 백색 도장

1 Red LED indirect lighting 2 Inside: app. white painting 3 App. wood 4 Purple LED indirect lighting 5 LED indirect lighting 6 Back side LED indirect lighting 7 Storage : app. white painting 8 Fire door : app. white painting 9 Black metal film sheet 10 Hot rolled steel sheet 11 App. white painting 12 Sliding door : silver mirror 13 App. white wallpaper/baseboard : app. bolon 14 Door : app. white painting 15 System furniture : app. white painting

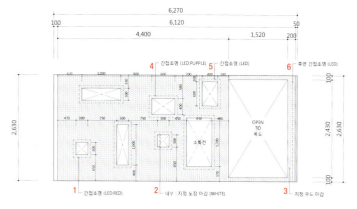

로비 입면 A / lobby elevation A

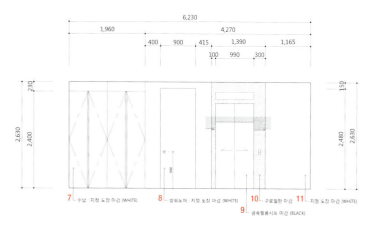

로비 입면 B / lobby elevation B

로비 입면 C / lobby elevation C

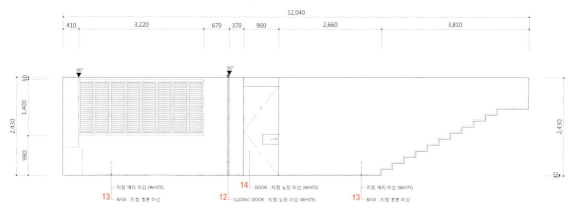

복도 입면 D / corridor elevation D

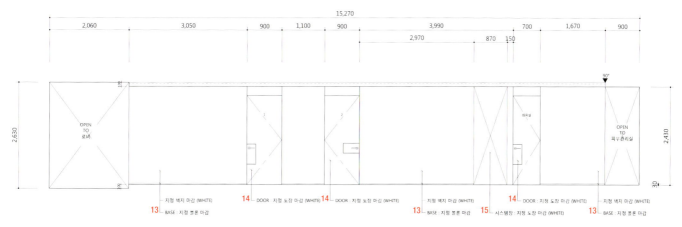

복도 입면 E / corridor elevation E

1 지정 백색 벽지 / 걸레받이 : 지정 볼론   2 LED 간접조명   3 문 : 지정 백색 도장   4 지정 백색 도장   5 미닫이문 : T11 강화유리   6 제작 가구 : 지정 볼론   7 가구 : 지정 백색 도장   8 걸레받이 : 지정 볼론   9 조명
10 투명 강화유리 위 시트 / 투명 강화유리   11 은경   12 가구 : 지정 볼론 / 가구 하부 : LED 간접조명

1 App. white wallpaper / baseboard : app. bolon   2 LED indirect lighting   3 Door : app. white painting   4 App. white painting   5 Sliding door : T11 tempered glass   6 Making furniture : app. bolon   7 Furniture : app. white painting   8 Baseboard : app. white painting   9 Lamp   10 Sheet on clear tempered glass / clear tempered glass   11 Silver mirror   12 Furniture : app. bolon / furniture bottom : LED indirect lighting

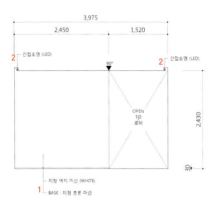

복도 입면 F / corridor elevation F

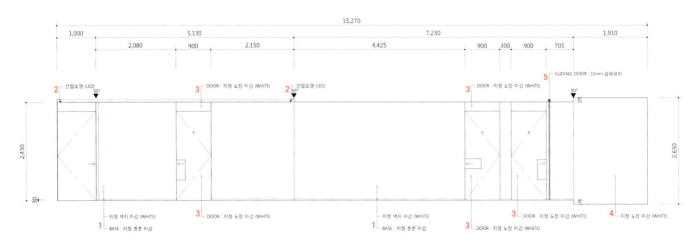

복도 입면 G / corridor elevation G

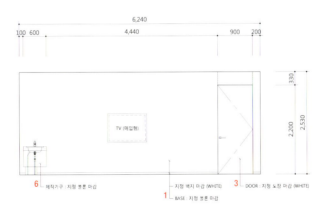

VIP실 입면 H / VIP room elevation H

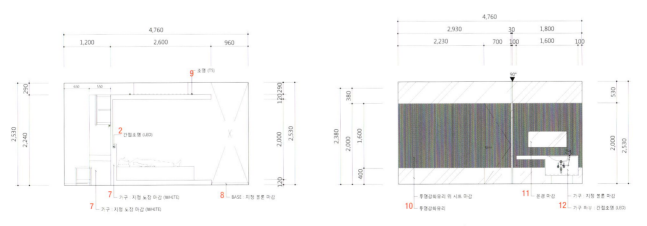

VIP실 입면 I / VIP room elevation I

VIP실 입면 J / VIP room elevation J

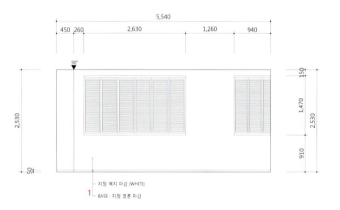

VIP실 입면 K / VIP room elevation K

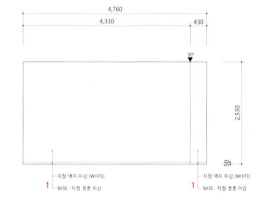

VIP실 입면 L / VIP room elevation L

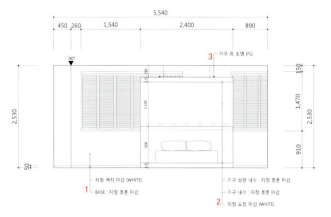

VIP실 입면 M / VIP room elevation M

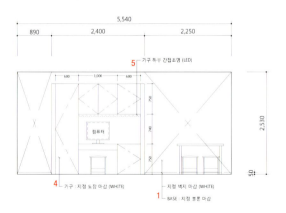

VIP실 입면 N / VIP room elevation N

1 지정 백색 벽지 / 걸레받이 : 지정 볼론   2 가구 상판 내부 : 지정 볼론 / 가구 내부 : 지정 볼론 / 지정 백색 도장   3 가구 위 조명   4 가구 : 지정 백색 도장   5 가구 하부 LED 간접조명   6 지정 타일   7 LED 간접 조명   8 가구 : 지정 볼론 / 가구 하부 : LED 간접조명 / 가구 하부 : 지정 타일   9 은경   10 스테인리스 스틸 헤어라인   11 샤워 부스 : 지정 강화유리   12 투명 강화유리 위 시트 / 투명 강화유리

1 App. white wallpaper / baseboard : app. bolon   2 Furniture top board inside : app. bolon / furniture inside : app. bolon / app. white painting   3 Lighting on furniture   4 Furniture : app. white painting   5 Furniture bottom LED indirect lighting   6 App. tile   7 LED indirect lighting   8 Furniture : app. bolon / furniture bottom : LED indirect lighting / furniture bottom : app. tile   9 Silver mirror   10 Stainless steel hairline   11 Shower booth : app. tempered glass   12 Sheet on clear tempered glass / clear tempered glass

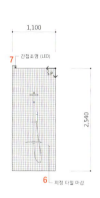 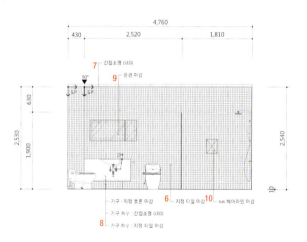

VIP실 화장실 입면 O / VIP bathroom elevation O   VIP실 화장실 입면 P / VIP bathroom elevation P

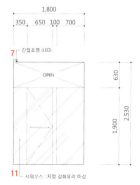 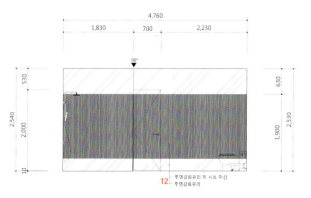

VIP실 화장실 입면 Q / VIP bathroom elevation Q   VIP실 화장실 입면 R / VIP bathroom elevation R

PYUNKANG ORIENTAL CLINIC_SEOMYUN

studioVASE | Jun Bum Jin

편강한의원은 폐를 맑게 하여 알레르기성 비염을 다스리는 '편강탕'이라는 약재로 잘 알려져 있는데, 여기 '맑다' 라는 단어에서 도출된 백(白)의 개념을 공간에 표현하고자 하였다. 물리적인 형태 없이 감성의 존재를 느낄 수 있고, 각기 다른 백색을 가진 디자인 장치로써, 모든 반짝이는 색의 근원인 빛, 촉감의 기억으로 인지되는 한지와 모시, 삼베, 매끈하면서도 둥근 형태의 달항아리를 사용하였다. 전실은 전이 공간으로써 백의 공간을 더욱 확장되어 보이는 효과를 준다. 내부 복도에 줄지어 서있는 가는 기둥은 매끈한 도자기와 같은 느낌을 주면서 공간감을 느낄 수 있는 요소가 된다. 대기실 천장에서 일정 높이까지 내려온 모시천은 공간을 구획하는 요소이자 은은한 빛과 함께 시각적으로 공간을 연장시킨다.

PyunKang Oriental Clinic is well known for its medicine Pyunkangtang which clears the lungs to treat allergic rhinitis. The clinic was designed to express the concept of 'white' drawn from the word 'clear.' As design units that respectively have different shades of white and make one feel the existence of emotions without physical form, the space design used light, which is the source of all shimmering colors, and traditional paper, ramie, and hemp that are perceived with memory of touch, along with moon pots that have smooth and round shape. The foyer as a transition space, has the effect of making the white space look all the more expanded. The slender columns standing in a row in the hall give the impression of smooth ceramics and becomes a design element that affect a sense of space. The ramie cloth in the waiting area hanging down from the ceiling to a set length serves as a design element that concurrently divides the space and visually expands the space with soft light.

디자인 전범진 / 스튜디오베이스
위치 부산광역시 부산진구 부전동 아이온시티 빌딩 17층
용도 한의원
면적 198.34㎡
마감 바닥 - 타일, 마루, 포천석, 롤 카펫 / 벽- 도장, 한지, 모시 / 천장 - 도장, 모시, 바리솔
완공 2013. 6
시공 스튜디오베이스
사진 박우진

Location 17F, Aion City building, Bujeon-dong, Jin-gu, Busan,
Use Oriental medical clinic
Area 198.34㎡
Finishing Floor - Tile, Flooring, Granite, Roll carpet / Wall - Painting, Korean paper, Ramie fabric / Ceiling - Painting, Ramie fabric, Barrisol
Completion 2013. 6
Photographer Park Woo Jin

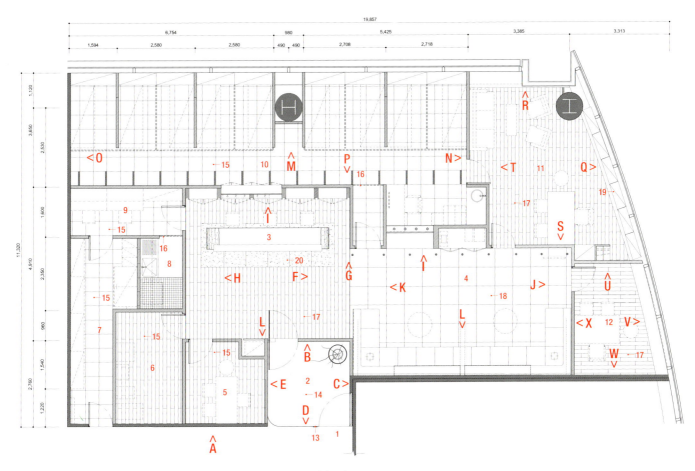

평면도 / floor plan

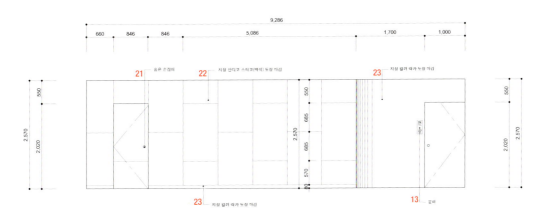

파사드 A / facade A

1 입구 2 전실 3 안내데스크 4 대기실 5 상담실 6 검진실 7 탈의실, 창고 8 다실 9 간호사실 10 침구실 11 원장실 12 부원장실 13 문패 14 지정 회색 롤 카페트 15 지정 P-타일 16 커튼 레일 17 지정 우드 플로링 18 지정 타일 19 약장 20 지정 화강석 21 숨은 손잡이 22 지정 백색 안티스투코 도장 23 지정색 래커 도장

1 Entrance 2 Foyer 3 Information desk 4 Waiting room 5 Counseling room 6 Examination room 7 Changing room, storage 8 Kichenette 9 Nurse's room 10 Acupuncture cure room 11 Director's room 12 Vice director's room 13 Doorplate 14 App. gray roll carpet 15 App. P-tile 16 Curtain rail 17 App. wood flooring 18 App. tile 19 Medicine cabinet 20 App. granite 21 Hidden handle 22 App. white antistucco painting 23 App. color lacquer painting

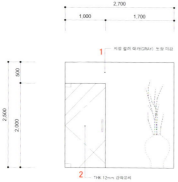

전실 입면 B / foyer elevation B

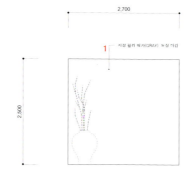

전실 입면 C / foyer elevation C

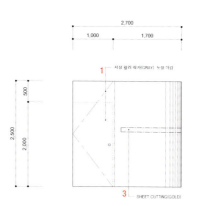

전실 입면 D / foyer elevation D

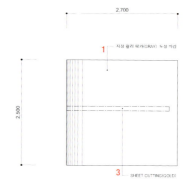

전실 입면 E / foyer elevation E

1 지정 회색 래커 도장 2 T12 강화유리 3 금색 시트 절삭 4 걸레받이 : 지정 도장 5 지정 포천석 6 소파 : 지정 무늬목 7 지정 비닐 페인트 도장 8 환봉 매입 9 지정 패브릭 10 줄눈 11 T5 철판 위 지정 도장 12 조명 매입 13 지정 회색 도장 / 지정 한지 위 도장 14 LED 조명 매입 15 T8 투명유리

1 App. gray lacquer painting 2 T12 tempered glass 3 Gold sheet cutting 4 Baseboard : app. painting 5 App. granite 6 Sofa : app. wood veneer 7 App. vinyl painting 8 Circular bar embedded 9 App. fabric 10 Masonry joint 11 App. painting on T5 steel plate 12 Lighting embedded 13 App. gray painting / painting on app. Korean paper 14 LED lighting embedded 15 T8 clear glass

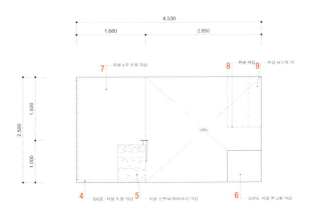

안내데스크 입면 F / information desk elevation F

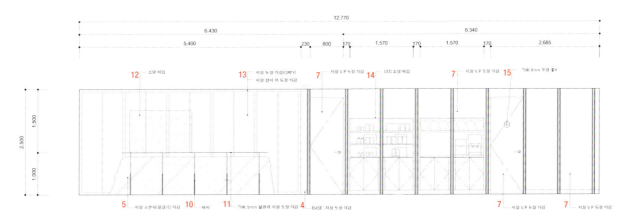

안내데스크 입면 G / information desk elevation G

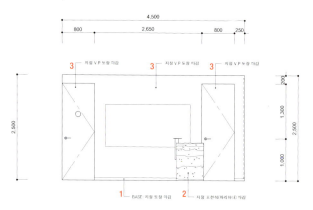

안내데스크 입면 H / information desk elevation H

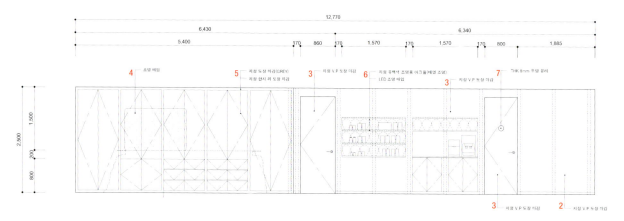

안내데스크 입면 I / information desk elevation I

1 걸레받이 : 지정 도장 2 지정 화강석 3 지정 비닐 페인트 도장 4 조명 매입 5 지정 회색 도장 / 지정 한지 위 도장 6 지정 유백색 조명용 아크릴(배면 조명) / LED 조명 매입 7 T8 투명유리 8 지정 무늬목 / 소파 : 지정 인조 가죽 / 지정 무늬목 9 조명 박스 : 상부 방향 조명 10 지정 패브릭 11 환봉 매입 12 소파 : 지정 인조 가죽 13 지정 무늬목 14 지정 패브릭 / 환봉 매입 15 지정 비닐 페인트 도장 / 상부 방향 조명 16 스탠드 조명 17 T12 강화유리

1 Baseboard : app. painting 2 App. granite 3 App. vinyl painting 4 Lighting embedded 5 App. gray painting / painting on app. Korean paper 6 App. milk white acrylic for lamp (on rear side) / LED lighting embedded 7 T8 clear glass 8 App. wood veneer / sofa : app. artificial leather / app. wood veneer 9 Lighting box : up lighting 10 App. fabric 11 Circular bar embedded 12 Sofa : app. artificial leather 13 App. wood veneer 14 App. fabric / circular bar embedded 15 App. vinyl painting / up lighting 16 Standing lighting 17 T12 tempered glass

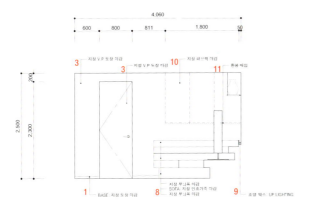

대기실 입면 J / waiting room elevation J

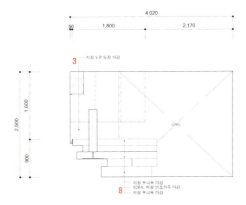

대기실 입면 K / waiting room elevation K

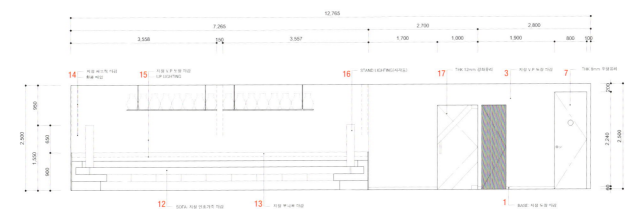

대기실 입면 L / waiting room elevation L

1 걸레받이 : 지정 시트 2 걸레받이 : 지정 도장 3 지정 시트 4 건축 창호 5 지정 벽지 6 지정 커튼 부착 7 블라인드 매입 8 싱크 상부장 : 지정 도장 9 지정 비닐 페인트 도장 10 싱크장 : 지정 도장 11 지정 도장 12 지정 커튼 부착 13 은경 부착

1 Baseboard : app. sheet 2 Baseboard : app. painting 3 App. sheet 4 Architectural window 5 App. wallpaper 6 App. curtain attached 7 Blind embedded 8 Sink upper storage closet : app. painting 9 App. vinyl painting 10 Sink storage closet : app. painting 11 App. painting 12 App. curtain attached 13 Silver mirror attached

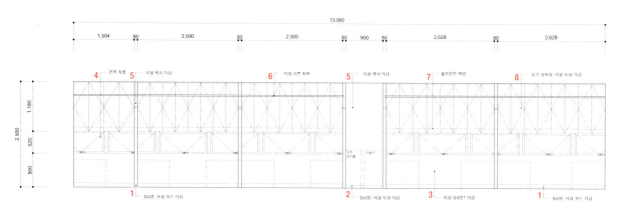

침구실 입면 M / acupuncture cure room elevation M

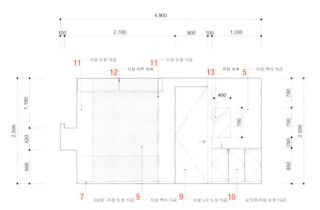

침구실 입면 N / acupuncture cure room elevation N

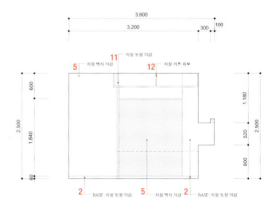

침구실 입면 O / acupuncture cure room elevation O

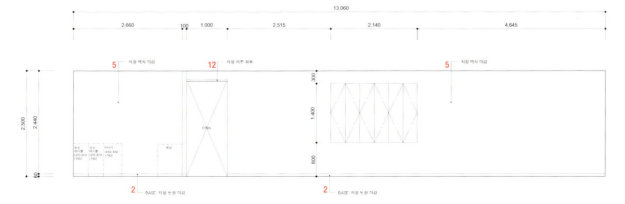

침구실 입면 P / acupuncture cure room elevation P

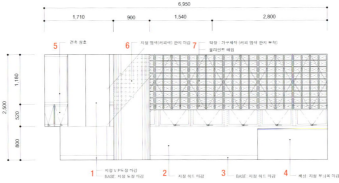

원장실 입면 Q / director's room elevation Q

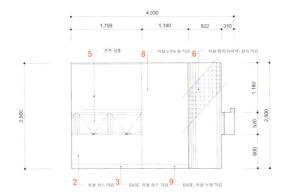

원장실 입면 R / director's room elevation R

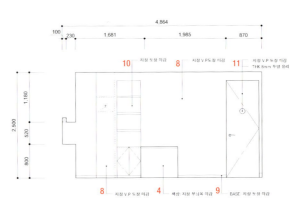

원장실 입면 S / director's room elevation S

1 지정 비닐 페인트 도장 / 걸레받이 : 지정 도장 2 지정 시트 3 걸레받이 : 지정 시트 4 책상 : 지정 무늬목 5 건축 창호 6 지정 커피색 염색 한지 7 약장 : 가구 제작(커피색 염색 한지 부착) / 블라인드 매입 8 지정 비닐 페인트 도장 9 걸레받이 : 지정 도장 10 지정 도장 11 지정 비닐 페인트 도장 / T8 투명유리 12 지정 벽지

1 App. vinyl painting / baseboard : app. painting 2 App. sheet 3 Baseboard : app. sheet 4 Desk : app. wood veneer 5 Architectural window 6 App. coffee color dye Korean paper 7 Medicine cabinet : making furniture (coffee color dye Korean paper attached) / blind embedded 8 App. vinyl painting 9 Baseboard : app. painting 10 App. painting 11 App. vinyl painting / T8 clear glass 12 App. wallpaper

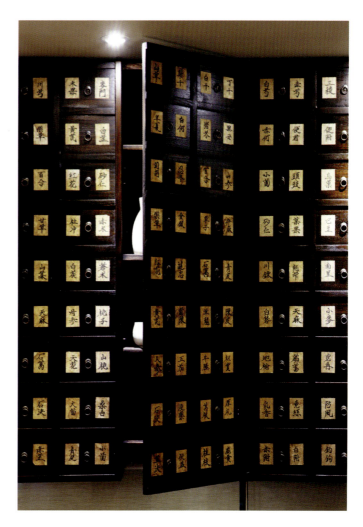

원장실 입면 T / director's room elevation T

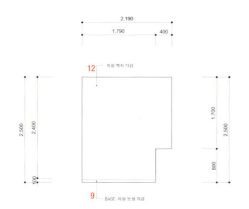

부원장실 입면 U / vice director's room elevation U

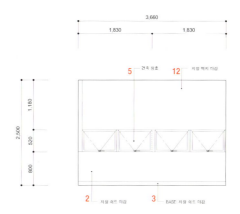

부원장실 입면 V / vice director's room elevation V

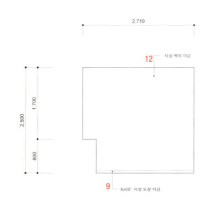

부원장실 입면 W / vice director's room elevation W

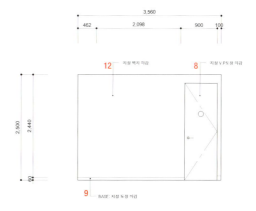

부원장실 입면 X / vice director's room elevation X

SUUM SLEEP CLINIC

BALSANG Inc. | Lee Kyu Hyuk, Park Ji Yoon

숨 수면클리닉은 사용자들의 수면유도를 위해 장식적인 요소를 배제하고 미니멀한 연출을 통해 벽체와 창으로 전달되는 시각적, 청각적 자극에 의한 소음을 차단하고자 하였다. 사용자가 처음 대면하는 출입구를 비롯한 대기실은 안정적이고 고요한 분위기를 유도하기 위해 담백한 크림 화이트 컬러를 사용하여 은은한 조도와 어우러지게 하였다. 또한 공간을 한 번 더 감싼 형태의 접이식 구조로 공간의 변화가 안정감으로 융합되어 사용자를 자극하지 않으면서도 지루하지 않은 공간의 미를 창출하였다. 전체적으로 정해진 시간에 잠을 자야만 하는 환자들의 긴장감 완화를 위해 각 공간은 사용자의 섬세한 심리적 해석을 바탕으로 한 감성 디자인으로 완성되었다.

In order to induce sleep of the users, Suum Sleep Clinic attempted to block the noise created from visual and auditory stimuli that are transmitted through the walls and windows by eliminating decorative elements and presenting a minimal look. The entrance and the waiting area where the users first come into contact with the clinic are designed to draw a calm and peaceful atmosphere using simple cream white color fused with soft light. Also, with a folded shape that is shaped like a space which is double wrapped, variations in space is fused with stability without irritating the users nor boring them out, and thus creating beauty. Overall, in order to relief the tension of the patients who have to fall asleep at a designated time, each room is completed with sensible design details based on careful psychological interpretation of the user.

디자인 이규혁, 박지윤 / (주)발상
위치 서울특별시 강남구 논현동 5번지 페이토빌딩 10층
용도 병원
면적 305.5㎡
마감 바닥 – 폴리싱 타일, 데코 타일 / 벽 – 유리, 하이글로시 보드, 래커, 그래픽 시트 / 천장 – 비닐 페인트 도장
완공 2013. 5
디자인팀 조현자, 이윤정, 이강선
시공팀 임진수
사진 (주)발상 제공

Location 10F, Peitho Building, 5, Nonhyeon-dong, Gangnam-gu, Seoul
Use Hospital
Area 305.5㎡
Finishing Floor - Polishing tile, Deco tile / Wall - Glass, High glossy board, Lacquer, Graphic sheet / Ceiling - Vinyl painting
Completion 2013. 5
Photos offer BALSANG Inc.

평면도 / floor plan

1 입구 2 안내데스크 3 대기공간 4 차트실 5 진료실 6 소독실 7 의사실 8 수술실 9 입원실 10 검사실 11 린넨실 12 조정실 13 직원 소지품 보관함 14 샤워실 15 CT 실 16 주사실 17 상담실

1 Entrance 2 Information desk 3 Waiting area 4 Chart room 5 Consulting room 6 Disinfecting room 7 Doctor's room 8 Operating room 9 Patient's room 10 Examination room 11 Linen room 12 Control room 13 Staff locker room 14 Shower room 15 CT room 16 Injection room 17 Counseling room

AGAON FERTILITY CLINIC

MD SPACE Co., Ltd. | Cha Seung Hee, Kim Bo Kyung

아가온 여성의원은 그 이름처럼 아기를 기다리는 부부의 소망이 담겨있는 곳이다. 디자인 개념은 출산을 준비하는 부부들이 마치 자궁 안에 있는 것처럼 편안함을 느낄 수 있도록 하는 것이었다. 가장 먼저 보이는 안내데스크의 이미지월은 곡면을 활용하여 커다란 그릇(자궁)을 형상화하였고, 안내데스크에서 검사실로의 길은 생명의 길(탯줄)과 같이 희망적인 공간으로 표현하였다. 복도의 이미지월은 검사실과 진료실을 구분하고, LED 조명의 부드러운 색 변화를 통한 편안함과 생동감을 유도하였다. 일반진료실과 검사실은 식재 및 나무색을 사용하여 심리적 안정감을 제공한다. 무균실은 전문병원으로서의 신뢰도를 높이기 위해 짙은 월넛목 바닥재와 흰색 벽으로 모던함을 강조하였다. 또한 기능적인 면을 고려하여 출입구에서부터 분리된 동선과 친환경 도료 마감으로 환자와 실내의 쾌적함을 도모하였다.

Agaon Fertility Clinic is a place that embodies the clients' wish for babies to come, which is what the word 'agaon' means. The design concept for the clinic was to create a space where prospective parents would feel comfortable as if they were in a mother's womb. The image wall on the information desk, a spot that first comes in view when clients step into the clinic, is visualized into a huge bowl (womb) using curves, and the path from the information desk to the testing room is expressed as a hopeful space like a passage to life(umbilical cord). The image wall in the hallway separates the testing room and the doctor's consulting room, and induces comfort and liveliness through soft color changes of LED lighting. The regular consulting room and the testing room are styled with plants and wooden colors to provide psychological stability to the visitors. To heighten the trust for the clinic specializing in fertility, the aseptic room is finished with walnut flooring and white wall emphasizing modernity. Also, the moving line, which is separated from the main entrance giving thought to the functional aspects of the clinic, and the use of eco-friendly varnish heighten the comfort of patients and the interior.

디자인 차승희, 김보경 / (주)MD SPACE
위치 서울특별시 구로구 구로1동 1124-72 조영빌딩 8층
용도 산부인과
면적 567.5㎡
마감 바닥 – 폴리싱 타일, 자기 타일, 데코 타일 / 벽 – 안티 스투코, 친환경 도장, 무늬목 / 천장 – 실크 벽지
시공 (주)MD SPACE
사진 (주)MD SPACE 제공

Location 8F, Joyoung Building, 1124-72, Guro 1-dong, Guro-gu, Seoul
Use Obstetric and Gynecology Clinic
Area 567.5㎡
Finishing Floor - Polishing tile, Porcelain tile, Deco tile / Wall - Antistucco, Eco-friendly painting, Wood veneer / Ceiling - Silk wallpaper
Photos offer MD SPACE Co., Ltd.

천장도 / ceiling plan

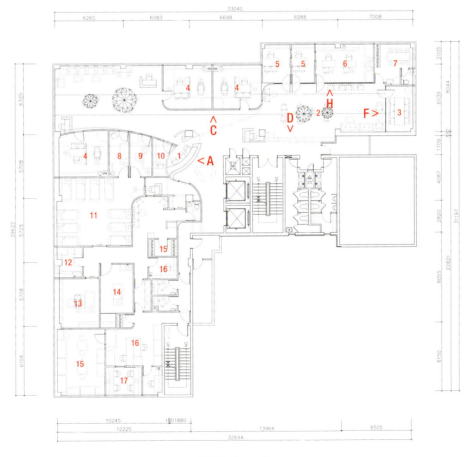

평면도 / floor plan

1 리셉션 2 대기공간 3 세미나실 4 진료실 5 상담실 6 채혈실 7 직원실 8 입원실 9 인공수정실 10 원무과 11 회복실 12 소독실 13 채취실 14 수술실 15 무균실 16 연구실 17 연구원실

1 Reception 2 Waiting area 3 Seminar room 4 Examination room 5 Counseling room 6 Specimen collection room 7 Staff room 8 Patient room 9 Artificial insemination room 10 Admission and discharging office
11 Recovery room 12 Disinfecting room 13 Colletion room 14 Operating room 15 Bioclean room 16 Laboratory 17 Researcher's room

1 자동문 2 지정 도장 3 지정 무늬목 4 ALC 블록 위 도장 5 점검구 6 T5 아크릴 (확산시트 부착) 7 T5 간접조명 8 간접조명 9 지정 벽지 / 지정 필름 10 지정 목재 위 도장 / 지정 조명용 인조대리석 11 지정 무늬목 위 도장 12 지정 집성목 13 LED 조명 14 조명용 인조대리석 15 무늬목 도어

1 Auto door 2 App. painting 3 App. wood veneer 4 Painting on ALC block 5 Access hole 6 T3 acryl (diffusion sheet attached) 7 T5 indirect lighting 8 Indirec lighting 9 App. wall paper / app. film 10 Painting on app. wood / mock marble for app. lighting 11 Painting on app. wood veneer 12 App. laminated timber 13 LED lighting 14 Mock marble for lighting 15 Wood veneer door

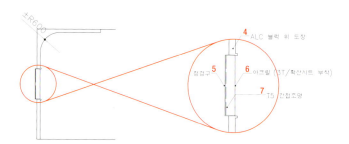

벽 단면 B / wall section B

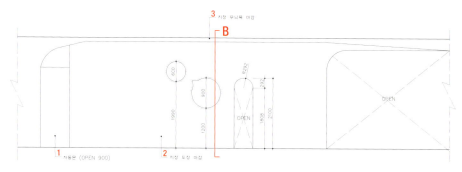

리셉션 입면 A / reception elevation A

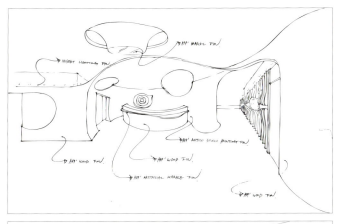
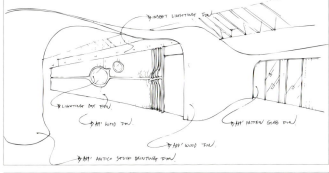
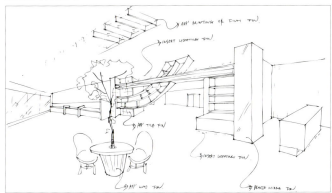

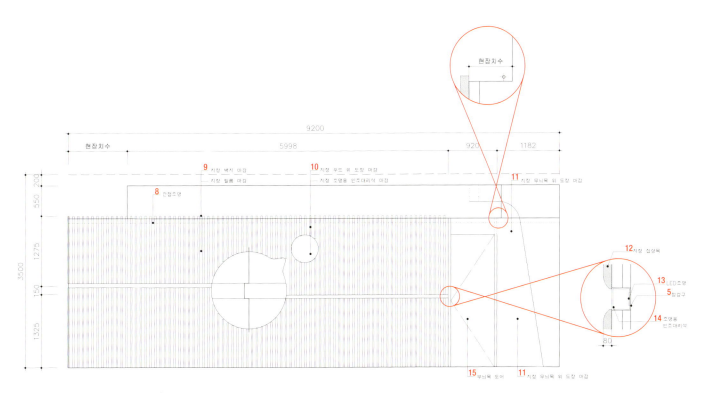

복도 입면 C / corridor elevation C

1 지정 타일 2 지정 필름 3 브론즈 미러 4 간접조명 5 지정 목재 위 스테인 도장 6 지정 우드 플로링 7 지정 벽지 / 지정 목재 8 LED 조명 9 지정 무늬목 도어 10 지정 벽지

1 App. tile 2 App. film 3 Bronze mirror 4 Indirect lighting 5 Stain painting on app. wood 6 App. wood flooring 7 App. wall paper / app. wood 8 LED lighting 9 App. wood veneer door 10 App. wall paper

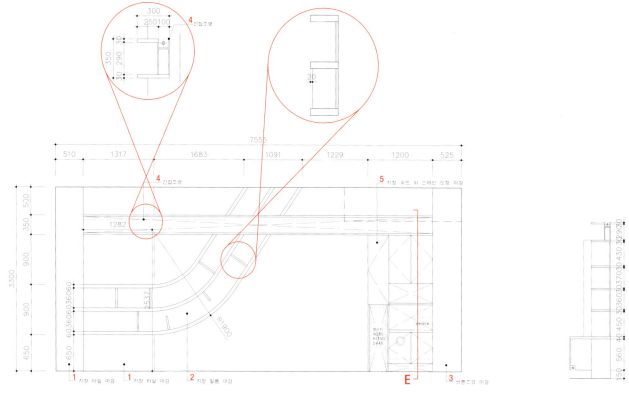

대기실 입면 D / waiting room elevation D

가구 단면 E / furniture section E

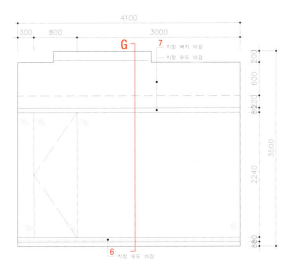

홀 입면 F / hall elevation F

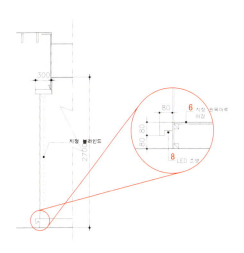

벽 단면 G / wall section G

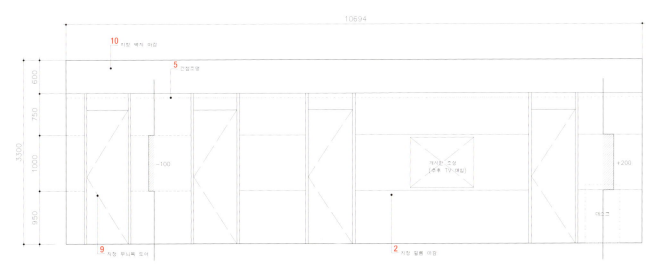

홀 입면 H / hall elevation H

SEOUL BEST DENTAL CLINIC

Friend's Design | Yang Jin Young, Kwon Il Kwon

서울 베스트 치과는 기존 병원들과는 확연히 다른 차별성을 주어 편안하면서도 다시 찾고 싶은 병원으로 설계하고자 하였다. 도시적 느낌과 자연을 결합하여 전체적으로 편안함과 따뜻함을 강조하는 동시에, 재료를 통해 고급스럽고 세련된 느낌의 공간을 연출하였다. 가장 먼저 접하게 되는 안내데스크는 덩어리 형태의 석재를 사용하여 공간의 무게감을 주고자 하였다. 공간 속에 또 다른 공간을 관입시키는 개념으로 디자인된 세미나실은 집의 형태를 적용하여 대기공간과 분리시킴으로써 독립적이면서도 개방적인 공간으로 계획하였다.

Seoul Best Dental Clinic attempted a design that is clearly differentiated from those of existing clinics. It is designed as a comfortable place where clients would want to visit again. Combining an urban look with nature, the overall design emphasized comfort and warmth and, at the same time, staged a space that gives a high-end and sophisticated impression by the materials. The information desk that comes in view at first is made of a block of stone to give a sense of weight to the space. The seminar room which is designed with the idea of interpenetrating another space in a space separates the atmosphere by applying the form of a house so as to build a space that is independent and open at the same time.

디자인 양진영, 권일권 / (주)프랜즈디자인
위치 경기도 수원시 영통구 이의동 1325-4번지 경현빌딩 2층
용도 치과
면적 123㎡
마감 바닥 - 타일, 데코 타일 / 벽 - 도배, 도장, 무늬유리, 금속 / 천장 - 도장, 도배
완공 2013. 2
디자인팀 정연이, 노지은, 이아람
사진 최정복

Location 1325-4, Iui-dong, Yeongtong-gu, Suwon, Gyeonggi-do
Use Dental clinic
Area 123㎡
Finishing Floor - Tile, Deco tile / Wall - Wallpaper, Painting, Patterned glass, Metal / Ceiling - Painting, Wallpaper
Completion 2013. 2
Photographer Choi Jeong Bok

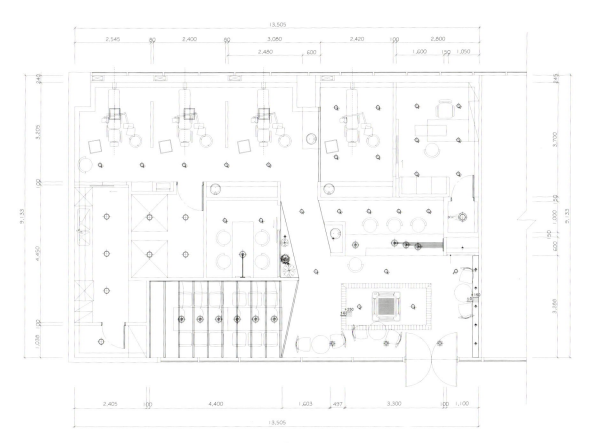

천장도 / ceiling plan

평면도 / floor plan

1 입구 2 대기공간 3 접수대 4 원장실 5 VIP실 6 진료실 7 촬영공간 8 간호사실, 준비실, 기공실 9 X-ray실 10 상담실 11 세미나실 12 기계실 13 샤워실 14 이동식 카트 15 모니터

1 Entrance 2 Waiting area 3 Reception 4 Director's room 5 VIP room 6 Consulting room 7 Photo zone 8 Nurse's room, preparation room, dental laboratory 9 X-ray room 10 Counseling room 11 Seminar room 12 Machine room 13 Shower room 14 Mobile cart 15 Monitor

접수대 입면 A / reception elevation A

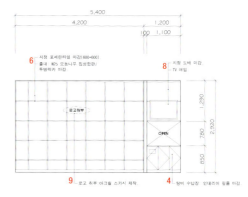

접수대 입면 B / reception elevation B

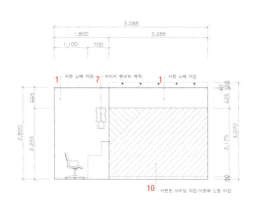

접수대 입면 C / reception elevation C

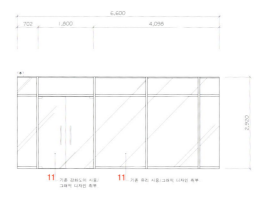

대기공간 입면 D / waiting area elevation D

1 지정 도배 2 상판 : 지정 판재 / 지정 고재 3 접수대 상판 : 지정 대리석 / 지정 흑두기석 4 식음대 수납장 : 인테리어 필름 5 아크릴 위 글자 시트 커팅 6 지정 포세린 타일 / 졸대 : 오동나무 집성 합판, 투명 래커 7 이미지 펜던트 8 지정 도배 / TV 매입 9 로고 부착 : 아크릴 문자 커팅 10 시멘트 사이딩, 지정색 도장 11 기존 강화문 사용, 그래픽 디자인 부착 12 지정 도배(포인트색) 13 투명유리 14 640X1,940 행거문 타공 후 지정 모양 문살 시공

1 App. wallpaper 2 Top board : app. plank / app. old wood 3 Reception top board : app. marble / app. granite 4 Beverage storage closet : interior film 5 Text sheet cutting on acrylic 6 App. porcelain tile / wood lath : paulownia laminated plywood, clear lacquer 7 Image pendant 8 App. wallpaper / TV embedded 9 Logo attached : acrylic letter cutting 10 Cement siding, app. color painting 11 Using existing tempered door, graphic design attached 12 App. wallpaper (point color) 13 Clear glass 14 App. shape of paper sliding door construction after 640X1,940 hanger door perforated

상담실 입면 E / counseling room elevation E

상담실 입면 F / counseling room elevation F

상담실 입면 G / counseling room elevation G

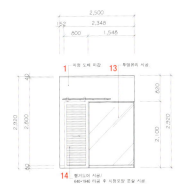

상담실 입면 H / counseling room elevation H

1 38X140 구조목, 투명 래커 2 투명유리 3 아크릴 위 글자 시트 커팅 4 지정 백색 유리 5 조경 6 640X1,940 행거문 타공 후 지정 모양 문살 시공 7 지정 도배 8 지정색 도장 9 이미지 팬던트 10 그래픽 디자인 부착 11 기존 창 사용 12 H:150 물받이 / 수납장 : 지정 인테리어 필름 13 선반 : 오동나무 집성 합판, 투명 래커 / 수납장 : 지정 인테리어 필름 14 지정 타일 / 거울 15 수납장 : 지정 인테리어 필름 16 파티션 17 허니콤 블라인드 18 지정색 유리 / 수납장 : 지정 인테리어 필름 19 지정 모양 CNC 가공 / 20X40 각파이프 위 지정색 도장

1 38X140 structural wood, clear lacquer 2 Clear glass 3 Text sheet cutting on acrylic 4 App. white glass 5 Landscaping 6 App. shape of paper sliding door construction after 640X1,940 hanger door perforated 7 App. wallpaper 8 App. color painting 9 Image pendant 10 Graphic design attached 11 Using existing window 12 H:150 downpipe / storage closet : app. interior film 13 Shelf : paulownia laminated plywood, clear lacquer / storage closet : app. interior film 14 App. tile / mirror 15 Storage closet : app. interior film 16 Partition 17 Honeycomb blind 18 App. color glass / storage closet : app. interior film 19 App. shape CNC cutting / app. color painting on 20X40 square pipe

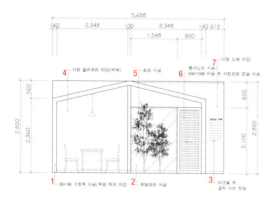

세미나실 입면 I / seminar room elevation I

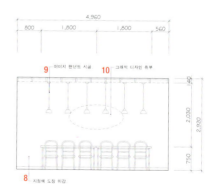

세미나실 입면 J / seminar room elevation J

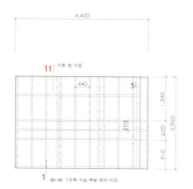

세미나실 입면 K / seminar room elevation K

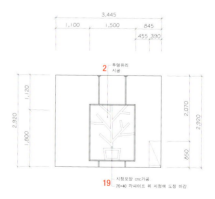

진료실 파티션 측면 L / consulting room partition side view L

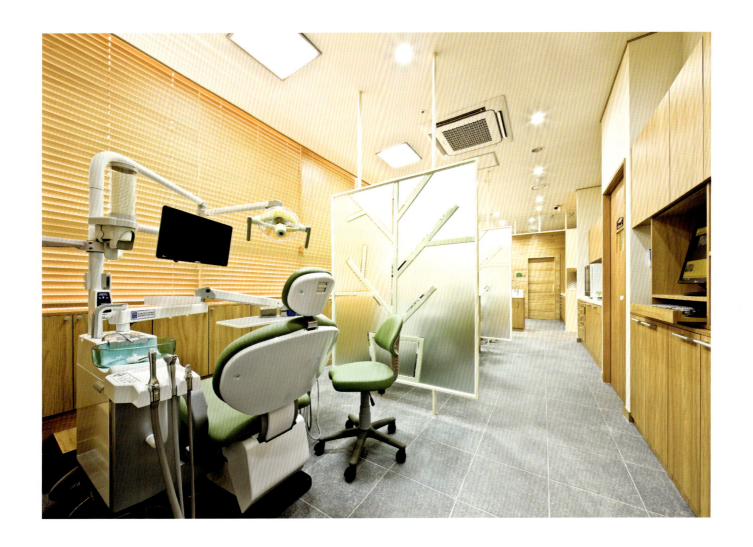

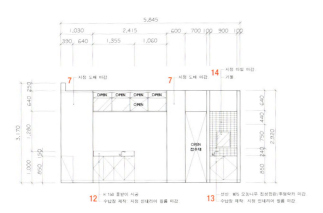

진료실 입면 M / consulting room elevation M

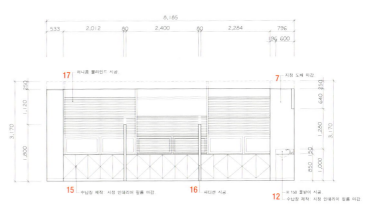

진료실 입면 N / consulting room elevation N

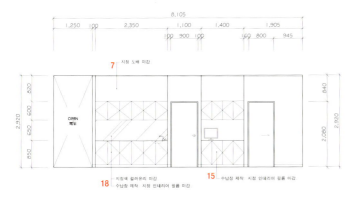

진료실 입면 O / consulting room elevation O

진료실 입면 P / consulting room elevation P

1 수납장 : 지정 인테리어 필름 2 허니콤 블라인드 3 300X1,400 창문, 투명유리 / 선반 : 오동나무 집성 합판, 투명 래커 4 오동나무 합판, 투명 래커 5 840X2,050 문 6 지정색 유리 / 수납장 : 지정 인테리어 필름 7 지정 도배 8 H:150 물받이 / 수납장 : 지정 인테리어 필름 9 목구조 틀 위 부분 투명유리, 그래픽 시트 10 기존 창문 사용 11 소지품 보관함, 책꽂이 : 인테리어 필름 12 740X2,050 문 13 300X1,400 창문, 투명유리

1 Storage closet : app. interior film 2 Honeycomb blind 3 300X1,400 window, clear glass / shelf : paulownia laminated plywood, clear lacquer 4 Paulownia plywood, clear lacquer 5 840X2,050 door 6 App. color glass / storage closet : app. interior film 7 App. wallpaper 8 H:150 downpipe / storage closet : app. interior film 9 Partial clear glass on wooden structure frame, graphic sheet 10 Using existing window 11 Locker, bookshelf : interior film 12 740X2,050 door 13 300X1,400 window, clear glass

VIP실 입면 Q / VIP room elevation Q

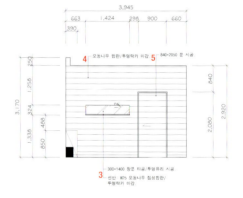

VIP실 입면 R / VIP room elevation R

VIP실 입면 S / VIP room elevation S

VIP실 입면 T / VIP room elevation T

원장실 입면 U / director's room elevation U

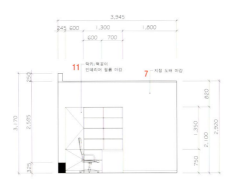

원장실 입면 V / director's room elevation V

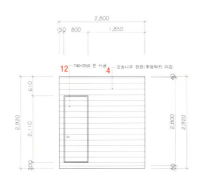

원장실 입면 W / director's room elevation W

원장실 입면 X / director's room elevation X

DREAM DENTAL CLINIC

R.Republic + mtom design | Kim Jin Guk

드림 치과는 압구정역 메디컬구역의 특성과 연예인 전속 병원이라는 대표성을 부각시키기 위해 심플하지만 세련된 공간과 효율적인 동선을 갖도록 구성하였다. 엘리베이터에서 보이는 둥근 형태의 데스크는 일반 보철과 교정 파트 환자의 동선을 분리한다. 각 파트별 복도에는 별도의 상담실과 파우더룸이 두어 직원 및 의료진의 업무가 편리하도록 배치하였다. 전체적으로 백색의 벽체로 구성하고, 부분적으로 드림메디컬그룹을 상징하는 파란색이 사용되어 다양한 마감과 그래픽에 의해 드림치과만의 아이덴티티를 드러내고자 하였다. 병원이 추구하고자 하는 '한발 앞서 가는 병원'이라는 이미지를 강조하기 위해 깔끔하게 정돈된 색과 다양한 그래픽으로 마감하였다.

Dream Dental Clinic was designed to have simple but sophisticated spaces and efficient circulation in order to highlight its representative characters of being located in the Apgujeong Station medical district and serving as an exclusive clinic for celebrities. The curved information desk that comes in sight from the elevator separates the flow of patients who come for regular prosthodontics from those who come for orthodontics. In the hallway for each part, a counseling room and a powder room are arranged for the work convenience of the staff and doctors. The interior is overall composed of white walls, while the color blue, which symbolize the Dream Medical group, is used partially so that the overall design shows off the identity of the Dream Dental Clinic through a variety of finishing materials and graphics. In order to emphasize the image of the clinic as 'one that is a step ahead of others' the interior is finished with clean and neat colors and a variety of graphics.

디자인 김진국 / 알리퍼블릭 디자인 + 엠투엠 디자인
위치 서울특별시 강남구 신사동 603-2 CGV빌딩 9층
용도 치과
면적 325㎡
마감 바닥 – 폴리싱 타일 / 벽– 도장, 실사 이미지, 컬러 유리 / 천장 – 도장
시공 팀 황문구
사진 황문구

Location 9F, CGV building, 603-2, Sinsa-dong, Gangnam-gu, Seoul, Korea
Use Dental clinic
Area 325㎡
Finishing Floor - Polishing tile / Wall - Painting, Actual image, Color glass / Ceiling - Painting
Photographer Whang Mun Goo

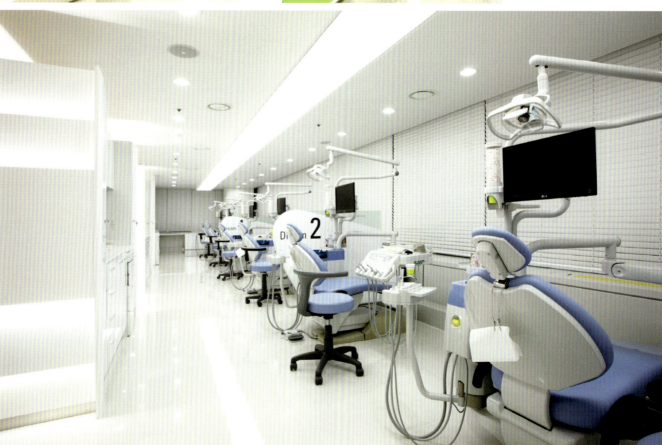

천장도 / ceiling plan

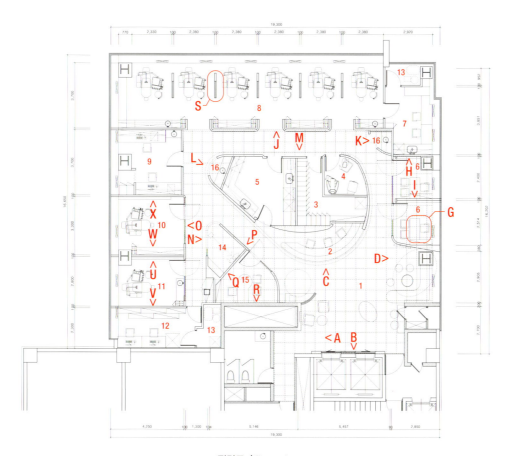

평면도 / floor plan

1 대기공간 2 리셉션 3 직원실 4 X-ray 실 5 소독실 6 상담실 7 기공실 8 진료실 9 원장실 10 수술실 11 특진실 12 창고 13 기계실 14 촬영실 15 원장 상담실 16 파우더룸 17 지정 바리솔(조명형)
18 지정 도장 19 지정 도배

1 Waiting area 2 Reception 3 Staff room 4 X-ray room 5 Disinfecting room 6 Counseling room 7 Dental laboratory 8 Consulting room 9 Director's room 10 Surgery room 11 Special consulting room 12 Storage
13 Machine room 14 Photo zone 15 Director's counseling room 16 Powder room 17 App. barrisol (lamp type) 18 App. painting 19 App. wallpaper

1 지정 실사 이미지 / 걸레받이 : 스테인리스 스틸 헤어라인 2 T12 투명유리 / 지정 필름 3 T5 컬러 유리 4 지정 필름 5 지정 필름 / 걸레받이 : 스테인리스 스틸 헤어라인 6 지정 도장 / 걸레받이 : 스테인리스 스틸 헤어라인 7 자석판 부착

1 App. actual image / baseboard : stainless steel hairline 2 T12 clear glass / app. film 3 T5 color glass 4 App. film 5 App. film / baseboard : stainless steel hairline 6 App. painting / baseboard : stainless steel hairline 7 Magnet board attached

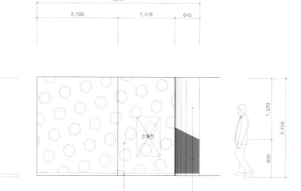

입구 입면 A / entrance elevation A

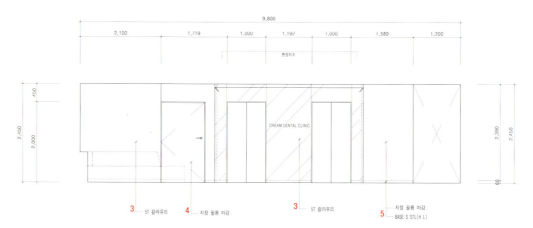

입구 입면 B / entrance elevation B

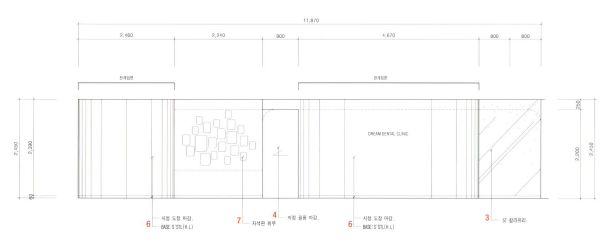

리셉션 입면 C / reception elevation C

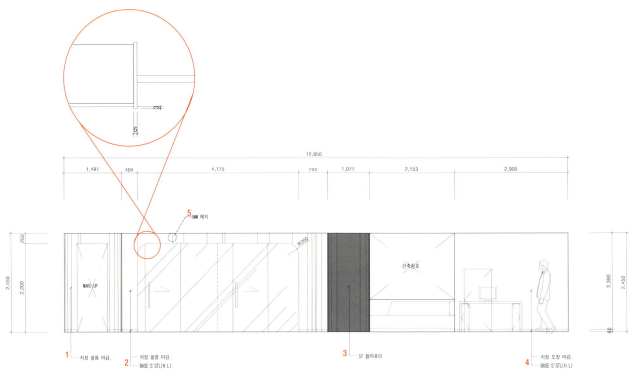

대기공간 입면 D / waiting area elevation D

1 지정 필름 2 지정 필름 / 걸레받이 : 스테인리스 스틸 헤어라인 3 T5 컬러 유리
4 지정 도장 / 걸레받이 : 스테인리스 스틸 헤어라인 5 6mm 줄눈 6 지정 벽지 /
걸레받이 : 지정 필름 7 T5 은경 / 지정 필름 8 지정색 도장 9 지정 백색 도장

1 App. film 2 App. film / baseboard : stainless steel hairline 3 T5 color glass
4 App. painting / baseboard : stainless steel hairline 5 6mm masonry joint 6 App.
wallpaper / baseboard : app. film 7 T5 silver mirror / app. film 8 App. color painting
9 App. white painting

상담실 테이블 평면 E /
counseling room table top view E

상담실 테이블 측면 F /
counseling room table side view F

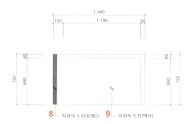

상담실 테이블 정면 G /
counseling room table front view G

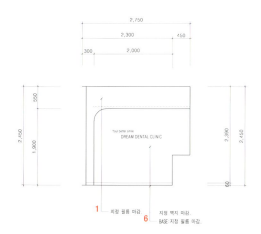

상담실 입면 H / counseling room elevation H

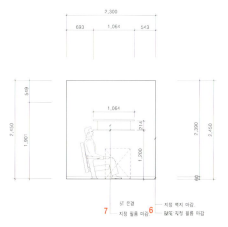

상담실 입면 I / counseling room elevation I

219

1 지정 필름 / 걸레받이 : 스테인리스 스틸 헤어라인   2 지정 필름   3 자석판 부착   4 지정 도장 / 걸레받이 : 스테인리스 스틸 헤어라인   5 T5 은경, 그라데이션 시트   6 컬러 유리   7 인조대리석   8 지정 타일

1 App. film / baseboard : stainless steel hairline   2 App. film   3 Magnet board attached   4 App. painting / baseboard : stainless steel hairline   5 T5 silver mirror, gradation sheet   6 Color glass   7 Mock marble   8 App. tile

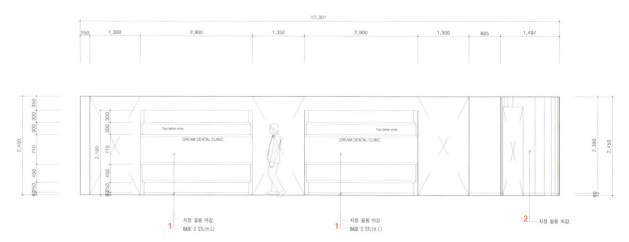

복도 입면 J / corridor elevation J

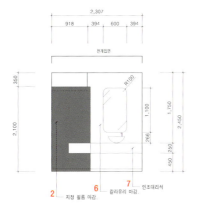

파우더룸 입면 K / powder room elevation K

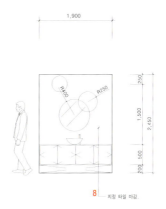

파우더룸 입면 L / powder room elevation L

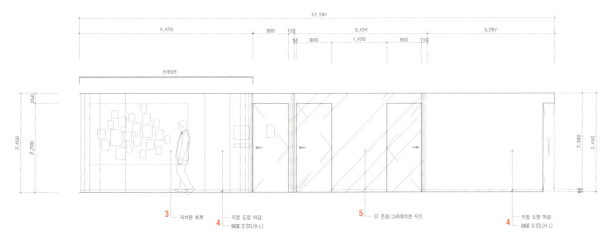

복도 입면 M / corridor elevation M

1 지정 필름 / 걸레받이 : 스테인리스 스틸 헤어라인   2 HPL 유광 문   3 지정 필름   4 T5 컬러 유리   5 6mm 줄눈   6 컬러 유리 10mm 단차   7 지정 벽지   8 걸레받이 : 지정 필름   9 간접조명   10 지정 벽지 / 걸레받이 : 지정 필름

1 App. film / baseboard : stainless steel hairline   2 HPL glossy door   3 App. film   4 T5 color glass   5 6mm masonry joint   6 Color glass with 10mm height difference   7 App. wallpaper   8 Baseboard : app. film   9 Indirect lighting   10 App. wallpaper / baseboard : app. film

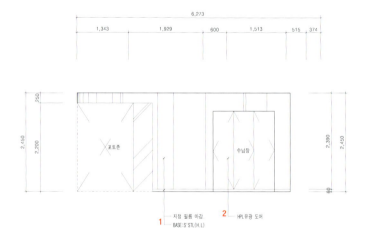

복도 입면 N / corridor elevation N

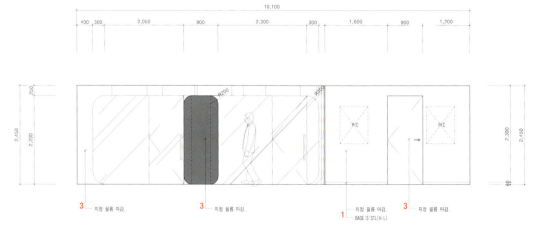

복도 입면 O / corridor elevation O

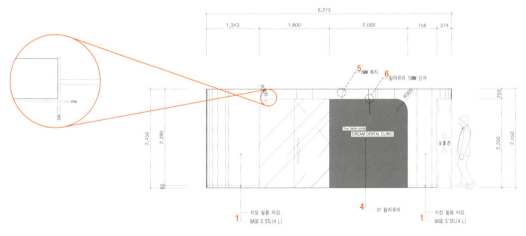

복도 입면 P / corridor elevation P

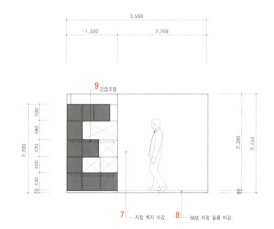

원장 상담실 입면 Q / director's counseling room elevation Q

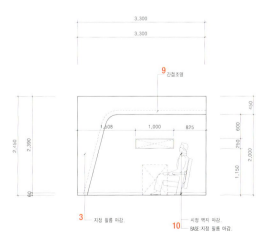

원장 상담실 입면 R / director's counseling room elevation R

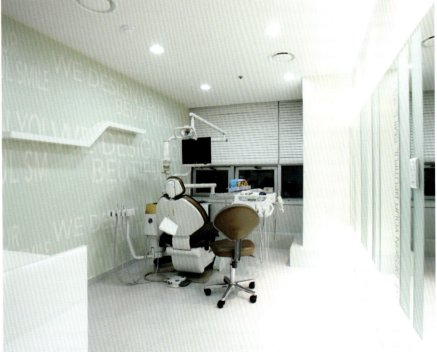

진료실 파티션 평면 S /
consulting room partition top view S

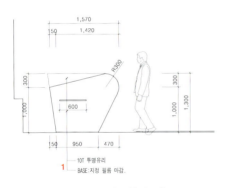

진료실 파티션 측면 T /
consulting room partition side view T

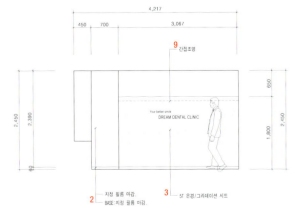

특진실 입면 U / special consulting room elevation U

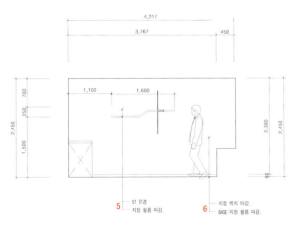

특진실 입면 V / special consulting room elevation V

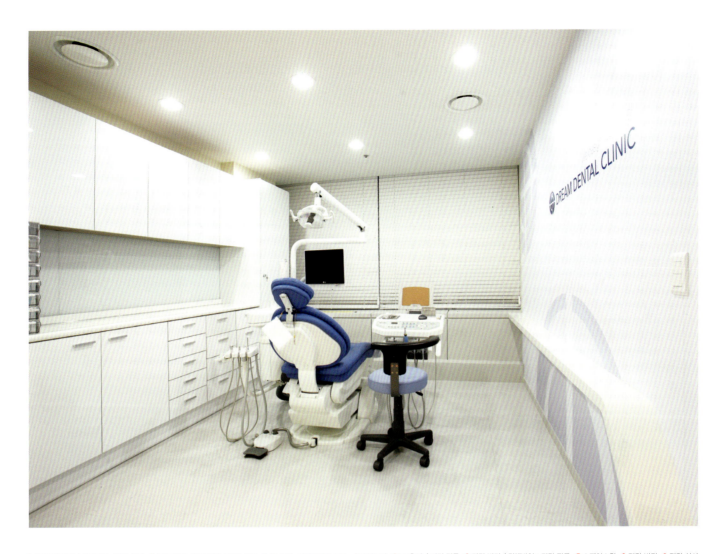

1 T10 투명유리 / 걸레받이 : 지정 필름 2 지정 필름 / 걸레받이 : 지정 필름 3 T5 은경, 그라데이션 시트 4 간접조명 5 T5 은경 / 지정 필름 6 지정 벽지 / 걸레받이 : 지정 필름 7 스페이스월 8 지정 벽지 9 지정 실사 이미지

1 T10 clear glass / baseboard : app. film 2 App. filme / baseboard : app. film 3 T5 silver mirror, gradation sheet 4 Indirect lighting 5 T5 silver mirror / app. film 6 App. wallpaper / baseboard : app. film 7 Space wall 8 App. wallpaper 9 App. actual image

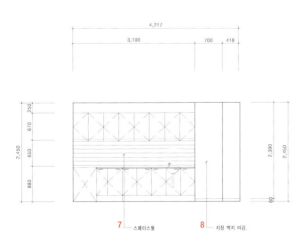

수술실 입면 W / surgery room elevation W

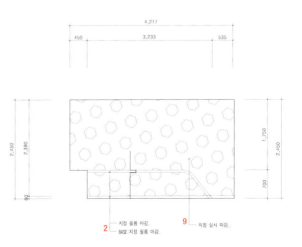

수술실 입면 X / surgery room elevation X

KOWON PLASTIC SURGERY

Limtaehee design studio | Lim Tae Hee

코원 성형외과는 기대와 두려움을 가지고 병원을 방문하는 사람들에게 아름다움에 대한 욕망을 실현할 수 있는 공간으로 계획하였다. 입구의 'ㄱ'자 공간에는 몇 개의 뚫린 문들이 연속으로 나열되어 있는데 이를 통해 진료실, 원장실 그리고 수술실로 이르는 작은 복도를 만든다. 뚫린 문과 겹쳐 보이는 벽면은 사선의 검은색 목재 패널을 사용하여 백색의 리셉션 공간과 반전되는 인상을 주도록 하였다. 여기에 금색 도료를 뿌려 구름 덩어리처럼 걸쳐놓아 반짝거림과 함께 환자가 기대하는 욕망의 형상을 표현하였다. 또한 리셉션의 데스크 및 공간 곳곳에 예각을 사용하여 세련된 느낌으로 구성하였다.

Kowon plastic surgery was designed to provide a place that realizes the desire for beauty of the people who visit the hospital with expectations and anxiety. The inverted L shape entrance area is lined up with a series of openings on the wall, which form a small hallway that leads to the consulting room, the director's office, and the surgery room. The wall surface that overlaps with this wall of openings is finished with black wooden panels with diagonal stripes to give a reversed impression of the white reception area. Here, gold paint is sprinkled on the surface making it seem as if patches of clouds are hanging in space, along with the glitter, it expressed the form of the desire the patients expect to realize. In addition, acute angles are used on the reception deck and all over the space to compose a space with a sophisticated look.

디자인 임태희 / 임태희디자인스튜디오
위치 서울특별시 강남구 신사동 592-4
용도 성형외과
면적 179.85㎡
마감 도장, 안티스투코, 도배
설계기간 2013. 4 ~ 2013. 5
공사기간 2013. 5 ~ 2013. 7
디자인팀 박동은, 신은혜
사진 박영채

Location 592-4, Sinsa-dong, Gangnam-gu, Seoul
Use Plastic surgery
Area 179.85㎡
Finishing Painting, Anti stucco, Wallpaper
Design period 2013. 4 ~ 2013. 5
Construction period 2013. 5 ~ 2013. 7
Photographer Park Young Chae

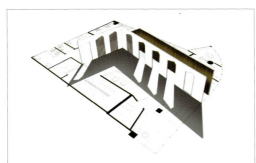
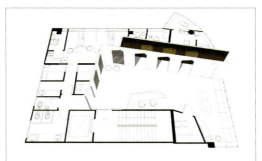

평면도 / floor plan

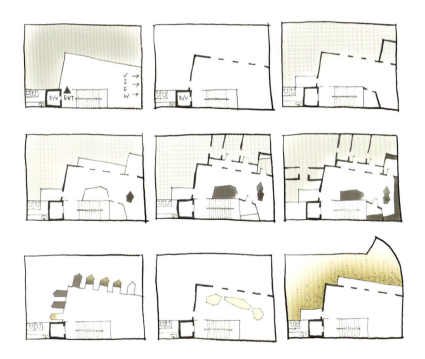

공간 시퀀스 / spatial sequence

1 입구 2 로비 3 대기공간 4 상담실 5 진료실 6 원장실 7 차트실 및 창고 8 치료실 9 준비실 10 수술실 11 소독실 12 회복실 13 간호사실 14 파우더룸 15 남자화장실 16 여자화장실 17 목재 & 패브릭 가구 18 폴리싱 타일 19 P-타일

1 Entrance 2 Lobby 3 Waiting area 4 Counseling room 5 Consulting room 6 Director's room 7 Chart room & Storage 8 Cure room 9 Preparation room 10 Surgery room 11 Disinfecting room 12 Recovery room 13 Nurse's room 14 Powder room 15 Men's toilet 16 Women's toilet 17 Wood & fabric furniture 18 Polishing tile 19 P-tile

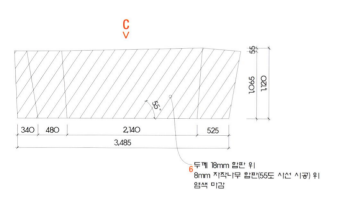

리셉션 데스크 정면 B / reception desk front view B

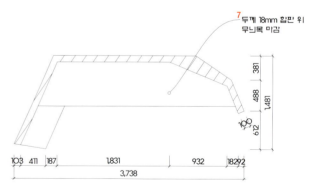

리셉션 데스크 평면 C / reception desk top view C

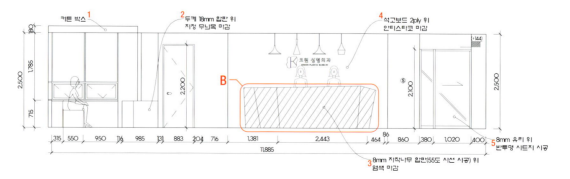

로비 입면 A / lobby elevation A

1 커튼 박스 2 T18 합판 위 지정 무늬목 3 T8 자작나무 합판(55°사선 시공) 위 염색 4 석고보드 2겹 위 안티스투코 5 T8 유리 위 반투명 시트지 6 T18 합판 위 T8 자작나무 합판(55°사선 시공) 위 염색 7 T18 합판 위 무늬목 8 T5 동경 위 시트지 사선 시공 9 패브릭 가구 제작 및 설치

1 Curtain box 2 App. wood veneer on T18 plywood 3 Dyeing on T8 birch plywood (55° diagonal line construction) 4 Antistucco on gypsum board 2ply 5 Translucent sheet paper on T8 glass 6 Dyeing on T8 birch plywood (55° diagonal line construction) on T18 plywood 7 Wood veneer on T18 plywood 8 Sheet paper diagonal line construction on T5 brass mirror 9 Fabric furniture making & installed

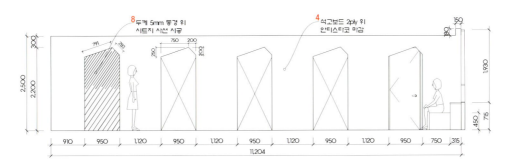

로비 입면 D / lobby elevation D

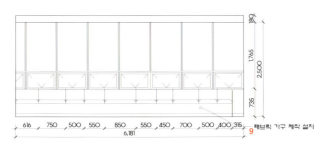

로비 입면 E / lobby elevation E

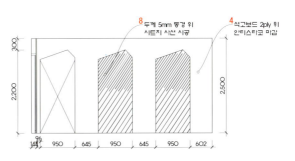

로비 입면 F / lobby elevation F

1 석고보드 2겹 위 T8 자작나무 패널(55°시공) 위 금분 페인트 그라데이션 2 자작나무 패널 55°시공(문 프레임 숨김) 3 제작 문 위 T8 자작나무 패널 55°시공(염색) 4 석고보드 2겹 위 안티스투코 5 T18 합판 위 지정 무늬목 6 TV 케이블선 및 전기선 벽체 매입 7 석고보드 2겹 위 지정 안티스투코 8 T18 합판 위 타공(유리크기), T5 투명유리 시공 후 전체 무늬목 마감 9 정수기 배수 구멍 타공 10 전선 구멍 타공 11 휴지통 뚜껑

1 Gold dust paint gradation on T8 birch panel (55° construction) on gypsum board 2ply 2 Birch panel 55° construction (hiding door frame) 3 Birch panel 55° construction on making door (dyeing) 4 Antistucco on gypsum board 2ply 5 App. wood veneer on T18 plywood 6 TV cable line and electrode lead embedded in wall 7 App. antistucco on gypsum board 2ply 8 Perforating on T18 plywood (glass size), total wood veneer finish after T5 clear glass construction 9 Water purifier drain hole perforated 10 Wire hole perforated 11 Rubbish bin cap

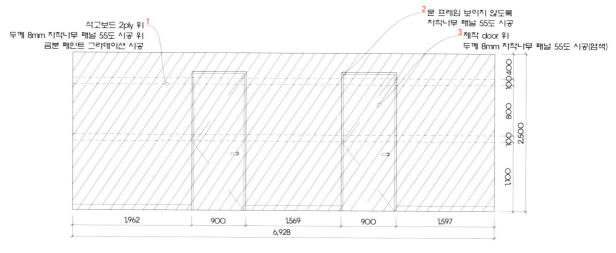

복도 입면 G / corridor elevation G

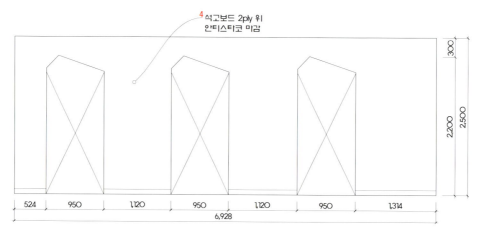

복도 입면 H / corridor elevation H

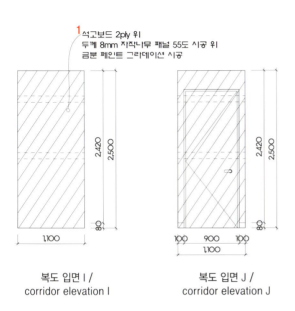

복도 입면 I / corridor elevation I

복도 입면 J / corridor elevation J

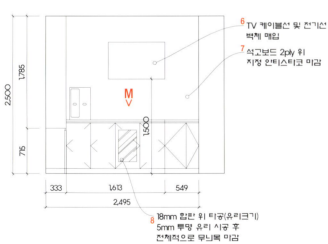

대기 공간 입면 K / waiting area elevation K

대기 공간 입면 L / waiting area elevation L

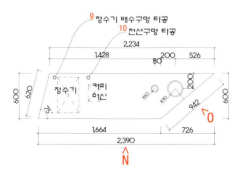

서비스 테이블 평면 M / service table top view M

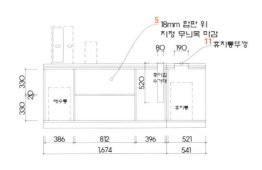

서비스 테이블 정면 N 내부 / service table front view N inside

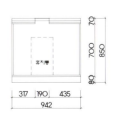

서비스 테이블 측면 O 내부 / service table side view O inside

SHINSEGAE DENTAL CLINIC

PEOPLE WHO WORK | Ann Si Ne

신세계 치과의 진료실은 모든 환자가 VIP라는 느낌을 받을 수 있도록 방으로 구성하였는데, 자칫 답답함을 줄 수 있는 방의 전면과 측면을 유리로 구획하여 개방감을 주었다. 공간의 개방과 폐쇄의 혼합을 위해 벽체에 투명유리와 불투명 유리를 사용하여 의료진과 환자의 심리적 안정을 도모하였다. 대기공간은 가볍고 거친 느낌의 시멘트 모르타르로 마감하였고, 천연 대리석의 안내데스크와 화려한 조명을 배치하였다. 에폭시 바닥은 고급스러운 느낌을 연출하고, 모노 점보타일 위 백색 도장 마감으로 질감을 살려 어두울 수 있는 대기공간에 밝고 세련됨을 더하였다. 환자의 접근성을 고려하여 진료실 입구에 상담실을 배치하였고 편안한 느낌으로 상담을 받을 수 있도록 외부 창을 계획하였다.

The consulting rooms in Shinsegae Dental Clinic were designed as rooms so that all patients can feel they are treated as VIPs. The front and the sides of the rooms are planned with glass to give a sense of openness to the space that could have felt rather cramped. For a combination of open and closed effect, clear glass and frosted glass are used, thus promoting psychological stability of the patients as well as the doctors and staff. The waiting area is finished with cement mortar that has a light and coarse effect and is arranged with marble information desk and colorful lightings. Epoxy flooring produces a sophisticated look, and the white seal finishing on the mono jumbo tile that highlights the texture of the tiles adds bright and stylized ambiance to the atmosphere which could have been otherwise dark. Taking into account patients' accessibility, the counseling room was arranged in front of the consulting room. Also, the window facing the outdoor was styled so that patients can feel comfortable during consultations.

디자인 안시내 / 일하는 사람들-나는김정현이다
위치 충청남도 천안시 동남구 신부동 461-1
용도 치과
면적 263㎡
마감 바닥 - 셀프 레벨링 위 투명 에폭시, 폴리싱 타일 / 벽 - 모노 점보타일, 석고, 수성 페인트, 모르타르 / 천장 - 콘크리트 위 수성 페인트
완공 2013. 10
사진 김정현

Location 461-1, Sinbu-dong, Dongnam-gu, Cheonan, Chungcheongnam-do
Use Dental clinic
Area 263㎡
Finishing Floor - Clear epoxy on self leveling, Polishing tile / Wall - Mono jumbo tile, Plaster, Water paint, Mortar / Ceiling - Water paint on concrete
Completion 2013. 10
Photographer Kim Joung Hyun

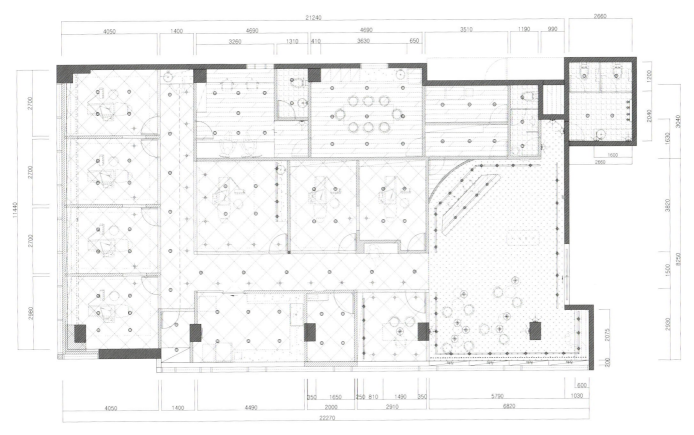

천장도 / ceiling plan

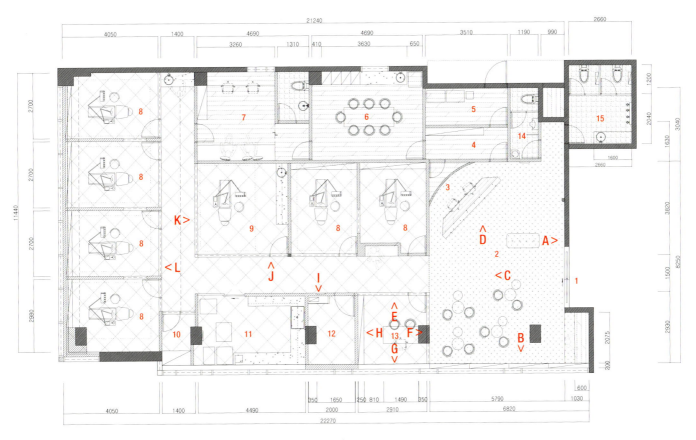

평면도 / floor plan

1 입구 2 대기공간 3 안내데스크 4 차트실 5 기계실 6 세미나실 7 원장실 8 진료실 9 수술실 10 주사실 11 공급실 12 X-ray 실 13 상담실 14 여자화장실 15 남자화장실

1 Entrance 2 Waiting area 3 Information desk 4 Chart room 5 Machine room 6 Seminar room 7 Director's room 8 Consulting room 9 Surgery room 10 Injection room 11 Supply room 12 X-ray room
13 Counseling room 14 Women's toilet 15 Men's toilet

1 지정 파벽돌 위 백색 도장 / 지정 문 MDF 위 도장 2 지정 시멘트칠 / 상판 : 지정 집성목, 문 MDF 위 도장 3 소화전 4 유리 5 지정 집성목 / 지정 회색 파벽돌 위 백색 도장

1 White painting on app. broken brick / painting on app. door MDF 2 App. cement painting / top board : app. glued-laminated wood, painting on door MDF 3 Fireplug 4 Glass 5 App. glued-laminated wood / white painting on app. gray broken brick

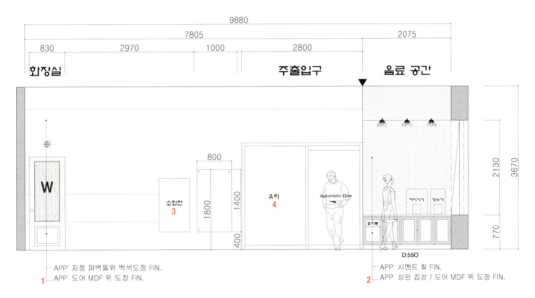

입구 입면 A / entrance elevation A

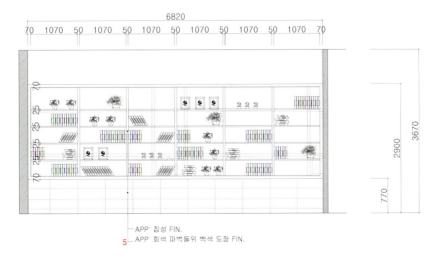

대기공간 입면 B / waiting area elevation B

1 지정 MDF 위 지정 몰딩 / 지정 벽면 시멘트칠(모르타르)   2 지정 파벽돌 위 백색 도장 / 지정 문 MDF 위 도장   3 지정 벽면 시멘트칠(모르타르) / 지정 대리석   4 지정 문 MDF 위 도장   5 지정 파벽돌 위 백색 도장

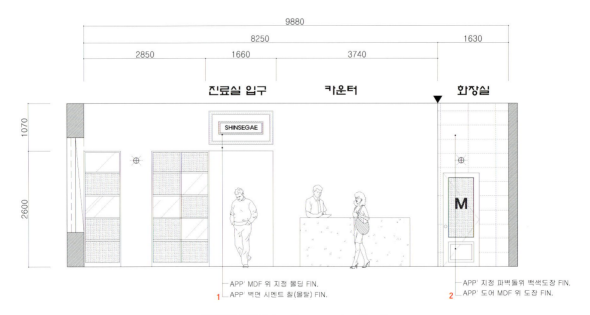

대기공간 입면 C / waiting area elevation C

1 App. molding on app. MDF / app. cement painting on wall (mortar) 2 White painting on app. broken brick / painting on app. door MDF 3 App. cement painting on wall (mortar) / app. marble 4 Painting on app. door MDF
5 White painting on app. broken brick

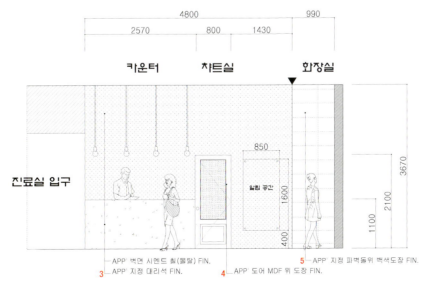

안내데스크 입면 D / information desk elevation D

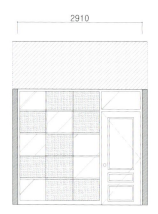

상담실 입면 E / counseling room elevation E

상담실 입면 F / counseling room elevation F

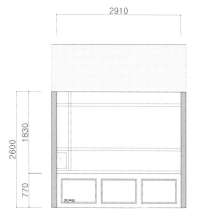

상담실 입면 G / counseling room elevation G

상담실 입면 H / counseling room elevation H

1 커튼 박스(창높이까지) **2** 액자 레일 : T110 프레임 몰딩 **3** T30 MDF 위 지정 몰딩 / 걸레받이 몰딩 / 문 내부 선반 **4** 지정 투명유리 / 지정 문 MDF 위 도장 **5** 지정 투명유리 / T30 지정 각파이프 / 지정 고방유리 **6** 지정 백색 도장

1 Curtain box (to height of window) **2** Frame rail : T110 frame molding **3** App. molding on T30 MDF / baseboard molding / shelf in door **4** App. clear glass / painting on app. door MDF **5** App. clear glass / T30 app. square pipe / app. grid-patterned glass **6** App. white painting

복도 입면 l / corridor elevation l

1 지정 MDF 위 지정 도장 / 지정 백색 도장 / 상판, 측면 : 지정 ㄷ형 인조대리석 / 지정 고방유리 2 지정 투명유리 / T30 지정 각파이프 / 지정 고방유리 3 지정 투명유리 / 지정 문 MDF 위 도장 4 지정 백색 도장 / 지정 고방유리 / 지정 문 MDF 위 도장 5 지정 벽면 시멘트칠(모르타르) / 지정 고방유리 / 지정 문 MDF 위 도장 6 지정 투명유리 / T30 지정 각파이프 7 지정 석고 벽체 / 지정 MDF 위 지정 도장

1 App. painting on app. MDF / app. white painting / top board, side : app. C-type mock marble / app. grid-patterned glass 2 App. clear glass / T30 app. square pipe / app. grid-patterned glass 3 App. clear glass / painting on app. door MDF 4 App. white painting / app. grid-patterned glass / painting on app. door MDF 5 App. cement painting on wall (mortar) / app. grid-patterned glass / painting on app. door MDF 6 App. clear glass / T30 app. square pipe 7 App. plaster wall / app. painting on app. MDF

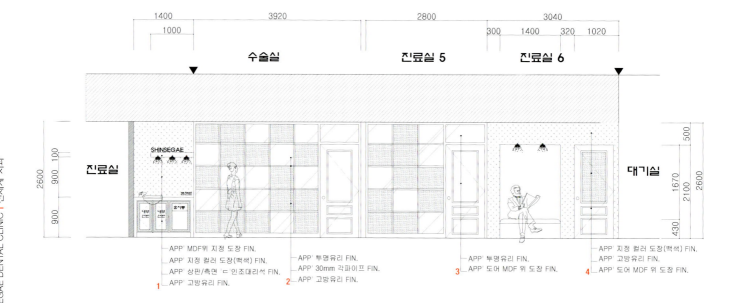

복도 입면 J / corridor elevation J

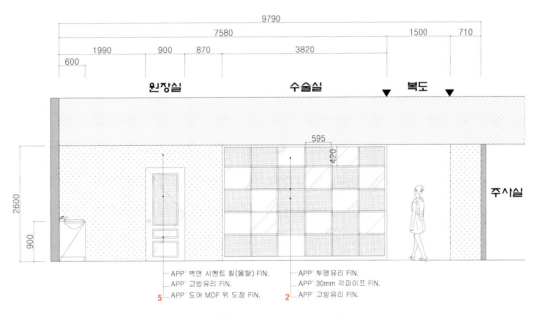

복도 입면 K / corridor elevation K

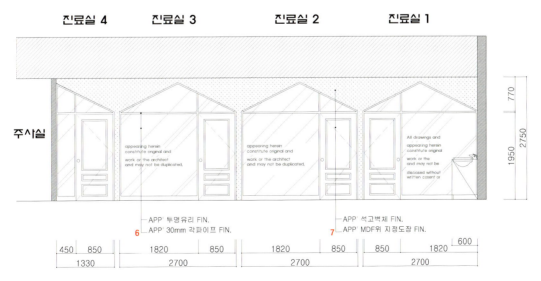

복도 입면 L / corridor elevation L

S PEDIATRICS (HOUSE IN HOUSE)

Limtaehee design studio | Lim Tae Hee

S 소아과는 공간이 아이들의 정서발달에 좋은 영향력을 줄 수 있는 디자인으로 계획되었다. 먼저 아이들에게 3차원의 공간적 경험을 유도하기 위해 공간 속에 또 다른 공간을 디자인하였다. 아이들의 흥미를 유발시키기 위해 두 가지 집 형태의 공간을 비틀어진 각도로 배치하였으며, 파생되는 잉여공간은 안내데스크와 대기공간으로 계획하였다. 두 개의 집은 독립된 방의 개념일 뿐만 아니라 공간과 공간을 이어주는 매개공간이 된다. 둘째, 색을 이용한 다양한 자극과 경험이 가능하도록 원색이 아닌 고급스럽고 차분한 색을 사용하여 편안하고 자연스러운 분위기를 조성하였다. 그 밖에 다양한 형태의 작은 집 형태로 구성된 책장을 두어 여러가지 볼거리와 함께 파티션으로도 사용할 수 있도록 하였다.

S Pediatrics was designed so that the space can have positive effects on children's emotional development. First, in order to draw a three-dimensional spatial experience for the children, another space within a space is incorporated in the design. Two kinds of house-shaped spaces are arranged in a twisted angle to spark the interest of the children, and the remaining space derived from this arrangement is planned out for the information desk and waiting area. Hence, the two houses not only fulfill the concept of independent room but also serve as a mediated space that connects one space with another. Second, the design used sophisticated and calm non-primary colors forming a comfortable and natural ambiance to facilitate various stimulations and experiences. In addition, a bookcase made of various shapes of small houses is installed to provide a variety of visual attractions and also serve as a partition.

디자인 임태희 / 임태희디자인스튜디오
위치 서울특별시 성동구 옥수동
용도 소아과
면적 108.8㎡
마감 도장, 도배
설계기간 2012. 11 ~ 2012. 12
공사기간 2013. 1 ~ 2013. 3
디자인팀 박동은, 오소라
사진 박영채

Location Oksu-dong, Seongdong-gu, Seoul
Use Pediatrics
Area 108.8㎡
Finishing Painting, Wallpaper
Design period 2012. 11 ~ 2012. 12
Construction period 2013. 1 ~ 2013. 3
Photographer Park Young Chae

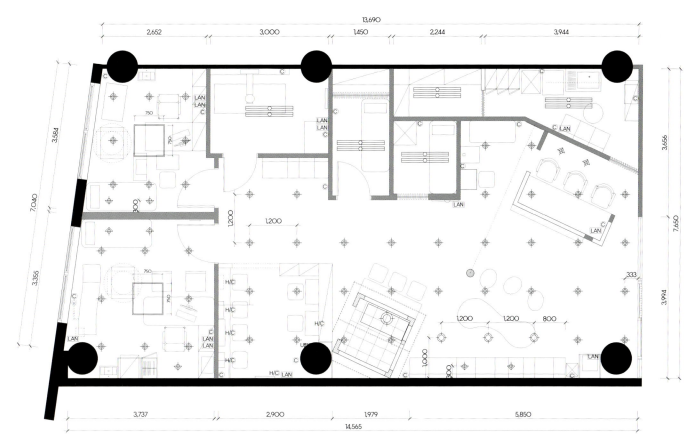

천장도 / ceiling plan

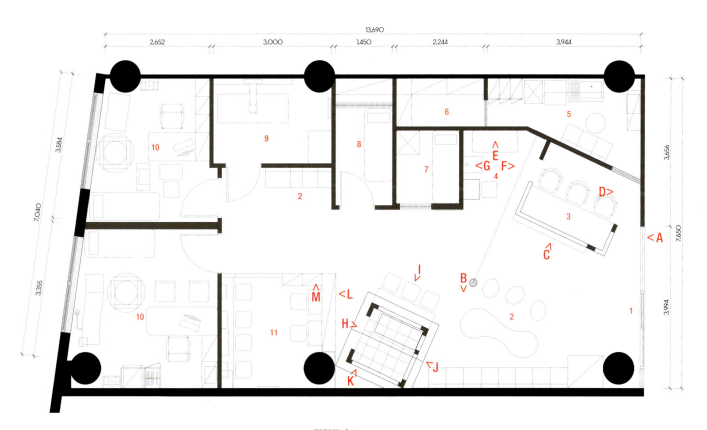

평면도 / floor plan

1 입구 2 대기공간 3 리셉션 4 측정실 5 간호사실 6 창고 7 입원실 8 수액실 9 X-ray 실 10 진료실 11 호흡기 치료 & 성장검사실

1 Entrance 2 Waiting area 3 Reception 4 Measurement room 5 Nurse's room 6 Storage 7 Hospital room 8 Infusion solution room 9 X-ray room 10 Consulting room 11 Respiratory care & growth examination room

1 콘크리트 블록　**2** 콘크리트 블록 위 도장　**3** T18 합판 위 지정색 도장(측면 색상 다르게)　**4** T18 코어 합판 루버 위 투명 도장　**5** 석고보드 2겹 위 지정색 도장　**6** T15 자작나무 합판 2겹 위 투명 도장　**7** T8.5 자작나무 합판 55°시공 위 투명 도장

1 Concrete block　**2** Painting on concrete block　**3** App. color painting on T18 plywood (side color differently)　**4** Clear painting on T18 core plywood louver　**5** App. color painting on gypsum board 2ply　**6** Clear painting on T15 birch plywood 2ply　**7** Clear painting on T8.6 birch plywood 55° construction

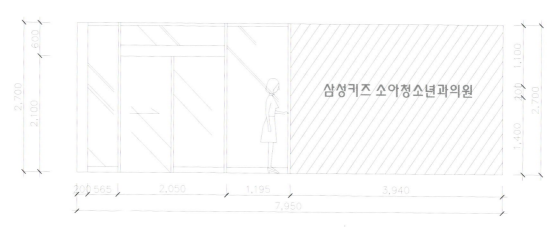

입구 입면 A / entrance elevation A

대기공간 입면 B / waiting area elevation B

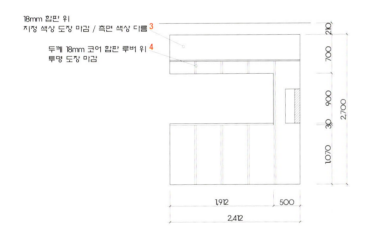

리셉션 입면 C / reception elevation C

리셉션 입면 D / reception elevation D

측정실 입면 E /
measurement room elevation E

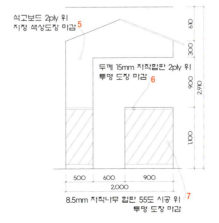

측정실 입면 F /
measurement room elevation F

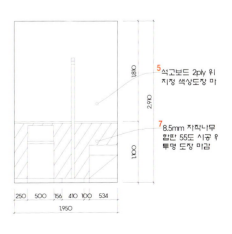

측정실 입면 G /
measurement room elevation G

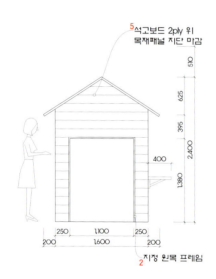

집 속의 집 좌측면 H / house in house left side view H

집 속의 집 정면 I / house in house front view I

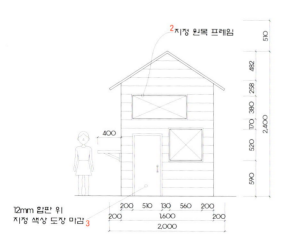

집 속의 집 우측면 J / house in house right side view J

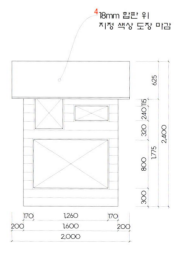

집 속의 집 후면 K / house in house rear view K

1 석고보드 2겹 위 목재 패널 지단 마감   2 지정 원목 프레임   3 T12 합판 위 지정색 도장   4 T18 합판 위 지정색 도장   5 T8.5 합판 위 지정색 도장   6 T18 코어 합판 위 투명 도장

1 Base painting finish on wood panel on gypsum board 2ply   2 App. hardwood frame   3 App. color painting on T12 plywood   4 App. color painting on T18 plywood   5 App. color painting on T8.5 plywood   6 Clear painting on T18 core plywood

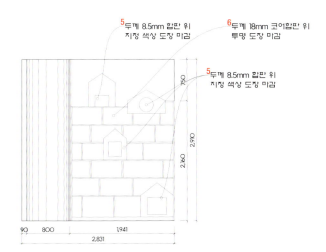

높은 책장 입면 L / high bookshelf elevation L

낮은 책장 입면 M / low bookshelf elevation M

2014 ANNUAL INTERIOR DETAIL

HOTEL · HOUSING

250 HOTEL MANU
마누 호텔

266 FUNCTION HOUSE
기능적인 집

276 YANGPYEONG HOUSE
양평주택

HOTEL MANU

CRE-ID | Choi Myung Koo

사무실 건물을 비즈니스 호텔로 개조한 마누 호텔은 가공되지 않은 재료 본연의 가치와 멋을 중시하는 '로가닉' 스타일을 기초로 감성적인 디자인을 유도하였다. 호텔 안내데스크의 전면은 포인트 벽으로 강조하였고, 뒷벽은 전통 한지로 커튼 패널을 연출하여 고요하고 은은한 이미지를 보여주고자 하였다. 라운지의 조명은 공간 스케일에 맞게 디자인하여 강한 이미지의 오브제로 연출하면서 외부의 시선을 유도할 수 있도록 하였다. 객실은 비즈니스 호텔의 특성을 고려하여 압축적이면서도 기능적인 공간으로 디자인하였는데, 최대의 공간을 확보하고 다양한 기능을 내장한 가구 디자인으로 편리함을 도모하였다. 또한 지중해의 청량한 느낌이 들도록 스파 및 체력단련실을 청색으로 연출하여 고객이 스트레스와 피로감을 풀며 휴식을 취할 수 있도록 하였다.

HOTEL MANU, a business hotel renovated from an office building, took on a sensuous design based on the 'rawganic' style that stresses the natural value and beauty of materials. The front of the hotel information desk is emphasized with a point wall, while the rear is staged with curtain panels made of traditional Korean paper, exhibiting a serene and soft image. The lightings in the lounge are designed in accordance with the scale of the space and are presented as strong images of objets to draw the attention from the outside. Taking into consideration the characteristics of business hotels, the guest rooms are designed as compact and functional spaces, securing maximum space and enhancing convenience through designing furniture that are equipped with various functions. Also, the spa and fitness room are finished with blue to give the refreshing impression of the Mediterranean and help the guests relieve their stress and fatigue and have a good rest.

디자인 최명구 / (주)크레이드
위치 서울특별시 중구 남대문로5가 84-16
용도 호텔
면적 3,200㎡
마감 바닥 - 대리석, 카펫 / 벽 - 무늬목, 대리석, 전통 한지, 특수도장 / 천장 - 도장, 고재 원목, 흡음 목재패널 / 가구 - 원목, 천연가죽
완공 2012. 11
디자인팀 이수현, 박건남, 오명심, 이승학, 송아롬
시공팀 장재용, 하동식, 한강석, 박지범
사진 이철희

Location 84-16, Namdaemunno 5-ga, Jung-gu, Seoul
Use Hotel
Area 3,200㎡
Finishing Floor - Marble, Carpet / Wall - Wood veneer, Marble, Korean paper, Special painting / Ceiling - Painting, Wood, Acoustic wood panel / Furniture - Natural wood, Natural leather
Completion 2012. 11
Photographer Lee Cheol Hee

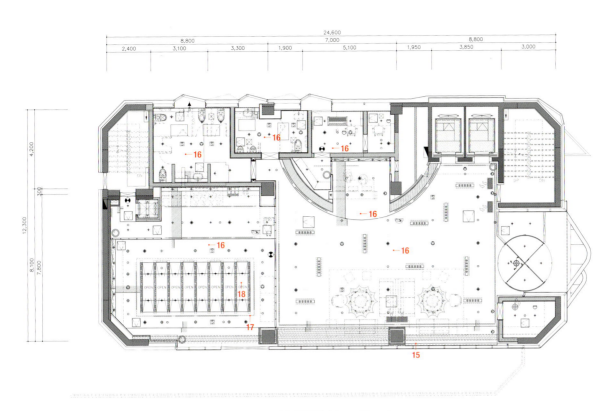

1층 천장도 / 1st ceiling plan

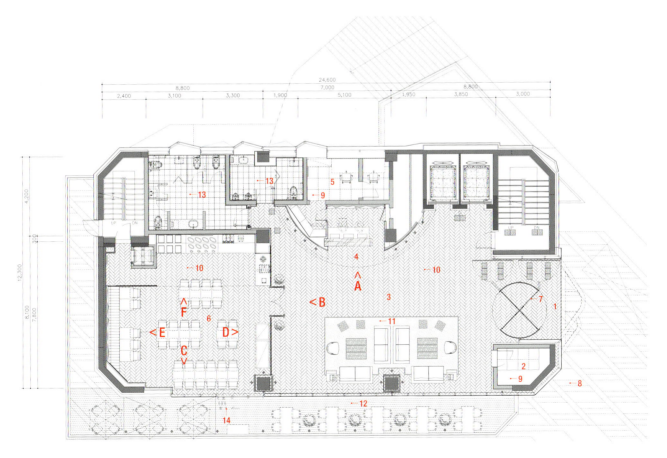

1층 평면도 / 1st floor plan

1 입구 2 짐 보관실 3 로비 & 라운지 4 프론트 5 안쪽 사무실 6 레스토랑 7 방풍실 8 지정 석재 9 지정 P-타일 10 지정 석재(헤링본) 11 지정 러그 12 지정 목재 데크 13 지정 타일 14 접이문 15 100X 150 롤블라인드 박스 : 지정 롤스크린 블라인드 16 지정 페인트 17 지정 원목 18 지정 검은색 페인트

1 Entrance 2 Luggage storage 3 Lobby & lounge 4 Front desk 5 Back office 6 Restaurant 7 Wind break area 8 App. stone 9 App. P-tile 10 App. stone (herringbone) 11 App. rug 12 App. wood deck 13 App. tile 14 Folding door 15 100X150 roll blind box : app. roll screen blind 16 App. paint 17 App. solid wood 18 App. black paint

1 지정 무늬목 / 걸레받이 : 지정 석재 2 지정 투명유리 및 서리 시트 / 프레임 : 지정 스테인리스 스틸 헤어라인 3 지정 강재 무늬목 4 지정 스펙트럼 페이퍼 / 지정 원목 / 지정 거울 5 지정 무늬목 6 지정 스테인리스 스틸 (진동) 7 바닥 조명 8 지정 화강석(표면) / 걸레받이 : 지정 석재 9 지정 경사 투명유리 / 지정 검은색 금속(밀랍처리)

1 App. wood veneer / baseboard : app. stone 2 App. clear glass with frost sheet / frame : app. stainless steel hairline 3 App. solid wood veneer 4 App. spectal paper / app. solid wood / app. mirror 5 App. wood veneer 6 App. stainless steel (vibration) 7 Floor light 8 App. granite (surface) / baseboard : app. stone 9 App. beveled clear glass / app. solid black metal (waxed)

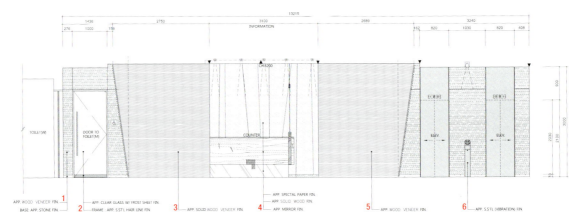

로비 입면 A / lobby elevation A

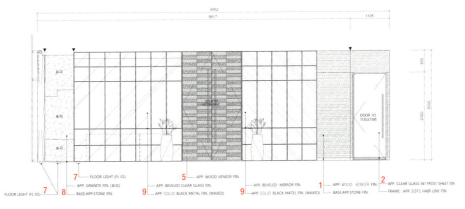

로비 입면 B / lobby elevation B

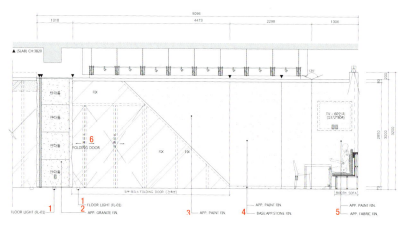

레스토랑 입면 C / restaurant elevation C

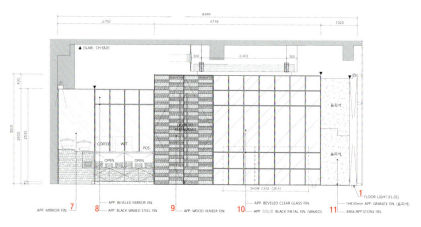

레스토랑 입면 D / restaurant elevation D

1 바닥 조명 2 지정 화강석 3 지정 페인트 4 지정 페인트 / 걸레받이 : 지정 석재 5 지정 페인트 / 지정 패브릭 6 접이문 7 지정 거울 8 지정 경사 투명유리 / 지정 검은색 방수 강철 9 지정 무늬목 10 지정 경사 투명유리 / 지정 검은색 금속(밀랍처리) 11 T30 지정 화강석(표면) / 걸레받이 : 지정 석재 12 지정 합판 및 스펙트럼 페이퍼 / 지정 패브릭 / 지정 무늬목 13 지정 거울 / 지정 검은색 금속(밀랍처리) 14 지정 페인트 / 100X200 지정 타일 15 지정 무늬목 / 걸레받이 : 지정 석재 16 지정 검은색 금속(밀랍처리) / 지정 거울 17 급배기

1 Floor light 2 App. granite 3 App. paint 4 App. paint / baseboard : app. stone 5 App. paint / app. fabric 6 Folding door 7 App. mirror 8 App. beveled clear glass / app. black waxed steel 9 App. wood veneer 10 App. beveled clear glass / app. solid black metal (waxed) 11 T30 app. granite (surface) / baseboard : app. stone 12 App. plywood with spectal paper / app. fabric / app. wood veneer 13 App. mirror / app. solid black metal (waxed) 14 App. paint / 100X200 app. tile 15 App. wood veneer / baseboard : app. stone 16 App. solid black metal (waxed) / app. mirror 17 Airing

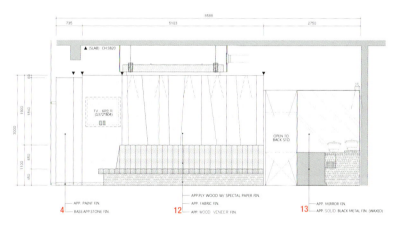

레스토랑 입면 E / restaurant elevation E

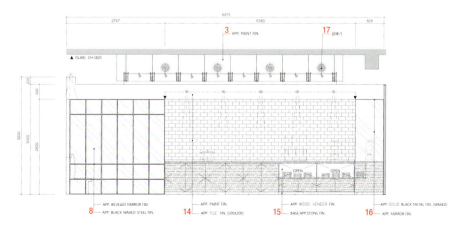

레스토랑 입면 F / restaurant elevation F

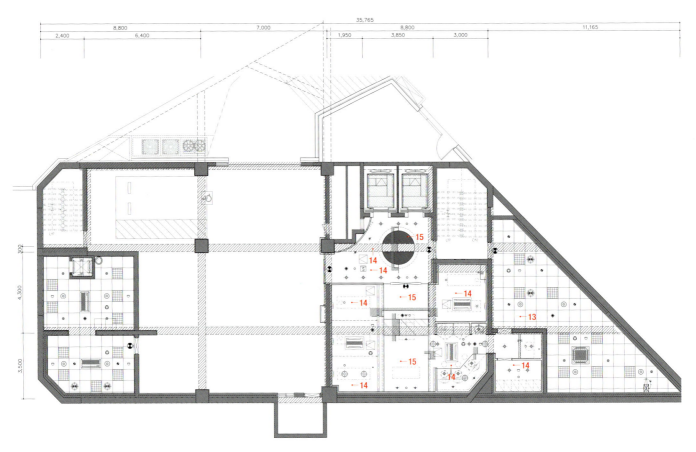

지하 1층 천장도 / 1st basement ceiling plan

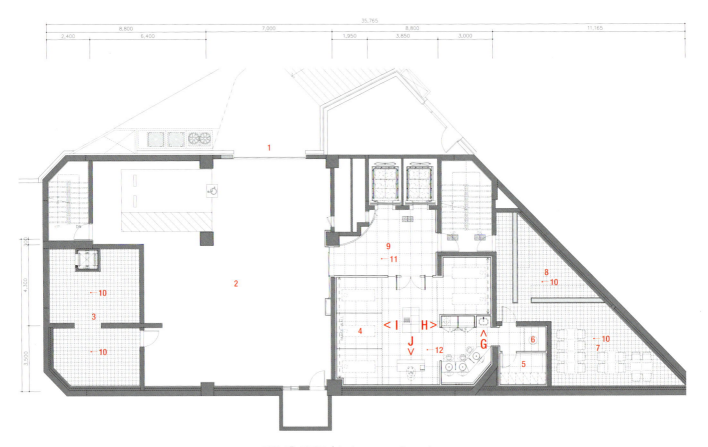

지하 1층 평면도 / 1st basement floor plan

1 입구 2 주차장 3 주방 4 휴게실 5 소지품 보관실 6 파우더룸 7 직원 식당 8 직원 주방 9 엘레베이터 홀 10 지정 타일 11 무광처리 지정 타일 12 연마처리 지정 타일 13 지정 SMC 14 지정 페인트 15 지정 청색 바리솔 16 지정 투명유리 및 지정 서리 시트 / 지정 벽 피복재 / 걸레받이 : 지정 목재 시트 17 지정 투명 유리 및 그라데이션 시트 / 지정 스테인리스 스틸 헤어라인 18 지정 커튼 19 지정 벽 피복재 / 걸레받이 : 지정 목재 시트 20 지정 거울 / 지정 인조대리석 / 지정 자작나무 합판 21 상부장 : 간접조명 22 지정 연마처리 스테인리스 스틸

1 Entrance 2 Parking lot 3 Kitchen 4 Relax room 5 Locker room 6 Powder room 7 Staff dining room 8 Staff kitchen 9 Elevator hall 10 App. tile 11 App. tile with matt finish 12 App. tile with polishing 13 App. SMC 14 App. paint 15 App. blue barrisol 16 App. clear glass with app. frost sheet / app. wall covering / baseboard : app. wood sheet 17 App. clear glass with gradation sheet / app. stainless steel hairline 18 App. curtain 19 App. wall covering / baseboard : app. wood sheet 20 App. mirror / app. mock marble / app. birch plywood 21 Top starage closet : indirect lighting 22 App. stainless steel with polishing

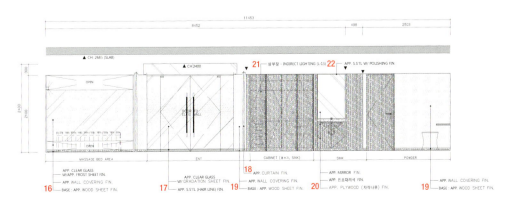

휴게실 입면 G / relax room elevation G

257

1 지정 그래픽 시트 / 걸레받이 : 지정 목재 시트   2 지정 벽 피복재 / 걸레받이 : 지정 목재 시트   3 지정 목재 시트   4 지정 자작나무 합판   5 지정 포인트벽 피복재 / 지정 아이보리 인조 가죽 / 지정 자작나무 합판
6 지정 거울 / 지정 젖빛 유리(조명 내), 후면 확산 시트 / 걸레받이 : 지정 연마처리 철제   7 지정 커튼

1 App. graphic sheet / baseboard : app. wood sheet   2 App. wall covering / baseboard : app. wood sheet   3 App. wood sheet   4 App. birch plywood   5 App. point wall covering / app. ivory artificial leather / app. birch plywood
6 App. mirror / app. milk glass (in lighting), back side diffusion sheet / baseboard : app. steel polished   7 App. curtain

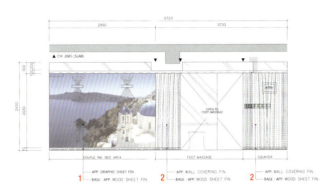

휴게실 입면 H / relax room elevation H

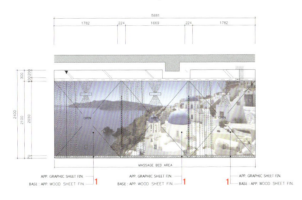

휴게실 입면 I / relax room elevation I

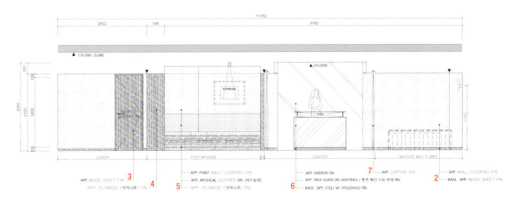

휴게실 입면 J / relax room elevation J

지하 2층 천장도 / 2nd basement ceiling plan

지하 2층 평면도 / 2nd basement floor plan

1 엘레베이터 홀 2 회의실 3 대표실 4 사무실 5 문서고 6 휴게실 & 소지품 보관실 7 다리미 방 8 피트니스 실 9 발전기실 10 물탱크실 11 지정 카펫 12 지정 디럭스 타일 13 지정 P-타일 14 지정 타일 15 지정 우드 플로링 16 지정 고무매트 17 이미지월 18 지정 페인트 19 지정 진청색 페인트 20 지정 흡음보드 21 지정 페인트 / 걸레받이 : 지정 목재 시트 22 지정 투명유리 및 서리 시트 / 프레임 : 지정 스테인리스 스틸 헤어 라인 23 지정 그래픽 시트 / 걸레받이 : 지정 목재 시트 24 버튼 판 : 수퍼 미러 / 지정 거울 / 걸레받이 : 지정 목재 시트 25 지정 목재 시트 26 걸레받이 : 지정 목재 시트

1 Elevator hall 2 Meeting room 3 President room 4 Office 5 Document room 6 Lounge & locker room 7 Iron room 8 Fitness room 9 Generator room 10 Water tank room 11 App. carpet 12 App. deluxe tile 13 App. P-tile 14 App. tile 15 App. wood flooring 16 App. rubber mat 17 Image wall 18 App. paint 19 App. dark blue paint 20 App. acoustic absorption board 21 App. paint / baseboard : app. wood sheet 22 App. clear glass with frost sheet / frame : app. stainless steel hairline 23 App. graphic sheet / baseboard : app. wood sheet 24 Button plate : super mirror / app. mirror / baseboard : app. wood sheet 25 App. wood sheet 26 Baseboard : app. wood sheet

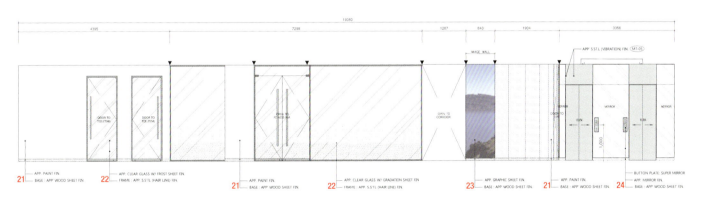

피트니스 실 복도 입면 K / fitness room corridor elevation K

피트니스 실 복도 입면 L / fitness room corridor elevation L

261

3 ~ 10층 평면도 / 3 ~ 10th floor plan

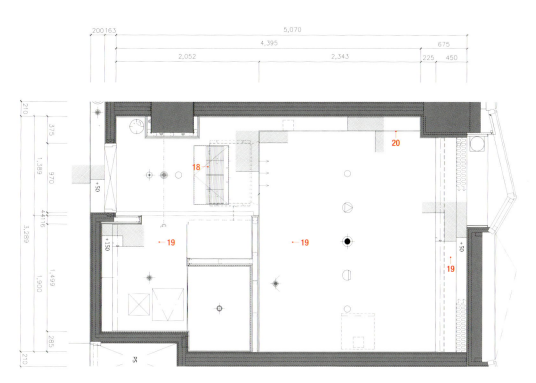

일반 객실 천장도 / guest room ceiling plan

일반 객실 평면도 / guest room floor plan

1 복도 2 객실 3 린넨실 4 지정 카펫 5 현관 6 화장실 7 침실 8 옷장 9 거울 10 짐 받침대 11 책상 12 예술품 13 미니 바 14 지정 목재 시트 15 커튼 : 지정 패브릭 16 지정 타일 17 1,000X2,000X600 싱글 침대 18 점검문 19 지정 페인트 20 10mm 리빌

1 Corridor 2 Guest room 3 Linen room 4 App. carpet 5 Foyer 6 Bathroom 7 Bedroom 8 Wardrobe 9 Mirror 10 Luggage rack 11 Desk 12 Art work 13 Mini bar 14 App. wood sheet 15 Curtain : app. fabric 16 App. tile 17 1,000X2,000X600 single bed 18 Access door 19 App. paint 20 10mm reveal

1 지정 벽 피복재 / 지정 카펫　2 지정 시트　3 지정 무늬목　4 간접 LED 조명 / 지정 무늬목　5 배출구　6 지정 비닐 패브릭, 모서리 : 지정 스테인리스 스틸　7 카드키 수납함 / 화장실 스위치　8 차임벨　9 데스크 넷박스 / 배출구　10 거울

1 App. wall covering / app. carpet　2 App. sheet　3 App. wood veneer　4 Indirect LED lighting / app. wood veener　5 Outlet　6 App. vinyl fabric, edge : app. stainless teel　7 Key card holder / toilet switch　8 Chime bell　9 Desk netbox / outlet　10 Mirror

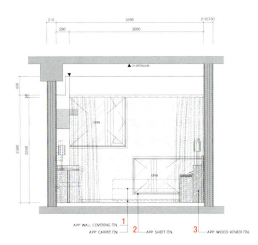

객실 입면 M / passenger room elevation M

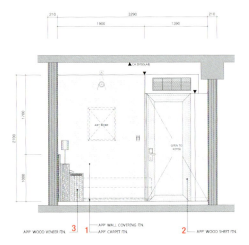

객실 입면 N / passenger room elevation N

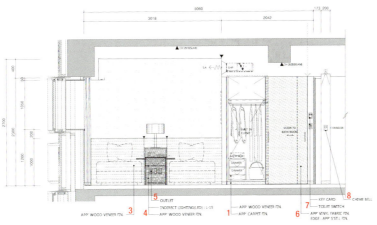

객실 입면 O / passenger room elevation O

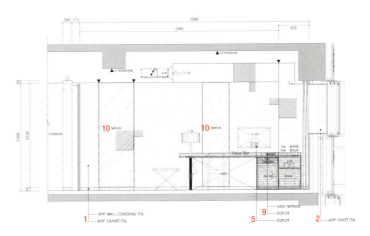

객실 입면 P / passenger room elevation P

FUNCTION HOUSE
jay is working. | Jang Soon Gak

이 집은 기존의 오래된 아파트에 '공간 속의 공간,' 그리고 '기능이 미를 만든다' 라는 두 가지 개념을 적용하여 계획하였다. 입구 왼편에 위치한 10개의 수납장 문이 마감재를 대신하고, 손잡이는 공간 속의 리듬감을 형성한다. 진입동선의 긴 축을 따라 배치된 오른편의 수납 및 전시모듈은 깨끗한 앞면의 순수성에 깊이감을 형성하고 벽부조명으로 기능한다. 동선축의 오른편에는 거실, 식사공간, 부엌이 있고, 다른 색으로 마감된 '공간 속의 공간' 이 관입되어 공용공간과 사적공간을 분리한다. 이 관입공간은 부부 침실과 옷방, 그리고 부부 화장실이 있는 사적인 전이공간이다. 평면 계획에서는 두 개의 큰 통로축으로 공간을 나누고 관입시켰으며, 각종 기능적인 가구와 모듈들의 디테일을 이용하여 공간의 미를 구축하였다. 공장에서 제작된 철제 장식장은 도장 후 설치하였고, 다리 없이 공중에 떠 있는 듯한 켄틸레버 구조의 식탁은 거실 디자인의 중심을 이루고 있다.

This house is designed by applying two ideas, 'space within a space' and 'function creates beauty,' to an old apartment. The doors of ten storage closets to the left of the entrance serve as a finishing material and their handles generate a sense of rhythm in space. The storage and display modules, arranged to the right side and along the long axis of the entrance moving line, embody a sense of depth from the purity of their clean facade and function as wall lighting. The living room, dining area, and the kitchen are arranged to the right side of the moving line. The public space is separated from the private space as 'space within a space' finished with different colors penetrates this section. The penetrated space is the private transition space where the master bedroom and dressing room, and the master bathroom are located. In the floor plan, two large passage axes divide and penetrate the space, while the beauty of the space is constructed through the use of various functional furniture and details of modules. The steel display cupboard made at the factory is painted and then installed, and the dining table, which has the structure of a cantilever as if floating on air without legs, forms the center of the living room design.

디자인 장순각 / (주)제이이즈워킹
위치 서울특별시 서초구 서초동 1330-16 나산 스위트
용도 주거
면적 137.95㎡
마감 바닥 - 복합 타일, 볼론, 원목 바닥 / 벽 - 하이글로시 패널, 패브릭 알판, 지정 도장 / 천장 - 바리솔, 벽지, 지정 도장
완공 2012. 10
디자인팀 채원우, 김태형
시공팀 채원우, 김태형
사진 (주)제이이즈워킹 제공

Location Nasan Sweet, 1330-16, Seocho-dong, Seocho-gu, Seoul
Use Housing
Area 137.95㎡
Finishing Floor - Composite tile, Bolon, Hardwood floor / Wall - High glossy panel, Fabric plate, App. painting / Ceiling - Barrisol, Wallpaper, App. painting
Completion 2012. 10
Photos offer jay is working.

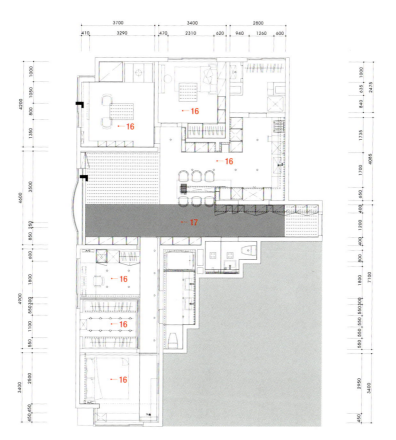

천장도 / ceiling plan

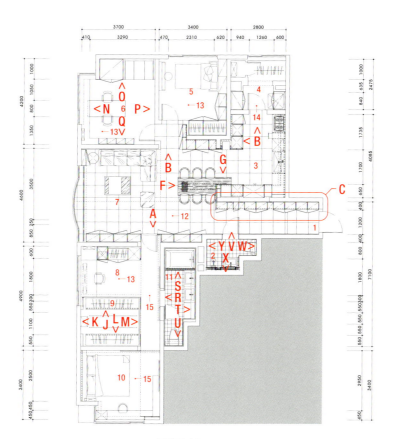

평면도 / floor plan

1 현관 2 욕실 3 주방 4 다용도실 5 침실 6 공부방 7 거실 8 집무실 9 옷방 10 부부 침실 11 부부 욕실 12 지정 복합타일 13 지정 원목마루 14 지정 타일 15 지정 볼론 16 지정 비닐 페인트 17 지정 바리솔

1 Entrance 2 Bathroom 3 Kitchen 4 Utility room 5 Bedroom 6 Study 7 Living room 8 Office 9 Dressroom 10 Master bedroom 11 Master bathroom 12 App. composite tile 13 App. hardwood floor 14 App. tile 15 App. bolon 16 App. vinyl paint 17 App. barrisol

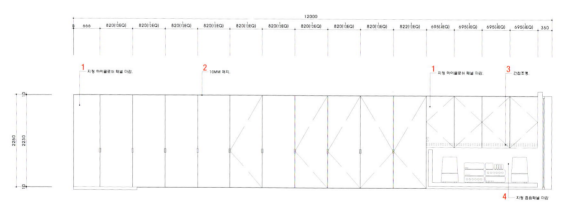

복도 입면 A / corridor elevation A

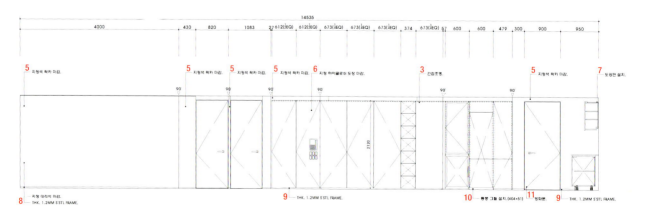

복도 입면 B / corridor elevation B

벽 수납장 평면 D / wall closet top view D

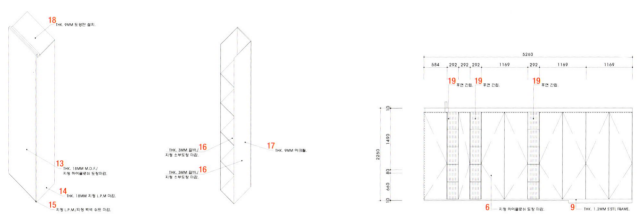

벽 수납장 아이소메트릭 / wall closet isometric

벽 수납장 입면 E / wall closet elevation E

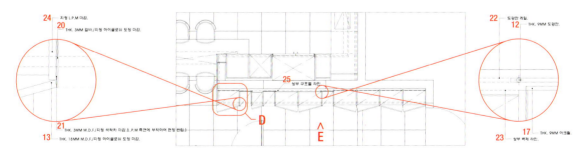

현관 공간 부분 평면 C / entrance area partial plan C

1 지정 하이글로시 패널 2 10mm 줄눈 3 간접조명 4 지정 흡음패널 5 지정색 래커 6 지정 하이글로시 도장 7 도광판 설치 8 지정 대리석 / T1.2 스테인리스 스틸 프레임 9 T1.2 스테인리스 스틸 프레임 10 404X51 통풍 그릴 설치 11 방화문 12 45° 절삭 13 T18 MDF, 지정 하이글로시 도장 14 T18 지정 LPM 15 지정 LPM, 지정 백색 시트 16 T3 갈바륨, 지정 분체도장 17 T9 아크릴 18 T9 도광판 설치 19 후면 간접조명 20 T3 갈바륨, 지정 하이글로시 도장 21 T3 MDF, 지정색 래커 22 도광판 레일 23 상부 벽체 라인 24 지정 LPM 25 상부 구조물 라인

1 App. high glossy panel 2 10mm masonry joint 3 Indirect lighting 4 App. acoustic absorption panel 5 App. color lacquer 6 App. high glossy painting 7 Light guide plate 8 App. marble / T1.2 stainless steel frame 9 T1.2 stainless steel frame 10 404X51 ventilation grill installed 11 Fire door 12 45° cutting 13 T18 MDF, app. high glossy painting 14 T18 app. LPM 15 App. LPM, app. white sheet 16 T3 galvalume, app. powder coating 17 T9 acrylic 18 T9 light guide plate 19 Back side indirect lighting 20 T3 galvalume, app. high glossy painting 21 T3 MDF, app. color lacquer 22 Light guide plate rail 23 Top wall structure line 24 App. LPM 25 Top structure line

1 지정색 래커 2 간접조명 3 후드 매입 4 지정 하이글로시 도장 5 T1.2 스테인리스 스틸 프레임 6 지정 건식 무늬목, 지정 투명 래커 7 T5 지정 색유리 8 T1.6 30X30 각파이프 9 T15 평철 10 T6 합판, T6 지정 인조대리석 11 T6 합판 12 T6 지정 인조대리석 13 T6 합판, 지정색 래커

주방 입면 F / kitchen elevation F

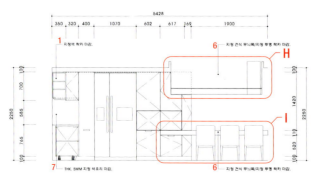

주방 입면 G / kitchen elevation G

1 App. color lacquer **2** Indirect lighting **3** Hood embedded **4** App. high glossy painting **5** T1.2 stainless steel frame **6** App. dry wood veneer, app. clear lacquer **7** T5 app. color glass **8** T1.6 30X30 square pipe **9** T15 flat steel **10** T6 plywood, T6 app. mock marble **11** T6 plywood **12** T6 app. mock marble **13** T6 plywood, app. color lacquer

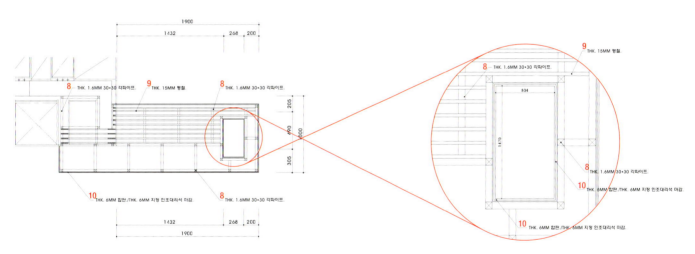

단면 상세 H / section detail H

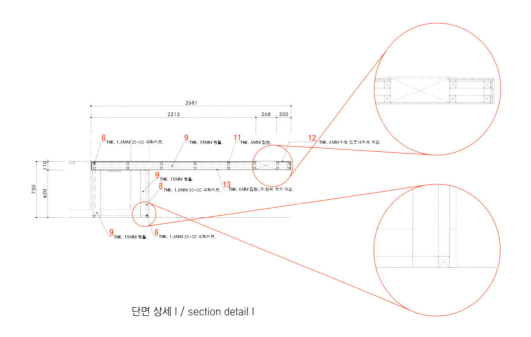

단면 상세 I / section detail I

1 지정색 래커 **2** 지정색 도장 **3** 채널 설치 **4** 지정색 하이글로시 도장 **5** 지정 패브릭 **6** 지정 벽지 / T1.2 스테인리스 스틸 프레임 **7** 지정색 백페인트 유리

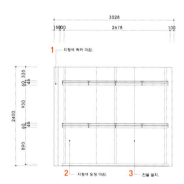

옷방 입면 J / dressroom elevation J

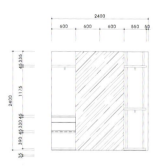

옷방 입면 K / dressroom elevation K

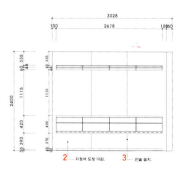

옷방 입면 L / dressroom elevation L

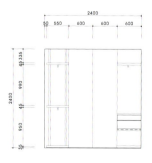

옷방 입면 M / dressroom elevation M

1 App. color lacquer **2** App. color painting **3** Channel installed **4** App. color high glossy painting **5** App. fabric **6** App. wallpaper / T1.2 stainless steel frame **7** App. color back painted glass

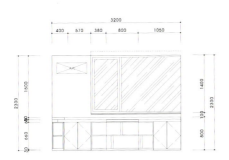

공부방 입면 N / study elevation N

공부방 입면 O / study elevation O

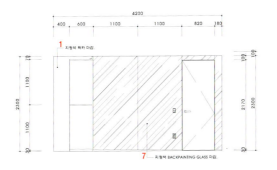

공부방 입면 P / study elevation P

공부방 입면 Q / study elevation Q

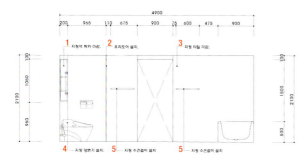

부부 욕실 입면 R /
master bathroom elevation R

부부 욕실 입면 S /
master bathroom elevation S

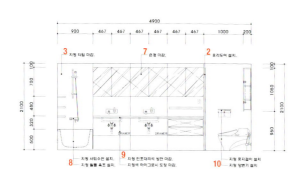

부부 욕실 입면 T /
master bathroom elevation T

부부 욕실 입면 U /
master bathroom elevation U

1 지정색 래커 2 유리문 설치 3 지정 타일 4 지정 양변기 5 지정 수건걸이 6 지정 월풀 욕조 설치 / 하부 트랜치 매입 7 은경 8 지정 샤워 수전 / 지정 월풀 욕조 설치 9 지정 인조대리석 상판 / 지정색 하이글로시 도장 10 지정 휴지걸이 설치 / 지정 양변기 설치 11 지정 LPM 바디, 은경 문 / 지정 인조대리석 / 지정 인조대리석 12 지정 휴지걸이 설치 13 지정 수건걸이 설치 / 지정 인조대리석 상판 14 지정 LPM 바디, 은경 문 15 지정 인조대리석 상판 / 지정 건식 무늬목 도장 / 지정 인조대리석 16 지정 LPM 바디, 은경 문 / 하부 트랜치 설치

1 App. color lacquer 2 Glass door installed 3 App. tile 4 App. toilet bowl 5 App. towel rack 6 App. whirlpool bath installed / bottom trench embedded 7 Silver mirror 8 App. shower faucet 9 App. mock marble top board / app. color high glossy painting 10 App. paper holder installed / app. toilet bowl installed 11 App. LPM body, silver mirror door / app. mock marble / app. mock marble 12 App. paper holder installed 13 App. towel rack / app. mock marble top board 14 App. LPM body, silver mirror door 15 App. mock marble top board / app. dry wood veneer painting / app. mock marble 16 App. LPM body, silver mirror door / bottom trench installed

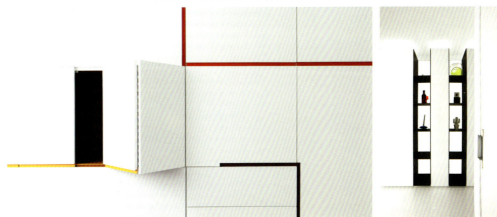

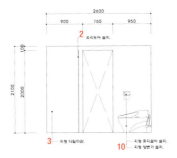

욕실 입면 V / bathroom elevation V

욕실 입면 W / bathroom elevation W

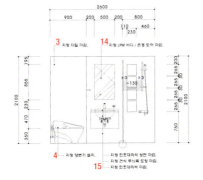

욕실 입면 X / bathroom elevation X

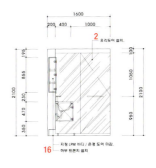

욕실 입면 Y / bathroom elevation Y

YANGPYEONG HOUSE

MIDAS DESIGN | Lee Sung Min

양평주택은 남한강 경치가 한 눈에 들어오는 언덕 위의 집을 콘셉트로, 두 필지의 대지에 스킵플로어와 같은 1층과 2층, 다시 1층 위에 3층이 있는 구조로 공간을 분할을 하고 모던하면서 심플한 느낌을 강조하고자 하였다. 강이 보이는 쪽에 벽체가 없는 시스템 창호로 마감하여 열린 시야와 함께 단열을 고려하였다. 1층 거실과 현관은 검은색과 백색의 조화와 함께 이태리산 원목을 사용하여 온화하면서도 식상하지 않는 느낌이 들도록 마감하였으며, 아일랜드 형태의 부엌은 백색의 깔끔한 느낌으로 구성하였다. 2층의 안방은 전체를 백색으로 구성하여 주문제작 침대와 함께 남한강이 한눈에 내려다보이도록 설치하였다. 안방 욕실에는 황토 사우나시설과 함께 양쪽에 세면대를 배치하였다. 화실이 있는 3층 역시로 넓은 테라스와 함께 남한강을 조망할 수 있도록 계획하였다.

Yangpyeong House was based on the concept of a house on a hill, overlooking a view of Namhan River. The two lots were divided into structures of the 1st and 2ond floor, and the 3rd floor over the 1st floor, as in skip floors to create a modern and simple space. The wall to the river was built with system windows with no walls to open the view and insulate heat. The 1st floor living room and porch is finished by black and white harmoniously in Italian hardwood, for a gentle and exciting environment. The island kitchen was finished in white for a clean feeling. The 2nd floor bedroom is all white with a custom bed overlooking the river. The bathroom has a red clay sauna and a double sink. The 3rd floor has a studio and a big terrace with a view of the river.

디자인 이성민 / 미다스 디자인
위치 경기도 양평군 대심리
용도 주거
면적 265.62㎡
마감 바닥 – 백색 원목마루, 볼락스 대리석 / 벽 – 원목마루, 페인트, 대리석 / 천장 – 비닐 페인트 도장, 바리솔
완공 2013.11
디자인팀 미다스 디자인
시공 미다스 디자인
사진 홍인근

Location Daesim-ri, Yangpyeong-gun, Gyeonggi-do
Use Housing
Area 265.62㎡
Finishing Floor - White solid wood floor, Volakas marble / Wall - Solid wood floor, painting, Marble / Ceiling - Vinyl painting, Barrisol
Completion 2013.11
Photographer Hong In Geun

3층 평면도 / 3rd floor plan

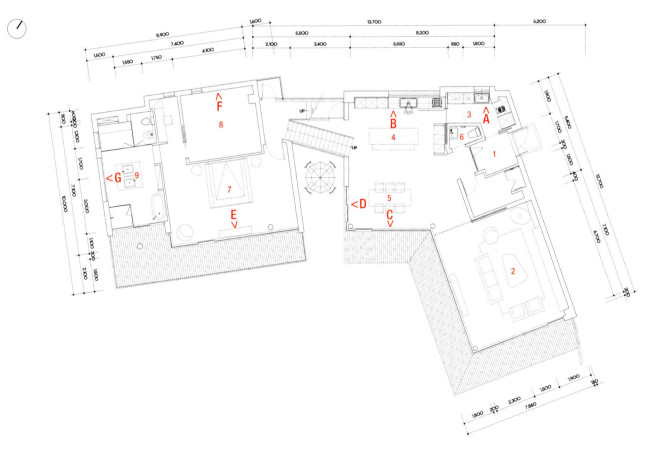

1, 2층 평면도 / 1st, 2nd floor plan

1 입구 2 거실 3 보조주방 4 주방 5 식당 6 화장실 7 안방 8 드레스룸 9 안방 화장실 10 화실 11 테라스

1 Entrance 2 Living room 3 Kitchenette 4 Kitchen 5 Dining room 6 Bathroom 7 Master bedroom 8 Dress room 9 Master bathroom 10 Studio 11 Terrace

INFORMATION

상업

원더플레이스_청주 | 때 | 서울특별시 용산구 한남동 남산맨션 726-731 | 02-792-4285

꾼 노리 | (주)프랜즈디자인 | 서울특별시 종로구 평창동 111번지 성림하우스 1층 | 02-744-9913

콴펜 2 | 비트윈스페이스디자인 | 서울특별시 성수1가2동 685-383 3층 | 02-6402-9665

봉봉루즈 루프탑 | 멜랑콜리 판타스틱 스페이스 리타 | 서울특별시 종로구 부암동 208-42 4층 | 070-8260-1209

재클린 | (주)디자인스튜디오 | 서울특별시 강남구 신사동 588-21 강남빌딩 9층 | 02-542-3580

헤어 마루니 | 엠에스에이엔디 | 서울특별시 서초구 잠원동 18-4 | 02-546-9578

엠블호텔 일라고 베이커리 & 와인숍 | (주)디자인 本홈 | 서울특별시 마포구 상수동 95-3 | 02-335-7120

마인츠돔 베이커리 | (주)쎄이어쏘시에이트 | 서울특별시 강남구 논현동 78-10 101호 | 02-514-2456

앙시 헤어숍 | (주)라움디자인 | 부산광역시 동래구 명륜동 605-6 | 051-583-9379

라쿠 | 엠에스에이엔디 | 서울특별시 서초구 잠원동 18-4 | 02-546-9578

살롱 드 에이치 | 미다스 디자인 | 서울특별시 강남구 압구정로42길 26 | 02-557-8982

저 집 | 스튜디오베이스 | 서울특별시 용산구 서빙고동 4-6 | 02-3444-5804

VB 다이어트 랩 | 파라스코프 | 서울특별시 용산구 한남대로42길 24 유림빌딩 1층 | 02-517-7273

나인 토파즈 | 코어 아이디 | 서울특별시 서초구 방배동 764-4 팔팔빌딩 202호 | 02-536-2993~4

의료

미래의료재단 건강증진센터 | (주)제이이즈워킹 | 서울특별시 성동구 왕십리로 222 한양대학교 한양종합기술원(HIT) 421호 | 02-597-5902

올리브성형외과 | (주)발상 | 서울특별시 강남구 역삼동 684-21 3층 | 02-567-5553

굿플라워 피부과 | 임태희디자인스튜디오 | 경기도 성남시 분당구 수내동 10-1 | 070-8249-5233

이음동물병원 | 멜랑콜리 판타스틱 스페이스 리타 | 서울특별시 종로구 부암동 208-42 4층 | 070-8260-1209

아이누리 한의원 | (주)프랜즈디자인 | 서울특별시 종로구 평창동 111번지 성림하우스 1층 | 02-744-9913

호산병원 산후조리원 | 윤공간디자인 | 서울특별시 서초구 양재동 96-16 주영빌딩 2층 | 02-575-8166

편강한의원_서면 | 스튜디오베이스 | 서울특별시 용산구 서빙고동 4-6 | 02-3444-5804

숨 수면클리닉 | (주)발상 | 서울특별시 강남구 역삼동 684-21 3층 | 02-567-5553

아가온 여성의원 | (주)MD SPACE | 서울특별시 강남구 논현동 266-1 더비트빌딩 3층 | 02-3445-2837

서울 베스트 치과 | (주)프랜즈디자인 | 서울특별시 평창동 111번지 성림하우스 1층 | 02-744-9913

드림 치과 | 알리퍼블릭디자인 + 엠투엠 디자인 | 서울특별시 서초구 양재동 117 1층 | 02-576-7105

코원 성형외과 | 임태희디자인스튜디오 | 경기도 성남시 분당구 수내동 10-1 | 070-8249-5233

신세계 치과 | 일하는 사람들-나는김정현이다 | 경기도 고양시 일산동구 풍동 1234-5 1층 | 070-4234-5545

S 소아과(집 속의 집) | 임태희디자인스튜디오 | 경기도 성남시 분당구 수내동 10-1 | 070-8249-5233

호텔·주거

마누 호텔 | (주)크레이드 | 서울특별시 강남구 도곡동 453-16 아성빌딩 2층 | 02-573-5364

기능적인 집 | (주)제이이즈워킹 | 서울특별시 성동구 왕십리로 222 한양대학교 한양종합기술원(HIT) 421호 | 02-597-5902

양평주택 | 미다스 디자인 | 서울특별시 강남구 압구정로42길 26 | 02-557-8982